STRANGER IN THE HOUSE

Women's Stories of Men Returning
from the Second World War

JULIE SUMMERS

**POCKET
BOOKS**

LONDON • SYDNEY • NEW YORK • TORONTO

First published in Great Britain in 2008 by Simon & Schuster UK Ltd
This edition published by Pocket Books, 2009
An imprint of Simon & Schuster UK Ltd
A CBS COMPANY

1 3 5 7 9 10 8 6 4 2

Simon & Schuster UK Ltd
1st Floor, 222 Grays Inn Road, London WC1X 8HB

www.simonandschuster.co.uk

Simon & Schuster Australia
Sydney

A CIP catalogue for this book is available
from the British Library.

ISBN: 978–1–41652–684–1

Typeset in Perpetua by M Rules
Printed by CPI Cox & Wyman, Reading, Berkshire RG1 8EX

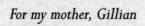

For my mother, Gillian

CONTENTS

CONTENTS

AUTHOR'S NOTE

The idea for *Stranger in the House* came to me on a train journey
from Oxford to London when I was on my way to meet an editor
about another book. I had not long published *The Colonel of
Tamarkan* and much of the correspondence I had received about
it dwelt upon the final chapter when I described the terribly difficult adjustment to post-war life experienced by my grandfather.
It struck a chord with many people and most of my correspondents were women, thanking me for tackling the thorny issue of
returning heroes. As I stared out of the window on to sodden
fields I suddenly began to think about what it must have been like
to welcome home a man who had been away for years; a man
who had experienced the horrors of war and who was now
expected to get on with life, to build a career, to take up with a
family he hardly knew any more and to live in a country ravaged
by years of war and rationing. Then I began to think about the
women. How did they cope? What kind of adjustment did they
have to make? How many of these women had any understanding at all of what was coming next?

Six months later I was standing on a riverbank talking to the
mother of one of my son's friends. She was about to take her
family to Australia on the family holiday of a lifetime. As we
perched on the steeply sloping bank feeling our heels sinking into

the soft grass I told her about the research I was doing for this book. She began to tell me the story of her family and the more she told me the more intently I listened. By the time she had finished my shoes were ruined but my interest was piqued to such an extent that we agreed to meet when she came back from her travels. Juliet Curry's life had been deeply affected by the war in a way that I had not come across before. Her father had not been in the forces but for him and his wife the dislocation caused by six years of separation had had extreme consequences. I realized then that this book was not just about the effect of returning service-men but about how the war affected family life, sometimes for ever, regardless of where a man had been.

So where to start and how to find people who would talk to me? In the first instance I wrote back to people who had written to me about *The Colonel* and asked if they would be interested in talking about their own experiences of men coming home. It was fertile ground and several important interviews stemmed from this including those of Di Elliott and Meg Parkes. I then approached people I knew who had indicated that they might have a story of interest. In this way I talked to Marion Platt and Chris Best, two women with completely different experi-ences from those I had gathered from my first round of research. After that people began to approach me, hearing about my research and wanting to tell their own stories. Two warm trans-atlantic friendships developed via email – with Jen Howe and Stephanie Hess – thanks to an introduction by Jonathan Moffatt. At the same time I read diaries and letters in the Department of Documents at the Imperial War Museum to flesh out the immediate post-war story. Through this rich source I met Hazel Watson, Janice Taylor and Barbara Sinclair. The invaluable diaries at the Mass Observation Archive at the University of Sussex in Brighton and their *Woman's Own* archive helped even further. Finally I decided I needed to spread my net so I wrote to the Women's Institute who kindly printed a letter in their newsletter. This produced a small avalanche of correspondence and added to the now burgeoning files in my office. As the stories began to take shape I discovered that women had often not talked in detail about their own experiences before or were surprised to be asked about how they had coped, rather than retelling the story of someone else's war.

My patient husband, Chris, who never gets to read my books until they are published but who is subjected to hours of pillow talk as I thrash out ideas, made some clever suggestions as to how the book might be structured. It was he who came up with the idea of dividing the book into the wife's tale, the daughter's tale and so on.

As a writer I am fascinated by the minutiae of everyday life. I like to think that a scratch-and-sniff approach reveals as much about the bigger picture as serious research into the important historical events that shape our lives. One of my favourite discoveries was in the Imperial War Museum in March 2006. There a file on a WAAF officer called Nancy Walton revealed the, to me, sensational snippet that Lord Nuffield had supplied the WAAF with sanitary towels for the entire duration of the war. These articles were newfangled and expensive but a vital aid to women. They were known as Nuffield's Nifties. Although this generous and imaginative act of Lord Nuffield's is perhaps little known and does not rate in the list of his enormously valuable benefactions, it was appreciated by the women on the receiving end and in the course of my conversations with ladies of a certain age I discovered that they all knew about Nuffield's Nifties and were extremely grateful to him. Other facts came to light as the research progressed such as the revelation by one of my interviewees that her mother used to cut up newspapers into squares to hang on a piece of string in the outside privy. Her aunt, however, who was a little grander, used to use pinking shears to give her squares a more pleasing outline.

When I began my research I wanted to learn how women had coped with their returning men and how they succeeded in balancing the combined pressures of family life and work with the added burdens of rationing, queuing and bringing up children. The research very quickly took on a life of its own as I realized it is impossible, in most cases, to isolate a returning man and examine just one relationship.

Eventually I interviewed over a hundred women and more than twenty men and spoke to many others. They came from a variety of different backgrounds, from a lady-in-waiting to the late Queen Mother to a widow from Yorkshire. I talked to friends and strangers, I wrote to people whose names were passed on via contacts and I met people on trains, in libraries and in unexpected places. Everyone I spoke to had a story to tell and many were willing to let their stories be reproduced in this volume.

Sometimes interviews took place face to face and at other times they were conducted over the telephone, by email or via letter. I travelled from Somerset to northern Scotland to collect material and I went to Australia in pursuit of tales from men who fought in almost every theatre of war from 1939 to 1945. I had help from individuals and institutions, from the WI and the War Widows Association, from the Commonwealth War Graves Commission and the ex-services mental health charity Combat Stress, from medical experts, psychologists and journalists.

The men we discussed – grandfathers, fathers, brothers, uncles, sons and nephews – had been all over the world during the war, from the Maritime Provinces of Eastern Canada to the jungles of Borneo. They had been prisoners of war in Germany, Italy and Poland, in Japan, Thailand and Malaya. They had flown over Norway and Malta, they had fought in North Africa, India, Palestine, they had sailed in the North and South Atlantic, the Pacific and the Mediterranean. Some men had had a 'good' war, others had returned injured in body and mind, some had just been relieved to get home and get on with life. For all these men there were women at the other end of their war – mothers, wives, girlfriends, sisters, aunts, daughters and carers.

I have shied away from making judgements about why people behaved in certain ways or did certain things because I felt that the stories should stand on their own without analysis. Often they developed over weeks of interviews so that the story slowly came out and took shape. I have tried to place the stories in the historical context and let the women speak for themselves. I am more convinced than ever that this period in our joint history had an enormous impact, and continues to have an impact on our lives today. I am certain that part of the current fascination with family history has to do with people trying to understand why they are like they are and what it was in their past that helped to shape their lives.

Everyone I have interviewed has been asked whether they are happy to be identified in the book. A small handful of women asked me to disguise their identities by giving them false names and locations. Where complete anonymity has been requested I have of course respected this. Every effort has been made to check facts and cross-reference dates. Any errors in the narrative are my responsibility. To everyone whose story is told in the following pages and to all the others not included but who contributed to the whole picture I give my sincere and heartfelt thanks.

Julie Summers
Oxford
April 2008

I

WAR WITHOUT END

> What we want now, at the end of this long period of adjustment, are not lectures on the sins of the past, but signposts for the future. Any fool can be destructive – it takes a clever and a wise person to be constructive.
>
> *Dame Barbara Cartland*

During the course of 1945 the Second World War ended. There was no single date in the calendar that people could point to, as there was after the First World War, and say 'it is over'. For the majority in Britain it came about with the announcement of the surrender of Germany and the VE Day celebrations on 8 May. For many, though, the war continued up to the surrender of Japan on 15 August.

Over a period of two years, more than 4 million servicemen came home and for the following months and in some cases years, they readjusted to life in the post-war world. So why, six decades on, does the end of the Second World War still matter? 'It takes a long time, I think, to understand a war,' the novelist

A. L. Kennedy said in 2008. 'We are almost at the point where we can have an overview of 1939–45.' I would go further and say that it takes even longer to understand the effect that war has on those caught up in its slipstream.

This book is a collection of reminiscences from women, largely, whose lives were affected by the fallout from that war. Some women were relieved that the war was over and they could get on with where life had left off in 1939. However, even for those who had no trouble assimilating after 1945 there was adjustment on some level. Britain was no longer the country it had been before the war. Life had changed in so many ways. There was less money, food and housing. There were more queues, rules and laws. The government had unprecedented levels of control over people's lives and it was a country almost bankrupt by six years of war.

The Second World War cut across the middle of the twenti-eth century. It tore at the fabric of society and at a generation. It brought turmoil in its wake, which was unprecedented in its ferocity. It damaged millions of lives beyond repair and caused the greatest mass migration in human history. It was total war, defined as a conflict of unlimited scope in which a faction mo-bilizes all available resources in order to destroy their rivals' ability to defend themselves. In total war there are no non-combatants: everyone, civilians and soldiers alike, is an acceptable target. Our national government took powers to control the country's human and material resources to confront the enemy in battle, to supply our armed forces and to feed and clothe the nation. Conscription extended beyond recruitment into the armed services to direct women into munitions work and the Land Army.

Sixty years on statistics for the Second World War vary but there were at least 15 million military deaths worldwide and probably double that number of civilian fatalities. The upheaval was worse in mainland Europe but in Britain alone countless families lost their homes. Over the summer and autumn of 1945 and on through the spring and summer of 1946 millions of men were demobbed and returned home. For many it was a serious challenge, for 'home' was not what they had known when they left to fight. For some it no longer existed physically – their homes had been bombed or lost. For others the loss was emotional: parents had died, wives and girlfriends had moved on, children had been born. For a fortunate few nothing much at home had changed. But these men had.

Sir Carol Mather wrote in his memoir *Aftermath of War*:

By the end of six years of war, one was totally satiated with the experience; one had lived, eaten, slept and dreamed 'war' to the exclusion of everything else. After it was over I put a cordon sanitaire around the whole affair and forgot about it. Then the years passed and a subtle change took place, as succeeding generations grew up. The episode passed, almost unnoticed, out of the realm of 'experience' and into the domain of 'history'.

'But what of the women?' The prolific novelist Dame Barbara Cartland posed this question in her autobiography *The Years of Opportunity 1939–1945*:

We were glad, but still our hearts refused to sing, the shadow of war still lay over us in a restriction of freedom, in controls and coupons. We had only to look at our empty larders, empty store cupboards and half-empty coal cellars to know war had not receded very far from our daily lives. To practically everyone in Great Britain the war had brought the loss of someone they loved – either man, woman or child – and for many there were crippled bodies or blinded eyes as a legacy from the nights of terror and fire.

Women had not fought in the front line but had been caught up in the war in almost every other way.

From every corner of the country came a sigh of relief that the war in Europe was over and VE Day was announced, but it was not until mid-August 1945 that Japan surrendered unconditionally, bringing the war to an end. As the photographer and designer Cecil Beaton observed on VE Day: 'Victory does not bring with it a sense of triumph – rather a dull numbness of relief that the blood-letting is over.' There was a sense of exhaustion that overrode the feelings of joy expressed in the street parties and victory parades. 'Everyone wants, above all things, a rest,' George Orwell had told American readers on a visit to the United States in the autumn of 1944.

What were people to make of it all? Men were uneasy with their freedom from order and discipline, thrown into a state of uncertainty about how they would fit back in to civilian society. They were confused by women who had grown older, who had become independent. Then there were the children who didn't recognize their fathers, who sometimes did not know their fathers as they had not yet met them, who were jealous of the attention now lavished on their mothers.

Where before there had been a certain harmony and rhythm, even in difficult times, there was now disruption and confusion. How could a woman ever understand what a soldier fighting in North Africa or Germany or France had experienced? How could a returning man comprehend what a woman had been through in the Blitz? For some it was the fact that they had grown up while they had been away, for others it was that people at home had changed. So much was unfamiliar and some things had moved on while others had stood still. All of this simmered away in family homes in cities, towns and villages throughout the country.

One initial reaction, after the relief of coming home, was surprise. A released prisoner of war from Germany, Lieutenant Frank Stewart, wrote in his diary:

> We were let loose at last on Thursday 10th May, armed with rail passes, ration books and clothing coupons, and even a little cash in our pockets. Our first stop was London and, for some reason or another, I and a few friends headed for Hyde Park Corner and sauntered through St James's Park. I remember how we were all surprised, and indeed shocked, by the blatancy of the couples on the benches and on the ground, as we thought back to pre-war days when holding hands in public was considered rather daring. Also, we noticed how many women now wore trousers . . . We moved on to Piccadilly Circus and stood there in silence recalling the scene. The lights weren't on again yet (it was too early in the day anyhow), but there was a great bustle of people. We thought they looked tired and drawn, as they had every reason to be after what they'd endured from the flying bombs and rockets. I wondered what the Londoner at that time would think if he knew of our less than vindictive feelings towards the Germans.

Kenneth Laing confessed in an article for the POWRA (Prisoner of War Relatives Association) newssheet in June 1945: 'A completely new generation has arrived. Strange people turn up among your acquaintances and you realize you left them as children. Now they're around everywhere. They're bewildering. They seem to have skidded out into life rather than to have grown up. They're a mixture of sheer worldliness and complete childish innocence. With them you really feel five years have passed.' But he was enchanted by children: 'I can't stop looking at them.' He wrote, 'At church the first Sunday I just stared and stared all through the service. They're so fresh and healthy and they have such wonderful colour on their cheeks. All the German children had what we called "potato complexion" – sallow and yellowish.'

Many boys had left home at eighteen and returned at twenty-three or four as men:

A young man is thrust into the army. He is conveyed to some un-familiar place suddenly, then, he is plunged into mortal combat. He does not know why. He does not understand. He is frightened; he loses control of the simplest bodily functions. But within the short space of a few hours, his spirit is carried through every degree of terror, horror, anger, pity, brutality, idealism, bravery, exultation, ecstasy. Then in some strange way it is over. He is back at routine. He finds himself bewildered. He looks about on the world and does not recognize it. He has been shaken and changed. He is, even after it is over, afraid. Terrible and wonderful pictures come into his brain at night. That is why we see so many men who were sensitive boys, before they entered the army, walking about the world with quiet, strange eyes.

The war had not been a terrible experience for all men. Some had found it to have been positive and their lives were enhanced by the camaraderie and excitement of their time in the services. But that did not necessarily make it any easier for the women and families they came home to. One woman wrote:

Imagine this, fifty years on my husband still tells anyone who will listen that the war years were the best years of his life. He had a wonderful war. He had adventures, he made friends, he saw incredible places that I can only dream of and when he came home he just went on and on about those days. Still does. That doesn't say much for our married life. There was no feeling for me and what I had been through with my little children. We'd had to live with my disabled mother and I spent the war looking after her and the children and trying to make ends meet. It was not glamorous at all and I didn't like having Alfred telling me how grand it had been for him while he took no notice of what I'd been through.

The feeling of dislocation and unease at the prospect of readjustment reached into almost every home. There was a sense that this had all been seen before, after the last war, and there was a determination within government that the mistakes that had been made then should not be repeated. The fiasco of demobilization in 1918 had subsequently been widely recognized as a scandal and the results had been in many cases tragic. Hundreds of thousands of men returned to a 'promised land fit for heroes' that turned out to be sadly less than able to cope with them owing to the approaching economic slump of the 1920s. A major problem too was the fact that so many men had suffered severe psychological damage as a result of the war and this was little understood. This time, the government knew, it would have to be different. There would be help for returning men and there would be advice on coping with the pressures of settling down.

All this was foreseen as early as 1942 at cabinet level. Churchill, focused on winning the war, at least agreed to appoint a minister of reconstruction to oversee this major task. The man charged with this was the great trade union leader Ernest Bevin, whom Churchill had appointed as minister of labour and national service in May 1940. No one in 1942 believed the war would last another three years so what might now seem somewhat premature, seeing that the peak of mobilization was not reached until 1943, made sense then. The government's planners began to consider a post-war future for its 'bombed-out, worn-out, rationed-out' people. Bevin understood all too well that housing was going to be of critical importance once the war was over. In a speech in Wigan in November 1943 he stated the case unequivocally: 'We must do it for the sake of the men who have married since the war, for two and a half million marriages have taken place since war broke out . . . Not more than 10 or 12 per cent have homes. They are living with their families or in furnished rooms . . . The one essential thing if you are going to stop moral disaster after the war is to enable these young folk to start off under reasonable conditions of home life as quickly as ever you can.'

The issue of housing focused the minds of the committee for reconstruction when they came to consider the hierarchy for demobilization. There were to be three categories of release: Class A for the longest-serving service personnel; Class B included construction and other key workers who could be called back to work in reconstruction; Class C was for compassionate cases. Bevin insisted that no consideration be taken of where a man had served or whether he was married, so that conceivably a single man who had served five years in Britain would be released before a married man who had served four years in the Middle East or India.

This was the sting in the tail as far as the forces were concerned and thus the reception of the plan was cool. In practice it had many hiccups, as this comment from a mother illustrates:

Young Sid's annoyed because he'll be in the army another 12 months. Because he was temporarily released from the army last year to do slating in London, the army's counted the time against him and put him back ten groups for demobbing. Sid's wild because he says that he's the sort of worker they'll need when

building houses. But I tell him not to be so daft. He's having an
easy time of it now, in the army, and if he applied for release under
the Class B scheme he'd be sent wherever the labour exchange
thought fit, and be worse off, paying out all his earnings in some
stinking lodgings.

There is a popular belief that the government and army had
made no provision for helping men to get back into the swing of
civvy street but, as will become clear, there was no shortage of
plans. As the end of the war drew closer a whole conflation of
documents and leaflets was published by the War Office, the
Ministry of Labour and the armed forces. The HMSO *Release and
Resettlement* advice booklet was handed out to every returning
serviceman urging them to contact their local Resettlement
Advice office to talk through issues with specially trained officers
who would address and advise on any topic, however unusual.

The weak point in the plan was the human element. 'The plan
was all paper, paper, paper – brilliant in theory but hopelessly
optimistic in assuming that individuals would surrender their
interests to the collective need.' No account, despite the experiences of the post-First World War era, was taken of the traumatic
psychological effect on men and women of the war. The medical
profession and public alike were inclined to underestimate the
results of delayed shock. A doctor giving lectures on First Aid
told his audience that in his opinion the biggest modern development from the medical science point of view was the treatment
of shock: 'In the last war, 1914–18, amazing strides were made
in surgery. In this war I believe the greatest advance is our realization that treatment for shock must take precedence over all
injuries.'

The army had its own psychiatrists who were working with the
services even during the war and one man in particular stood out

as someone who recognized the problems that men would have in readjusting to civilian life. His name was Thomas Forrest Main. Born in South Africa but educated in Britain and Ireland between the wars, he was taken on by the army in the Second World War. He said: 'The return of personal interest will be coupled with . . . complaints of unfairness; . . . indiscipline; depression; and epidemics of jealousy and resentment against different sections of the nation.' And he was right.

Bevin too understood the sensitive nature of repatriation and he insisted that the Resettlement Advice Service must 'have a human outlook and be patient in dealing with men who come to us. They have good reason to be unsettled and disturbed in their minds and we must, therefore, be sympathetic. There must be no "official" outlook or coldness of manner. Cases will vary greatly but we must not hesitate to give help or advice even if a case is not covered by instructions. Every man must be dealt with as an individual in need of help and advice.'

However, the truth was that there was little help offered to families who found themselves with marital difficulties and the experiences that Main and his colleagues encountered were not solved by well-intentioned official advice. The men and women who worked in the centres were not qualified to cope with intimate personal problems and men were often referred to voluntary bodies such as the British Legion, the Salvation Army and the Church who, it was felt, had more experience in dealing with these issues. Barbara Cartland, who worked as a welfare officer during the war, was dismissive of the ability of individual padres to deal with questions concerning sex and she told them so quite bluntly: 'Couldn't you speak to the men and tell them not to be upset if their married relationship is not quite normal – tell them that with patience and returning health things will adjust themselves?' She visited a group of returned prisoners of war from Germany and put the question to two priests.

> The padres looked at me goggle-eyed. 'We wouldn't have time to say that,' one remarked at length primly. What he meant was that he didn't want to talk about such things. But why not? Marriages are broken up every day through parties concerned being left in ignorance by people, who, however well-meaning, won't get down to brass tacks and talk in plain English about 'such things'. And whose job is it?
>
> The physical and spiritual are so closely related that it is no use Clerics and Medical Officers putting themselves into watertight compartments and trying to divide the indivisible. What is more, it is everybody's business and everybody's job to do what they can for the national happiness . . . Happiness is being destroyed and lost because we're too mealy-mouthed to tell young people what we know through experience.

The Marriage Guidance Council, set up in 1938, had centres in London and other big cities. It made a valuable contribution to helping married couples with problems but only, of course, for people who knew about the organization and were willing to talk to consultants. It was not yet widely accepted that marriage guidance could offer real help to couples, despite the government's acknowledgement in 1947 that early intervention by experts helped to save foundering relationships. It may also have been that men were simply unwilling to discuss more personal problems. For a man who had survived the war it was probably more than he could do to admit that he and his wife or family were finding it hard to settle down now that it was over, let alone discuss anything to do with sexual issues. Also, it is likely that some men saw their wider concerns not as a familial matter but more wrapped up in the way that society was developing after the war. Expressions of bafflement about the black market and the difficulties of civvy street were all too often heard and might have masked a great malaise at home.

Sydney Wootton, a prisoner of war from Thailand and Japan, kept all his resettlement papers in meticulous order after the war and they provide an overview of the advice given to men in 1945. One leaflet issued by the War Office (AMD (5) May 1945) was entitled *Hints on Diet during Recuperative Leave for Liberated POWs*. The advice was not to overload the stomach, 'to eat foods that were easy to digest such as eggs, fish and tender meat'. This was good advice but where might he obtain such foods? he wondered. 'Do not hurry your meals, chew your food carefully and avoid rush and hurry before and after meals.' For a man who had been starving for years this advice was not always welcome. As a Far Eastern prisoner of war he was given another envelope issued to men who had been in malarial areas. This was to be given to a GP who might not recognize the tropical diseases listed: malaria, dysentery (including amoebic dysentery), nutritional deficiencies, skin diseases and worm infestations.

In fact ex-POWs were bombarded with information from organizations that promised to help them to resettle: the Red Cross, the Indian Army, RAPWI (Recovery of Allied Prisoners of War and Internees) as well as the War Office and the government. There were instructions about what to do with enemy currency and how to exchange it, about obtaining clothes, leave, demob allowances, health and pensions. His Army Welfare Service officer wrote to him offering advice as well.

The Ministry of Labour and National Service sent him a *For Your Guidance* leaflet about what to do on leaving the services. 'To help you solve the many and varied problems which may arise when you reach home again, there will be a Resettlement Advice office in every town of any size. These offices have been set up especially to help you in this way – go to them with your problems whatever they may be and everything possible will be done to assist you.' But, after all that encouraging advice, this was principally concerned with getting men back to work in their old jobs, new jobs or apprentice schemes. The leaflet also instructed him what to do with his uniform (keep it clean in case there is another national emergency); it informed him about ration books and entitlements, about parliamentary registration, about railway concessions and what to do if he had contracted venereal disease.

So it was not that there was a lack of advice and help on hand. As this shows, it was there in plenty, but it was all designed to move things forward bureaucratically and, crucially, with the exception of the advice from his regimental association, it offered no emotional support.

The overriding message for ex-servicemen seemed to be to get on with the future, put the past behind you. Now was the time for the famous British stiff upper lip. And it is true that for every family who had problems they knew of others who were in a worse state, and that certainly had some bearing on people's desire to put up and shut up. How could a woman complain about her husband's strange new attitudes and anxieties when her friend had been widowed and another mother had lost her only son?

One group of returning men who were particularly hard hit were those coming back from the prisoner of war camps in the Far East. They came home to a world they barely recognized. Their war had ended so suddenly after the dropping of the atomic bombs on Hiroshima and Nagasaki that their initial reaction was one of shocked surprise that the end had come so quickly. This was summed up by Lieutenant Colonel Philip Toosey, who had been in charge of the officers' camp in Kanchanaburi in Thailand:

'My reaction? I was stunned. Stunned. You have to remember what we'd gone through. And then to be told, just like that, out of the blue, the whole thing was over. My mind was stunned. Completely. My feelings had been so numbed by some of the dreadful things that had gone on that I wasn't particularly easily moved by anything by then. But gradually my mind reacted to it and then it was a feeling of tremendous joy.' That joy was tempered by the fact that many of his men would not be coming home with him. Nearly a third of prisoners taken by the Japanese had died during captivity. Fit, fighting men, reduced to physical and mental shadows of their former selves, they had watched their colleagues die of disease and neglect in their thousands.

Quite apart from the shock of what they had seen and witnessed in the fighting and as prisoners, these men had been out of the frame for so long that the developments that had taken place in the meantime bewildered them: 'We are completely foxed by expressions such as D Day, VE Day, VJ day, SEAC, Alligators, Ducks, Pythons, RAPWI, buzz bombs, atom bombs, bazookers etc. Neither do we know who are Montgomery, Supremo, Ike or Bill Slim. I suppose we shall find out bit by bit,' wrote Lieutenant Louis Baume in early September 1945 as he became a free man again.

The concerns of men, women and families were expressed by many people not through official channels but via magazines and the letters pages of newspapers. There were four topics that were aired frequently: lack of decent food (rationing remained in place until 1954); lack of fuel – this was particularly serious during the freezing, snowy winter of 1947; housing shortages, the squalor of digs, shared accommodation; and finally, women: 'our wives are exhausted' one man in the Eighth Army wrote to the *British Legion Journal*, 'some neurotic and ill through war work, lack of essential food and queuing for hours'.

While men were sometimes able to find reassurance in the company of others who had had similar experiences, such as through regimental associations and the British Legion, for the women at home there were no such official bodies. The Women's Institute, the Townswomen's Guild and other such organizations provided welcome diversions and there were lectures on re-adjustment on a local level but they were not set up to provide anything other than informal assistance. Barbara Cartland was asked by an army educational officer to give a lecture to the ATS (Auxiliary Territorial Service) about readjustment:

> He had arranged a course of lectures and he said the first was to be on Town Planning. 'Have you seen those ATS?' I asked. 'How many of them do you expect to have the chance of planning a town? First things first. Let them learn to plan a home and as things are most of them will be lucky to get a shack.' The officer was really rather annoyed but after some argument I agreed to speak only if I could speak on the home. The lecture was called 'Design in the Home'. It was simple and practical, and the girls liked it. But I know the Educational Officer thought it was far too simple.

Cartland was unrepentant. She knew it was hopeless trying to encourage people to think about strategic matters when the basics were still all awry: 'If I want to treat a pimple on my nose I don't want to take a course in facial anatomy,' she wrote huffily. 'A home is made by the people in it and principally by the woman.'

The national women's weekly *Woman's Own* seems to have been well in tune with the Zeitgeist of the mid-1940s and the pages were full of good advice for women as well as romantic stories of love affairs, broken hearts and dirty-rotter characters who desert their damsels. What an invaluable source of advice this must have been for the readers. Among the knitting patterns and cookery recipes were editorials on specific topics about life in post-war Britain and of course the agony aunt pages were dominated by questions from women on how to cope with returning men. In January 1945 the magazine published an article by Norah C. James that got to the heart of the issue of how women should deal with men coming back from the war and what their role would be. Strikingly the emphasis was on the women's ability to make everything better. In 'Back to Real Life' James wrote:

What will be the most important among all the post-war problems for women? I think the central one will be the reinstatement of the home as a family unit. The home and the family have always been an essential part of our life and no war can alter that fact. What has happened to the average home since 1939? Chiefly, its dispersal. When peace comes that dispersal will not cease because the bells of victory ring out. It goes far deeper than the mere physical return of the family. It seems to me most essential that women should prepare themselves now for the future.

She warned women that husbands, sons and even daughters would come back changed. Husbands, who before they went away, had been happy to lead quiet, regular lives, would have faced the dangers of the battlefield 'and passed through experiences so gigantic that they are bound to have left their mark on them'. She conceded that women, too, would have changed: 'Quite possibly they have become more independent since their husbands went away. They have had to shoulder responsibilities that would not have been theirs in normal times. Some women may even have learned to enjoy the independence of salaries of their own. Giving these up may not be too easy.'

It was the long-term, slow-burn, below-the-surface problems that would cause families the greatest difficulties. James was not saying anything radical, after all, this had been the experience of women after the First World War, the mothers and sisters of the current generation, but she was putting the onus for tackling the post-war years on women. There was a sense that they held the key to making the future better for their men and children, that they had a duty of sacrifice in response to everything the men had fought for in the last six years: 'That is woman's main task in the reconstruction of life after the war. She will be the mainspring of a new and better way of living.' To women who were exhausted by having had to cope during the war years, who had brought children up alone, worried constantly about what was happening to their men, struggled with rationing and survived the Blitz, it seemed harsh that now they were expected by other women in positions to comment, as much as by the men in power, to pick up the post-war pieces and create stability in the aftermath.

The magazine's agony aunt from 1932 was the novelist and journalist Leonora Eyles, who became the trusted confidante of thousands of women who read her columns and wrote to her with their problems. She became the first famous agony aunt before Marjorie Proops and with her experience of living in poverty and difficult circumstances before the First World War she wrote with genuine kindness and understanding in response to her correspondents' concerns. One woman wrote to her addressing the topic that filled the agony pages of the magazine for the greater part of 1945: 'While my husband was a prisoner of war for over three years I just lived for him to come home and so did the children. But now that he is home I feel wretched. We do nothing but squabble; he seems a stranger to the children; and has lost all his nice ways with me. I am almost in despair.'

Leonora replied: 'So much depends on you, my dear, on your tact and gentle understanding. He has been through dreadful experiences which he probably won't talk about; the children probably hurt him too, because they formed a fairy-tale idea of him, and the poor man doesn't live up to it. I had a similar situation to face with my husband in the last war and if you care to let me have your address I will explain how I coped with a situation which often seemed beyond me.'

On 1 June 1945 another woman wrote to her: 'My husband is coming home after four years in a German prison; I lost my head two years ago, and had a baby. I made up my mind that I would keep it whatever happened, but now I have read about the sufferings of prisoners, I feel I cannot face my husband and let him know I was disloyal. He may forgive me in time but how can I greet him, ill and crippled, with this child?'

Leonora replied: 'I am glad you see that now; I know that few men in [his] state would be fit, physically or nervously, to face a story of infidelity. They are even nervous when we townsfolk ask them in to a meal. I urge you at once to find a foster mother through your local Welfare Officer and go to work to pay for the baby's keep. Later if your husband will forgive you, he may take the baby as his; or if you will write to me I will tell you on what terms some homes may take it.'

In the 22 June 1945 issue Leonora Eyles published an article about returning German prisoners of war. She dealt with the subject head on: 'Our town is at present full of repatriated prisoners and sometimes I feel sorry for them. They are all here because they are not yet well enough to go home, and when I talked to the Matron of their hospital recently she gave me some little sidelights on their needs.'

The first question was that of food and she reminded her readers that men who had been starving would have to be fed as if they were small children: 'his thinness is not only on the surface of his body, his digestive organs have also lost tone and power and cannot cope with the amount of food he craves. Small meals and often should be the rule. A drink won't hurt him, especially beer, but don't let his thoughtless friends give him too much.'

Men would have shattered nerves, she went on to explain, and would have to be treated with great care, as if they were an invalid. 'You wouldn't allow crowds in the house if your husband was ill with pneumonia, would you?' she asked them to consider. 'Well, treat him as carefully as you can by keeping crowds away.' This was all excellent advice and far more useful in many ways than the official advice published in documents that were distributed by the government.

She urged women to encourage men to talk about their experiences, something that was quite out of keeping with the army's recommendations to their returning prisoners, in particular. 'Let him get it off his chest,' she encouraged. 'If he sits silent and gloomy, let him alone. As a sick animal goes into a corner and wants to be alone, so does a man with a sick mind and body.'

'Lastly,' she wrote, 'there is the wife's side of the problem. She has been living in comparatively peaceful Britain – yes, I say "peaceful" in spite of bombs and overwork and queues. You have been looking forward to a new honeymoon, a little glamour, perhaps a little relaxation of your heavy burden of responsibility. But you can't have it yet.'

The educational psychologist K.M. Catlin wrote in similar vein in *Home & Country*, the Women's Institute magazine, in June 1945: 'Don't expect to pick up the threads just where you dropped them. It may be necessary to go back a bit – to get a little nearer your courting attitude when you weren't quite so sure of each other and couldn't afford to take things for granted, but rather set out to please and win the other's affection.'

There it was. The woman had her work cut out. Hers was to be the responsibility to create a new homely order out of the mess left behind by six years of war. She would have to be patient, caring and loving but above all practical. She would not be able to take a well-earned rest or expect to have the burden of responsibility lifted from her shoulders. One wife, now in her nineties, commented to a neighbour: 'When their war ended, our war began.'

2

AN IRON RATION OF LOVE: THE VALUE OF COMMUNICATION

Letters for us stand for love, longing, light-heartedness and lyricism. Letters evoke passion, tenderness, amusement, sadness, rejoicing, surprise. And none of this is possible without the Army Post Office.

Diana Hopkinson

The families who seemed to fare best in the immediate aftermath of the Second World War were those who had been able to communicate their thoughts and feelings during the long months and years of separation. It made no difference what background people came from, if they were able to share their day-to-day lives freely by whatever means, it helped them readjust to home life afterwards. Most communication during the war was by letter and some families exchanged hundreds of letters with their husbands, wives, children or parents. This chapter considers the importance of communication and looks at how it helped people to come back home and take up their places within the family and, in time, in society.

In the six years of war the army postal service handled thousands of millions of letters and parcels to and from conflict zones throughout the world. In every diary written during the war there are references to the arrival or non-arrival of the post. Crushing disappointment when nothing came, euphoria at the delivery of a letter from a loved one, smugness that you had one and your neighbour did not, sadness that he had one and you did not. And at home the post was just as eagerly awaited. 'No letter from Jack this week' or 'I am sure you have written but I haven't received any letters from you for a fortnight and I do so worry when I don't hear from you.' 'Bliss oh bliss! Four letters in one day. I jumped into bed, pulled the covers up to my nose and breathed in your news.' The value of postal communication and exchange of information between servicemen and women and their families is hard to overestimate.

It is easy to read unimaginable statistics describing numbers of letters sent to and from the United Kingdom during the war and to take the post for granted but perhaps a brief history of the army postal service, this vital line of communication that kept many relationships going, will help to underline the extraordinary organization of this vital link.

In 1795 an Act of Parliament was passed 'allowing seamen, NCOs and soldiers to "send and receive letters by the post on their own private concerns" at a special low rate of one penny per letter, which was to be paid when the letter was posted'. The overarching reason for the introduction of this generous gesture was in fact to prevent loss of revenue which resulted from soldiers being unable to pay the accumulated postage on readdressed letters when they caught up with them. The side effect, as it were, of this legislation, was to encourage men to write home.

Not many ordinary soldiers in the nineteenth century were literate but as literacy increased so the number of letters sent home increased too. The post was originally handled by civilian postal workers but this was phased out after the Crimean War and the army took responsibility for its own post.

In early 1913, eighteen months before the outbreak of the First World War, the Army Post Office Corps became a special reserve unit of the Royal Engineers. They took on the title of Royal Engineers Postal Section (REPS) and had, at the outbreak of war, 10 officers and 294 ORs (other ranks) which was sufficient for a force of six divisions. Of course, as the size of the army swelled during the early years of the Great War, so did the need for care to avoid military information about troop movements and so on falling into enemy hands. Censorship was introduced and the army issued a pamphlet entitled *Censorship Order and Regulations for Troops in the Field* in November 1916 which listed nine subjects that the censor would not permit, including 'comments on the effects of hostile fire, the physical and moral conditions of the troops and details of defensive works'.

By the outbreak of the Second World War the REPS was well organized and determined to keep post going under as many circumstances as it could. REPS personnel began to move to France on 4 September 1939, several weeks before the first troops of the British Expeditionary Force. The first post office was set up in Chanzy Barracks at Le Mans and in December that year a route from Folkestone to Boulogne was opened and the front-line troops received and sent their mail via Amiens.

Throughout the Phoney War the postal service worked remarkably well. When the Germans launched the Blitzkrieg on 10 May 1940 the REPS's prearranged contingency plans were put into effect but the speed of the German advance disrupted the rate at which the postal service could operate: 'The stationery office at Boulogne was destroyed by bombing on 19 May and the staff on duty there were killed. The following day the Germans reached the coast at Abbeville, thereby cutting off the Base PO at Le Havre from the troops fighting north of it, for whom on 27 May the postal authorities had 26,000 bags of undeliverable mail.' But in spite of the problems of the rapid German advance the average time for a letter posted in the United Kingdom to reach its addressee in France or Belgium was two and a half days.

As the war progressed, so did the extent of the REPS' work. In July 1940 personnel were sent to Egypt and Palestine to establish a Base Post Office. The Second World War was highly mobile and the Army Postal Service learned valuable lessons, which meant it was able to cope with the rapid advance through Italy. But perhaps its most spectacular planning came prior to D-Day in 1944. 'In the planning for operation OVERLORD it was decided that letters would be delivered in Normandy on D+1, newspapers on D+4 and parcels on D+6, using air transport as soon as airstrips became available.' According to Peter Boyden of the National Army Museum, the first REPS men arrived in Normandy by parachute on the morning of 6 June 1944 and by the end of D-Day the forty postal staff in France had opened three stationery post offices.

On D-Day itself a surgeon tending a badly wounded man on the beach heard his name spoken, looked up and was handed a buff envelope by a triumphant lance corporal who had located him with great difficulty. He opened it to find an income tax demand.

This extraordinary postal operation was planned by Brigadier James Drew on Montgomery's orders. In 1944 alone his unit succeeded in dispatching some 340 million letters, 95 million packets and 13 million parcels. James Norris Drew had entered the Post Office in 1933 as an assistant traffic superintendent (telephones). In 1938 he became assistant surveyor and as a Royal Engineer officer in the Army Supplementary Reserve he became closely involved with the Army Postal Service. Described as a tall, powerfully built man with an awe-inspiring handlebar moustache, Drew had an ability to achieve apparently impossible objectives which made him a legendary figure in the services.

The great success of this operation was due in part to the army's recognition of the importance to the morale of the servicemen of being in contact with their families. Tank crews in the desert, riflemen in the Burmese jungle, ambulance crews in France and Italy, and men in every part of the service could be sure that their mail would reach them. Certainly reading letters written during the war it is indisputable that this brought untold comfort and reassurance to men in the field, as indeed it did to their families back home. Naturally not all news was good and several hundred thousand families received a War Office telegram or letter to say that a serviceman had been wounded or killed.

The value of correspondence, especially for men who were away for years, was summed up by an editorial in *Woman's Own* in September 1945:

Those letters have transported me home every single day, writes an RAF reader, telling me how much, during his five years of service, his wife's faithful letters have meant to him. She used to apologize for having 'no real news' yet apparently her letters (1,825 of them he reckons!) have been entirely satisfactory to him. Not one day passed when she did not put down a line or two about the day's events.

Through her daily letters I have followed the progress of a chubby three-months-old babe I left, into the wiry schoolboy of five . . . Lately his adventures at the prep school have dominated, and the quaint philosophic musings of this five-year-old sage, while relating his daily doings over tea to his mother, have been good to read . . .

This RAF father almost could smell the flowers in his garden through his wife's vivid chronicles. She did not forget to tell him that she put the copper beech leaves in his favourite yellow vase. His home has been with him all the time, whatever his hardships.

Separation is not over yet, for many families – and the less eventful days of peacetime service probably move more slowly. I hope the pens at home are as busy and comradely as that of my correspondent's wife – who apologized for having no real news.

As the war began to draw to a close the nature of people's correspondence began to change. For now it was clear that people who had been living apart from one another for months and more often than not, years, would be reunited. As women turned their attention towards the future they also began to worry about what it would be like when the men came home, and indeed the men began to wonder what they would find when they came home.

Eve Boxall was married to an architect, Gordon, who served abroad, in Italy and Africa from March 1943 to November 1945. The couple had a daughter, Sally, born in June 1943. They lived on the Isle of Sheppey in Kent so that Eve was aware all the time of the proximity of the war to England. This gave Gordon great cause for anxiety and he was horrified when, in July 1944, he learned through her letters that she had had to move downstairs to sleep in the Morrison shelter in the dining room because of the threat of bombing. Being away from Britain he had no way of knowing how much danger his wife and daughter were in, so his letters of that period were full of concern for their safety. For her part Eve had no idea initially where her husband was posted and he was unable to tell her, but he dropped tantalizing hints in his first letters about blackberry bushes and lemon trees and other plants.

The two kept up a regular correspondence throughout the two and a half years he was abroad and there is a sense in the letters of the way their relationship matured while he was away. Eve's letters were full of tales on the one hand of how she was learning to cope living on her own and running the house and on the other of Sally's development: 'While I was playing with Sally today, patting her long brown legs I felt so sad that you're not here to hear her trying to talk,' she wrote, when Sally was just fourteen weeks old. Then she learned that Gordon had been fighting in Salerno, which made her feel proud of him: 'But the anxiety of it too, when I think that at this very moment that I'm lying in bed writing this you might be in some dangerous spot.' In another letter she wrote in ecstatic language having heard of his being awarded the Military Cross. Although this was all happening at a distance, there was a sense that she felt almost as if she were having a conversation with him: 'I feel quite sick with excitement. I just don't know how to write. I expect you know what I've heard. Oh darling, didn't you know anything about it? Listen to this: "for gallant and distinguished service in Italy Lieut (temporary captain) Gordon Charles Boxall RA Isle of Sheppey has been awarded the Military Cross." Again I've got that sick feeling as I write, oh <u>darling</u>.'

As the war progressed so the tone of Eve's letters became more intense. Gordon's letters to her were more than mere correspondence. They kept her going day to day:

Darling there you go again talking of boring me. You <u>can't</u> do, my sweet. But I <u>hate</u> the sound of the shelling of the road to . . . Hate it! Hate the rain, hate <u>everything</u> you have to put up with. But I feel happy my letters help & you keep saying they do. Well, I just can't describe the lovely warm feeling your letters give me. I take the pages to bed with me & they do make me flush & I just want to give and give and give. And I feel that I just want you to go on asking and asking what you want me to do, so that I can please you.

Gordon's letters, too, were full of his thoughts and dreams about their reunion which, at that stage, he hoped would be very soon, but Eve felt that it was bad luck to dream of such happiness. In November 1944 she wrote:

I never thought that this separation would last at least 2 years. Never. What a <u>mercy</u> we didn't know. Darling, I know I haven't changed and even if you think I have as you say, you can always change me back again and I'll soon change you back again. I think it inevitable that you will show signs of what you have endured, but darling I will be able to make you forget the horrors, won't I? I'm sure I will, I just won't let you remember. I shall only let you think of me, while you're lying back in my arms. I shall be most hurt if you don't think just about me. And Sally – oh she will give you joy, all being well, to hear her giggle, when she peeps under the table to say 'Bo'. She can play all those games indefinitely.

The separation was to continue. VE Day came and went without any news of when Gordon might be demobbed. He was suffering from anxiety and wrote on 16 June 1945:

I'm in poor shape mentally where you are concerned, darling, as I am anxious about you and I can see no answer to it until we are reunited. All I can say darling is to remind you that the time is approaching when I can be with you and when we can face all these crises together. I don't underrate the nervous strain under which we are living now – Indeed I recognize it to be a great

danger to our health – but at the same time we must defeat it as
we've defeated all the other strains.

By September he was still abroad but they believed he would
be home in weeks rather than months. Eve had moved house and
was now planning for his actual return. In amongst all the excitement she wrote very perceptively about what was to come and
how she had changed:

> . . . this rushing about I've done, this feverish sewing, is all for
> you. Amazing to think it's the same man that I was getting ready
> for 7 years ago; but what a difference this time. There's more
> depth in my feeling, we have Sally now, we've been through quite
> a lot, you so much more than me, we were almost children then,
> but it was very sweet. This time, oh I feel <u>years</u> older. I <u>have</u> got
> more confidence, but I've a <u>certain</u> feeling that it's <u>you</u> who's
> going to give me confidence when you come back, all being well.
> I know it because you are so sure of yourself now. Oh darling,
> honestly – together I have no fear of the future, with God's help.

Gordon Boxall was finally demobbed in November 1945 and the
correspondence stops there with no reference to how life settled
down after the war. One thing that was clear in the Boxall correspondence, which dates back to early 1943, was that one or
other of them had censored the most intimate letters before they
were given to the museum. They are nevertheless wonderful
because they present both sides of the story and the reader is able
to trace through the letters so many details about everyday life,
about the development of the war, about the introduction of
increasing restrictions and rationing and of course the relationship between Gordon and Eve.

Another husband and wife exchange was written up into a

wonderful memoir now in the IWM archives. In 1986 Diana Hopkinson wrote her story, with her husband's agreement, using their vast correspondence of over 500 letters that they had written to each other between 1941 and 1944. David Hopkinson had strained at the marriage leash while he was living in the Middle East for three years and the memoir is an honest account of how she came to terms with his affairs.

Diana and David had married before the war and in 1940 she was expecting their first child. 'I lived in a curious betwixt and between world. A wife by courtesy of such few hours of freedom as the Army allowed David, a visitor in someone else's house which freed me from those minor worries which at that stage of the war were all that rationing involved, and exempt from any of the women's services because of my pregnancy. Privileged I might be, yet I was still adrift on currents of war which carried millions all over Europe into seas forlorn.' David was in the army and his brother, Dick, in the RAF. Dick was shot down over Stavanger in Norway in July 1940:

> Thus we tasted the first bitterness of loss caused by a war in which it was still difficult wholly to believe. It was being said that this could not be a war of mass slaughter, like the last, and indeed the British losses never mounted to those catastrophic heights. But for us, this was the first of many sacrificial deaths amongst those dear and young. These losses have never ceased to be part of the life we subsequently lived. They left us totally bereft of our closest male friends, who never have been replaced.

Diana's son, Thomas, was born just before David left to go abroad. She was distraught with grief when he finally went. She packed up her possessions and prepared to move to her parents-in-law's house in the country. As she tidied what he had left behind she was struck by how little he had taken with him: 'It seemed to me that the personal possessions he had taken abroad were so minimal that he must be feeling as if he had shed his identity.' For the next three years she had to survive on letters. There were times, she wrote, when she felt a profound and sometimes devastating loneliness. 'The whole complicated pattern of messages which passed between us disturbed our sense of the sequence of events. A speedy aerograph would refer to the conclusion of some subject, long before we had received the letter which described its initiation. Time was stood on its head.' In 1942 David had a severe bout of malaria, complicated by dysentery, and was in hospital for several weeks. Diana was distracted with worry for him and wept bitter tears into the blueberry jam she was boiling. Their letters at this time were full of anxiety about how their emotional life was on hold:

> If we had lived in happier times our love might have spread wider but not been more intense. I mean that separation, wars and troubles cannot affect in any way the strength we have through the depth of our love though at other times we might have been able to spread it more widely, to indulge it, to make other people feel the benefit of it. Now everything is intense – an iron ration of love to be lived in a confined space; to love is a deep well in a desert, an air-raid shelter in a town, not to wander across cliffs and meadows, but to keep a small bright fire alight and a jet of water at a hidden spring.

When David came out of hospital he was sent to Jerusalem, given a commission and became an army educational officer. Life in the city disturbed him with its trappings of normality, European-style shops and constant reminders of what he was missing at home.

This deepens my personal sense of loss and sometimes centres it on a single point – the sexual deprivation. After all the physical is the one link of our love which has been cut off dead. In every other respect we exert some mastery over space, using mind, memory and imagination, sharing our thoughts in letters. But I cannot touch you . . . there is no sign with which I can seal you now. Nothing that paper will carry. You may remember that I have murmured, sinking into sleep beside you, 'Diana my precious, you are good, so good.' Then you had become like the earth, the sun or a river, little oasis of white flesh in a barren world, a principle, a function, an element, life-giving, healing, fertile.

In the summer of 1942 he wrote what she described as an ominous letter. He quoted Benjamin Franklin who had given advice to a young man saying that if he must take a mistress let it be a woman much older than himself as it will be a greater pleasure to her. Diana suddenly understood the significance of all his earlier letters when he had hinted that sex was the one thing that was missing in his life and indeed, in the next letter, he explained that 'fidelity or infidelity had no dominion in this tragic wartime situation. He had suggested that sexually we should go our separate ways finding what consolation we could derive, and what degree of satisfaction we could give, in relationships with others.' Diana became used to him mentioning brief encounters with women but it was his affair with an older married woman that really troubled her for she sensed that there was closeness in the relationship that threatened her own marriage. At home she was caught up with looking after her baby son and it was not easy for her to find another partner. Nor was she sure she wanted one. However in 1943 she had a brief affair, which she described as a disaster: 'All we had to give each other was affectionate pity as was soon revealed in that unsatisfactory and unsatisfying night together. I was left in no doubt that there could be no fulfilment for me until David returned.' She wrote and told David about the incident and it had a disturbing effect on him. He gave up his relationship with the older woman and made enquiries about whether he could be posted back to Britain.

In February 1944 Diana heard that David would be coming home imminently. Her joy was unbounded. She told Thomas, now three, that he would soon be seeing his daddy for the first time. 'Will he be coming after tea?' Thomas asked, and then a little later, after looking thoughtfully at David's photograph in the frame on the sideboard, said: 'How will he get out of his frame?' To David she wrote: 'Lord, oh Lord, how slowly the days pass now. Are you a mile – an hour – nearer me? As I clean my room, I wonder whether I am sweeping the bridal chamber. Your return has somehow a classical or biblical feeling. Ulysses? No – that is not a fortunate analogy. I haven't twenty suitors – not even one – and I weave no tapestry – except for the darns in my stockings.'

A few days later, she put on her smartest old petticoat and a flimsy dress under her Siberian coat and waited in a pub opposite the station in Hungerford:

When the train came in I was on the platform. A few huddled figures passed. At the far end I saw one tall figure hauling luggage out of the guards van. I ran up ready to throw myself into David's arms, but instead stumbled over his luggage which lay between us and nearly fell. Laughing he caught me up and murmured, as if he had rehearsed it, 'My bride, my darling . . .' I had never seen him wearing an officer's cap and his seemed quite different from anyone else's. His strange uniform, his strangely thin face, glimpsed in the dimmest light gave me a feeling of artificiality. Even in our kisses there was something unreal.

Only when we had reached Ivy Cottage and stood looking

down at Thomas, our sleeping son, unrecognizable to David from the baby he had left – did I begin to realize that we had at long last truly come together. But I was still to learn, before we slept, that there was to be a terrible sadness for him to overcome.

Diana had to tell him that his friend Pat had been killed. He had been a close friend of David's at Oxford and after going their separate ways after university they had begun writing to one another again during the war.

When I did so the effect on David was devastating. Joy and serenity went out of him; shock and horror took their place. He looked like a man grimly enduring trial by ordeal. Then he turned away from me in the bed and did not speak. I caught my breath in fear. Moments passed before I put my hand on his shoulder, lightly. When at last he turned towards me we made love as if we were partners in a solemn rite, strange, speechless but familiar.

Not everyone was able to correspond as freely or as frequently as the Boxalls and the Hopkinsons. The Army Postal Service worked well in Europe, North Africa, India and the Middle East, where by and large the terms of operating for the service had been agreed, even in enemy territory, and letters and parcels were sent and received in their millions. In the Far East the problems were formidable. The reason it is important to consider this situation is that for those who were unable to communicate with their families and sweethearts during the war, readjustment in the post-war years was generally more traumatic and difficult than for those who had been in regular contact.

Communication with Far Eastern prisoners of war was affected by the deliberate holding back of letters for the prison camps. Partly it was due to the complexity of handling the millions of letters destined for men in disparate camps all over South East Asia. In part it was due to the desire of the Japanese to censor the mail and the logistical problems that that threw up but it was also that the Japanese saw there was no reason to put their scarce human resources into helping the POWs. Apart from a postcard sent before leaving Singapore, it was not until late 1942 or early 1943 that most prisoners of war in Burma were given a postcard to send home with pre-printed sentences for the POWs to tick as appropriate and three lines for a personal message. In Thailand POWs were also given cards to send back to their loved ones and there were strict rules applied as to what could or could not be communicated. They could not, for instance, put a date or their POW number on the card and all the cards were censored, so that information had to be bland. Cards were on the whole sent through Tokyo and on via the Middle East so that the earliest delivery in the UK was in July and August 1943, a full eighteen months after the men had been taken prisoner. The Japanese in Burma would only allow working men to send cards home so that if a man were sick on the day the cards were distributed they would not have the opportunity to send a message to their families. The effect on the morale of the sick men can only be imagined. Communication, however imperfect, was a lifeline and this seemed to be a particularly cruel deceit to play on the prisoners.

Incoming mail from home was monstrously delayed in the Far East. Nevertheless a few letters did get through. To men who received letters they were a vital link with a world back home that many had not seen for years. To those who did not receive them it was a matter of enormous disappointment and often led to recriminations against those whose post had found its way through the vagaries of the system. The first significant consignment of letters for prisoners of war arrived in Singapore in

March 1943, 250,000 in total, many addressed to men who had already been transferred to Thailand. John Coast wrote in his memoir about his feelings when his first letter arrived: 'Well I remember sitting on the floor of Nut's tent, reading my first letter from home for fifteen months, tears in my eyes, and once again remembering that somewhere on the same earth people existed who did seem to mind what happened to you.'

For many men communication from home gave them something to hang on to, something to focus their minds on survival rather than giving in to the harsh circumstances. Alfred Allbury received five letters from home in July 1943. His wife had written in detail about the everyday goings-on at home and this thrilled him: 'I read that . . . my boy, not quite two, wanted to know when I was coming home to see him; that the beans were doing nicely in the garden. . . . There were other snippets, news of friends and relatives that left me quieted, softened and filled with nostalgic longing. There was much for me to get back to.'

Occasionally the Japanese used the mail as a form of punishment or torture. Major General Sitwell told his daughter Mollie that one of the cruellest things the Japanese ever did, in his opinion, was to burn unopened mail in front of prisoners on the parade ground. This same trick was played on prisoners in Burma. Seven men had attempted to escape from the camp but had been recaptured and the camp commandant, 'Captain Suzuki', called all the men to parade and told them:

'Today, for the first time we have received mail through the international Red Cross in Bangkok . . . No doubt many of you are wondering if there are letters for you amongst this mountain of mail. But it matters not in view of the very serious matter that has come to my attention [the escaped prisoners] . . . In view of what has happened, it becomes necessary for me to punish the whole camp by destroying those mailbags.' As the words sank in, an audible gasp of dismay went up from the POWs. Captain Suzuki beckoned forward two guards, who appeared with lighted torches and promptly plunged them into the twelve bags of mail, the POWs' only possible link with home, making sure they were entirely destroyed in the roaring inferno.

The importance of postal communication was emphasized again at the end of the war when POWs, for the first time, could write letters unhindered by censorship or fear of recrimination by the Japanese. For most men the delay before they got home was two and a half to three months. Often they were unable to write anything very much about their experiences – how indeed could three and a half years of suffering be summed up in a letter?

Two correspondents from the Far East were unusually perceptive about their post-release situations and made efforts to try to convey something of the essence of what they had been through to their wives back home. The letters would serve as an introduction to the 'new them' but also as a warning about what to expect. In 1945 Kenneth Davey was a 34-year-old regular army regimental sergeant major. He had been in the 18th Division that went out to Singapore in 1941, months after his marriage to Joyce 'Joy' Lloyd. Between 6 September and 19 October 1945 he wrote thirty-seven long letters that paint a vivid picture of the dawning realization of what freedom would mean to prisoners of war from the Far East.

RSM Davey was captured along with over 51,000 other Commonwealth and Allied troops by the Japanese in Singapore on 15 February 1942. For fourteen months he was held in Changi POW camp on Singapore Island until the Japanese called for 7,000 fit men to be sent up to Thailand to work on the railway that the Japanese were constructing between Bangkok and Moulmein in

Burma. Known to many as the Death Railway, the Thailand–Burma Railway ran for 415 kilometres through some of the most inhospitable jungle country on earth. It is said that a man died for every sleeper laid. A total of 12,619 Commonwealth, Dutch and American prisoners died during its construction. Davey and his men were told that they were to be sent to a country where they would have better food than in Singapore, where there would be plenty of space and recreation, a little light work and, above all, no marches. The reality for the prisoners of 'F' and 'H' Force who went up from Singapore to Thailand in April 1943 could not have been more different. After a four-day train journey in metal rice trucks up the Malaya peninsula the men, at least 30 per cent of whom were unfit to leave Singapore, let alone carry out any work, were marched 200 miles up into the jungle to a place close to the Thailand–Burma border called Songkurai, or Sonkrai, a name that for many prisoners became synonymous with death.

In May 1943 cholera broke out in the region and ripped through the jungle camps killing hundreds of British, Australian and Dutch prisoners as well as thousands of Asian labourers who had been forced by the Japanese to work on the railway. Here Davey witnessed men starving to death, dying of cholera, dysentery, malaria, beriberi and jungle ulcers. He watched as they gave up the fight for life and all the time he was completely alone. The role of a regimental sergeant major, even in the POW camps, was a solitary one, he told his wife in one of his first post-war letters: 'It's been lonely during all this time, horribly lonely – to exercise the leadership which has been my lot I have had to steer a straight monotonous course – never looking sideways for a moment – never letting up for a single second, and now I'm weary of it all – weary of the sweat, the toil and the blood – and very near to tears.' No communication other than his memories of Joy had been possible but it had helped, nevertheless:

Heaven bless you for your faith and courage, Joy – when things got pretty dark out here I assure you that you kept me going – the number of men who literally just gave up was terrible, many just lost heart, stopped eating the awful muck the Japs gave us and died. Particularly on the Railway, that awful bloody railway – bloody is the word – a life for every sleeper. The best literary description in the world could never cause the imagination of a person who was not there to understand what it was like. You will hear many stories in the press and so on and the ghastly thing is the stories can't be exaggerated. It's all horribly true.

After his release Davey had to wait weeks to be repatriated and during this time he stayed in a camp in Singapore and recuperated by eating, sleeping, writing and reading. 'Everything is fascinating and I haven't begun yet. I tore outside a few days ago to see a jeep and since then I think I've crawled all over one of them. I must have stood fully two minutes looking at a telephone until I realized how stupidly I was behaving – and any sudden noise and I'm halfway to the roof before it happens and that's odd because the air-raids here – the noise – didn't make me jump.'

The value of this correspondence is that it was written over a short and intensive period. His mood swings from utter euphoria . . . 'The shackles are off! That our freedom should be given so suddenly is simply staggering – I have to continually trot outside to make sure that the union jack is still on the flag mast, and I'm getting quite blue in places with pinching myself. The fact that I am writing to you Dear makes it more real – but I do feel a little giddy and light headed' . . . to anxiety and worry about the future: 'I'm trying so hard to be just like I was when you last saw me so that I won't scare you and you'll still love me but I'm afraid I look older and I'm worried that the privations of Sonkrai are in my face – and my manners. Oh Dear I'm scared stiff of girls and polite conversation and clever people – and my emotions.'

On 30 September he wrote:

> We've been studying very carefully the psychological reaction of everyone – including myself, on the effect that our freedom has caused and almost without exception we've all got an inferiority complex. I say 'almost' with the possible exception of Lt Col Dillon. It's rife among officers particularly and although it must be only a temporary handicap for us all it does cause some to do the oddest things. In my own case there is a shadow in the dim distance which insists that I am now quite beneath your notice – I did no great things in six years of war – whilst others have seen much of the scrapping and are the heroes. Oh well – I hope the feeling soon passes for me.

The temporary handicap he referred to turned out to be less temporary for many than he thought. The feeling, whether overt or subliminal, that the prisoners of war had suffered a humiliating defeat that would forever be on their records and conscience is one of the least discussed but widely felt aspects of their captivity. Another POW summed it neatly when he said: 'If my grandchildren ask me what I did during the war I shall have to tell them I ran like hell twice, and the second time we ran out of land.' He might have said it with a smile but it covered up a much deeper feeling of frustration.

Kenneth Davey's letters frightened Joy and although there are no copies of her responses in the collection, it is evident from his later correspondence that she was alarmed by the 'savage' that was about to appear in her life: 'Don't get scared,' he wrote to her on 14 October from the ship. 'There isn't a thing to be scared about – I'm your normal Ken and I love you and I'm going to make you very happy. I'll be ever so careful not to frighten you my darling and you'll be unfrozen before you know where you are – in fact you are going to be quite warm and never allowed to freeze again.' But then he added, in the same letter: 'Whilst it occurs to me Joy – I have developed a nervous habit of rubbing my hands together when I am not quite myself. I mean under some sort of nervous strain. If ever you see me doing that will you be my saviour and put your hand on my shoulder or steer the subject into other channels – please remember to do this for me.'

Kenneth Davey arrived in Britain at the end of October 1945 and reached home in Richmond in Yorkshire a few days later. The correspondence stops on his arrival but the remaining letters in the collection, written after the war, show that he very quickly slipped back into life at home. In 1946 Joyce gave birth to their first child, a daughter, Josephine Sonkrai Davey. Davey was determined that she would carry this name and had written about it to Joyce before he came back: 'If we have a daughter, darling, can her second name be SONKRAI (pronounced Song-Cry) as a memorial to all my men who won't be coming back this way and many of who sleep their long sleep at Sonkrai in the north jungles of Thailand.'

A son, Simon, was born in 1948 and Kenneth was sent out to Jamaica in 1949 with the army. Davey's letters had helped, the family was in no doubt, to prepare Joyce and his family for what to expect of him on his return. 'Joyce had been used to being told from the time of her marriage what she should do and to some extent what she should think,' explained Barbara Lamb. 'The letters home gave her all the information she needed about Kenneth so that she would be prepared and know what to expect when he came home.' In 1955 Kenneth Davey went into hospital for an operation on his liver and died unexpectedly on the operating table. He had almost never spoken to his children about his captivity and all that his daughter Jo knew was that Marmite had kept him alive and that palm oil had saved his sight. He had not even explained to her where her extraordinary middle name came from. It was not until she found the letters that she read the whole story. In 2004 Jo died of leukaemia. Before she died she visited her mother, who was in an old people's home suffering from dementia. She wanted to tell her mother how serious her illness was. The old lady could not really understand what her daughter was telling her but she suddenly began to cry and said to Jo: 'It was only one kiss you know. He was away for such a long time and I thought he would never come back.' It was only then that Jo understood that her mother had had a brief dalliance with another man during the war but it made her understand better the reassurances that her father had given Joy in his letters home.

On Saturday 18 August 1945 Charles Steel wrote his last letter as a prisoner. He had not, like some others, written a diary during his captivity, but had written letters to his wife, Louise, which he had kept successfully hidden from the Japanese for three and a half years:

So, my dear, at last it is over. There is every possibility now of you reading these letters very soon. I see that I managed my objective of one per week – 3½ years, that is 182 – and you have two over. At times, I was behind my average, at times in front . . . Our link with each other has not been broken. Tomorrow I shall write you my first letter as a free man. Soon I shall be writing you daily letters again . . . Soon our letters won't be necessary. Soon we shall be together again . . .

Over the next weeks Charles wrote regularly to Louise, revealing his hopes and dreams for his freedom but also dropping little hints about eccentricities she might be worried by: 'I am rather wary of hot baths at the moment,' he wrote, when he was offered one by the RAF, 'so went for a magnificent swim in the drain around the paddy field – probably my last swim in the nude.' Then he received a letter from Louise: 'Yesterday, I got your first letter and answered it straight away. Say, darling, did it give me a kick or didn't it!! I felt like pushing a house over.'

A week before Charles Steel sailed into Liverpool to meet his wife for the first time in four years he wrote her a long letter in response to her anxieties about whether they would get on with one another after such a period of separation:

Darling, let's clear up a point raised in one of your letters. It is about the 'altering' business during our separation. I know at first glance a difference in each other might have taken place and is likely – after all, for the last four years you have been mixing with the upper classes and I with the lower – but does this conclusion bear logical examination?

For the first 25 years of our lives we have been living very much the same lives. We come from similar middle class stock, we come from middle class families, we were both educated at secondary schools. We did similar types of work, we enjoyed similar types of pleasure. Our attitudes towards politics and religion are similar. Is this quarter of a century of similarity going to be completely affected by four years of different living? Of course it isn't.

And take another view. One of the most comforting things which your letters have told me is that you are still in close touch with our old friends and acquaintances. What is more, you are hoping to renew those friendships. Would this be the case if you had altered in any way or if some of your acquaintances, since you obtained a temporary commission, had blinded you with the lustre of the upper classes? Of course it wouldn't. To hear you talking about Iris and Albert, Jack Perkins, George Lane and the rest, means that you are still the Louie I love and not a person whose

43

exhilarating experiences of the last four years have gone to her head. To hear you talking about cooking for the family is as balm to my soul.

You see, I am sure that we shall come together quite naturally because I see, quite clearly, a scene in our garden in forty years' time. You will be reading these letters and I shall be gardening, and I shall come over to you with the loveliest rose I can find. As I pin it to your shawl, I can see you look up and hear you say, 'Darling, what silly children we were to think that a mere war would alter our love for each other!' And I shall kiss you, because I shall still love you . . .

Charles and Louise were married for over fifty years and made two trips to the Far East in the 1970s when Charles was able to show Louise where he had been a prisoner. Margaret, their daughter, remembers her mother telling her that when he was there he just lay on the ground in the cemeteries and wept. 'With hindsight those visits must have been hugely emotional.' His biographer, Brian Best, concluded: 'Far from being a broken man he put his experiences behind him and made his dreams during captivity come true.'

Margaret remembered her father as a particularly well-balanced man who never seemed to have a bad word to say about anyone. He would not allow her to read his letters to Louise while he was alive, however, and that was something she never understood. Occasionally he would let something slip about his past, but never with any bitterness, and sometimes these comments came out at strange times. 'The showstopper was one day in a September at my son's school when Daddy suddenly said: "Today was the date I should have been shot!" referring to the order given to the Japanese that all POWs would be executed in late September 1945.'

3

THE HOMECOMING AND THE IMMEDIATE AFTERMATH

Two and a half years! Back only a fortnight and she doesn't know what to do with him. He sits in the back room by himself. Won't speak to anybody, won't go out, won't read. Won't do nothing. She doesn't know what to do. There'll be trouble there!

Unnamed correspondent

For every individual family the homecoming was a significant event. One to look forward to in most cases, but there is a sense in many cases that the long-awaited day did not fulfil either side's hopes and expectations.

They came home in various moods. Some so weary they could hardly think straight, some so bitter and disillusioned it was almost like brain damage. Some came home cheerful, hopeful and raring to get back into civvy street. Actually they were the ones who suffered most. Civvy street, as they knew it, no longer existed. Civvy street was beaten into the ground by fear, shortages and sheer weariness.

Some had no homes to go to, no jobs, no families even. They couldn't drown their sorrows in drink because drink was in short supply. Cigarettes and sweets were hard to get too. Most of us had our little hoard where we painstakingly saved something out of our rations for when the boys came home. We put flags up for them, we had parties for them, but the boys that came back were not the boys who went away. They were men. Different men with different ideas, and they found us different too. The shy young girls they left behind became women, strong useful women with harder hearts and harder hands capable of doing jobs that men never dreamed women could do. Some of us were mothers, and the babies did not know their fathers and the fathers did not know their babies.

There was jealousy on both sides. The children who had had mum to themselves had to share her with a man who was almost a stranger. There were a lot of bedroom rows, I can tell you. A man who dreamed of lying in his own bed with his wife would have to fight a furious little son or daughter who thought they had a right to be there too.

Written some years after the end of the war by Margaret Wadsworth in Blackpool this letter gives an accurate oversight of the situation in the immediate aftermath of the war. Her emphasis on the differences encountered by men, women and children in almost every aspect of their lives points to the long-term effects of the war that would be felt for years.

Maurice Merritt arrived at his sister's house in London to find the key under the mat and a short note on the kitchen table inviting him to make a cup of cocoa and have the tin of pilchards in the larder if he felt peckish: '. . . bloody cocoa, after all that time in the desert. Pilchards! Ask any man who has been in the army what he thinks of pilchards and see what reply you get. Over six years of longing for this moment, yet now it had arrived, it was a little devoid of happiness and welcome. There was no one even to say hello – the cat couldn't wait to get outside for a wee.'

George Betts was a miner's son. He had been abroad for years and was anxious about how he would cope with coming home after such a long period away. He felt, he wrote in his memoir, a sense of utter despair and despondency as he sat on the train that would take him home. His stomach churned and thoughts tumbled around in his head as the train chugged along. Then he began to reflect how fortunate he was to be returning in one piece and how others were not coming home at all, or were injured and disabled by the war. 'And so, instead of moping about myself, I counted my blessings and resolved to devote myself to my family and my home that I had been privileged to live through the war for, and it was a happy occasion to be greeted by my wife and boys at the station, as they had received notification in advance, and we got a taxi home for happiness.'

Ray Ellis recalled his arrival at his parents' house:

The moment of walking through the door of my home, my return from war, was the culmination of all my hopes and dreams over the previous five years. I had every reason to be grateful that I had been spared to return unscathed, and I was deliriously happy to be safely home in the bosom of my family. My mother said that on the day of my return she was busy with a duster when the door bell rang. She answered the door to find me standing there and she never ever found that duster again. It was a day to remember, but so many things happened and the atmosphere was so emotionally charged that I only have fleeting memories of faces and places. It was a delight beyond belief to be back with my mother and father.

There were hugs and kisses in plenty, walks around the garden and the rooms of the house, astonishment in finding so many things unchanged and meals which were far too large for me to consume.

Charles Coles had been away for four years, two and a half of which he had spent as a prisoner of war in Germany. He delighted on arriving at an air force base in Bedfordshire at the smell of the hawthorn and birds singing in the hedgerows. His journey to London was full of familiar sights such as black cabs, London buses and Tube stations. Bombed-out London depressed him; girls in brightly coloured clothes excited him. He borrowed money from a friendly policeman to call home and warn his parents of his imminent arrival:

The phone call to my family was highly emotional – more than I had bargained for – and I won't dwell on it. My father answered, trying to sound his usual self, but his voiced seized up and he soon passed the phone over to my mother. She was in much the same state. I was an only son, and I had been away for over four uncertain years. However, she rallied . . . she always could. After the predictable opening remarks about health and what time I might be able to get home, my mother decided to get the bad news out of the way. Yes, our old dog had died a few weeks back; and yes, a succession of agonizing 'Dear John' letters had been sent to me over the last few months but – owing to the bombing in Germany – none of them had reached me. In fact my girlfriend was married. I closed my ears but was conscious of my mother doing her best with some gentle philosophizing.

The pain and sadness of such homecomings was felt as much by the family as by the returning men. Countless men came back to discover their girlfriends had not waited and for the families who might have been aware of this hurt to come it must have been difficult knowing how to deal with the bitterness and disappointment that marred their own delight.

For women the moment of homecoming was equally charged. Margaret Sullivan's husband returned from Italy wounded in the leg. 'All the joy and excitement I felt at the prospect of seeing Jim again drained away when I saw the look on his face as he stood on my doorstep. He had deep lines around his mouth and eyes, his skin had a grey pallor beneath the tan. He was clearly in pain and remained in constant pain for months. Far worse, however, was his fury that I had had to give up the house and move back to my family home. He didn't seem to want to get to know the children either. In the end we settled down but I did think about getting a divorce. It was all so hard and seemed so unfair.'

For some it lived up to expectations but there was often an element of surprise, as here for Winifred Beagan who wrote of her memories of that day sixty-three years after the event: 'I had been working seven days a week altering the aircraft to accommodate the bouncing bombs. It was four years since we had parted and – unbelievably – he arrived home at 10 pm just as I had started to wash my hair! I never have remembered how I put those 24 hair rollers in.'

When Edna Roper's husband, Stan, returned from the Far East she remembered being somewhat astonished:

When Stan walked off the train in Cambridge in November 1945 I looked at him and said, 'You <u>do</u> look well!' and he said to me 'You are well dressed.' Well, I wasn't. I was wearing a borrowed coat and my mother's hat. My skirt was at least six years old and I had turned it round so that the back was at my front and the sagging that had occurred after sitting down in the skirt was disguised under my cardigan. My underwear was patched but I had managed to get my hair done and Mother had lent me lipstick so I suppose on the face of it I looked quite presentable.

Jean Hammond recalled the moment when she first saw her father after the war: 'I remember seeing my father for the first time in my living memory. He was walking up the long garden path to our shared house in Sonning Common. My mother, Charlotte, was so overcome with emotion that she fell down the stairs when she saw him coming towards the house.' Fortunately she was uninjured but this dramatic reaction to her father's return stuck firmly in Jean's memory.

Dorothy White had been offered the chance to go to Southampton and meet her son Pat off the boat from the Far East, where he had been a prisoner of war in Formosa (Taiwan). She chose not to go, saying she would prefer to meet him at home. When he arrived at the house she did not recognize him. 'I just did not know who it was getting out of that car,' she told her daughter-in-law later. His eyesight had been affected by malnutrition and he was wearing glasses. He was also thinner than when she had last seen him. Pat White made a full recovery and was married not long after the war to a young woman called Jean who Dorothy had asked to help her son to find his feet again.

When Catherine Butcher's father came back from the Far East in November 1945 she and her mother met him on the doorstep of the house where they were billeted in Shorncliffe, outside Folkestone. 'He just appeared on the doorstep one day in November – a much thinner man, carrying a small suitcase. "Hello darlings," he said, as if he had never been away. It took my mother and father some time to settle down though. He had become quiet and withdrawn having been outgoing and full of life before the war. He just wanted a peaceful life, I think.'

Men who had been away for years in regular army postings

found life at home as difficult to accept as the wives and children who had to get used to them on their return: 'I don't relish the change much at present as I find London very different and twice as repulsive,' wrote Henry Anderson to his brigadier in February 1946. 'Since I came back I have been mainly "confined to home" as we have no servants and the children are a strong man's job alone – somewhere between a policeman and a zoo keeper.'

For him the biggest adjustment was rationing. He did not like it one bit and wrote bitterly of the woeful situation as he saw it:

> The most serious aspect of England and one which requires the best brains of the country is the question of drink. One bottle of gin a month is a laughable pittance, an insult to the drinking classes. It makes me wild to be offered port at 45/- a bottle when North Africa, and to a lesser degree Italy, are overflowing with good wine. I find I miss the stuff. It never occurred to me not to have a bottle of wine with dinner. I brought a case back from Italy but that lasted less than a week. I really think a self-respecting government should concentrate on getting some drink into the country at reasonable prices instead of all this long-range political stuff.

This may elicit a wry smile but it is symptomatic of the chasm that existed between those who had been living in Britain and some of those who had been away. In the army the men had in general been well fed and there was little experience for them of the rationing that had affected civilian Britain. For many it was a shock: 'The queues for food are ghastly. Be prepared for that,' one soldier warned his fiancée who was about to return home. 'Luckily eating in the mess we don't have those problems and we seem to have plenty of everything. Father ate all his marmalade ration for a month at one breakfast. He'd no idea of rationing after living in Cairo.'

It was not just men who were worried about rationing: 'From the really angry comments by women, I think the government had better do something about the food situation, if it doesn't want its delicate foreign policy to be sabotaged by half-nourished British people in this country,' wrote Jennifer Hill in her diary. She had heard that tinned salmon, which had been held back in 1939, was now on sale in Birkenhead. This had led, she wrote, to several people complaining it had upset their stomachs 'most likely because of the cans not having been completely airtight'. Food was a recurring theme in her diary throughout the summer months of 1945. In June she wrote: 'Miss B went for her lunch at noon, but rushed back five minutes later with laden carrier bags. She was excited, with news: "Quick, go round to Bowers! They've just got some potatoes in and the queue isn't very long. I'll mind the office and the phone for you."' Jennifer was concerned about people having to queue for food: '. . . I thought how humiliating a sight it was – a long queue of respectably dressed women (some of them white haired and shaky) standing like paupers, waiting for the beefy-looking owner of the shop to arrive in his car and unlock the shop door at 10 o'clock.'

All of this was unfamiliar to men who had been in the services for years. They found themselves confused by the black market that had grown up during the war and by the spivs that ran any number of scams. Thomas Hanley was newly married after the war and moved to Devon where he thought he would be happy to settle down to married life. He found that business was being run 'on chicanery and spivvery. In an atmosphere of rationing and shortages, interlopers like myself had a hard time. Helping hands were weighted with self-interest. Even persons of the utmost integrity, after six years of war, were motivated by self-preservation.'

Another man was shocked to discover that his seemingly unimpeachable wife had resorted to buying petrol on the black market. The owner of the local garage would call to say that 'the bicycle is repaired' and she would know that this was the hint that extra petrol was available and she would drive down to the village to fill up her car.

Amongst all the concerns about rationing, jobs, the black market and a general need for readjustment there were some lighter moments. Jennifer Hill recalled an event in September 1945 that brought a smile to her face:

We went to spend the day with Doris and Alf, and played records, some of which we took, for hours as a background to talk. Later his sister came in with [her] husband just home from Italy after 4 years, with an acquired taste for opera (which they all seem to get) which doesn't please [his] wife who prefers boogie-woogie. An odd couple – very possessive female with a love of public love-making which amused us. The young man seemed to think he had a way with ladies – possibly he had with Italian ladies.

Time spent in Italy had clearly affected others too. One wife wrote in bewilderment: 'For goodness' sake tell me how to become intellectual quickly! Before he went away, John was quite content to potter about the garden, and go to the pictures occasionally, but since he's been in Italy he's crazy about opera and art. I have to listen for hours to music I find faintly comic, and stand raptly before pictures I don't understand. The only thing of which I am conscious is my poor tired feet.'

For others the jolt came from seeing the state of their homes. 'We eventually arrived in Liverpool, and the heavily bombed city looked very dismal and desolate. After our stay in the US, everything at home here looked small, cars, lorries, vans and railway rolling stock all looked so small.' Even for men whose houses had been undamaged there was a sense of some things decaying while

others had remained unaltered. 'I found the family and everything at home in good order and condition and give my wife very
high marks. The place looks pretty shabby but it is intact. One of
the few places practically unchanged is the office. When I cleaned
my room out I found most things exactly as I had left them 6½
years ago. There was a letter from 1939 in my filing tray.'

The question of employment was a very serious one and even
those who had been fortunate enough to have their jobs held
open for them found that big changes had taken place in the years
they had been away: 'In business I found everything in good
shape, though my colleagues are inclined to treat me occasionally
as if I were a demented child who does not know the first thing
about government procedure, various by-laws, and the means of
circumventing them. Business is certainly very different from
what it was, but the essentials remain the same, and gradually I
am getting up quite a lot of interest in various tasks which the war
period has left behind.'

Kenneth Laing found that settling down to work was not easy:

When I eventually started to work a fortnight ago, I found the
actual work no more tiring than before the war. The first four or
five days, though, I was curiously restless. Again, it's an awful thing
to say: in a prisoner of war camp one got a broader view of
mankind than in one's job. One met all sorts and conditions of
men in the most peculiar and intimate circumstances and one had
plenty of time to talk to them. One is apt to miss this at first but
one soon adjusts oneself. There is no doubt in my mind that work
has a healing power. It absorbs one's nervous energy, which was
more or less frustrated in a prisoner of war camp. At the same
time, I am fortunate in living away from it and can get relaxation
and other interests in the evening. I really feel now that I'm getting back to a normal life.

For others their leave was cut short by their employers, necessitating a very quick adjustment to life in Britain. A. H. Gibbs wrote to his former commanding officer in August 1946:

> . . . Owing to the fact that my previous employers were very anxious to have me back I was able to take only three weeks of my release leave, most of which was taken up in endeavouring to fix my house in some resemblance of order and weather-worthiness. I have settled down fairly well and quickly but I notice a deplorable lack of 'team spirit' in business which was never the case in '37. Regarding home life, I am, of course, very glad to be able to spend time with my wife and son but at the same time I very much miss my very pleasant association of Vange [his regiment's HQ in Essex].

An all-male environment had become the norm over the years of the war and for some it was a wrench to give up that sense of camaraderie and forged friendships.

> Many could not settle down, for the continuous activities that had encompassed different countries in their travels abroad had instilled a very restless feeling in some men. Army life, though often sworn about and maligned by a serving soldier, had taken care of many aspects that he was now responsible for and did not always welcome. His civilian life confined him in a much smaller orbit, which proved a source of partial frustration and sometimes had a bad influence on domestic life.

K. M. Catlin, writing in *Home & Country* in June 1945, recognized that adjusting from the services to home life with its everyday humdrum would be difficult: 'Most of the folk who have been away during the war have been leading, for good or ill, more exciting lives than are possible in peacetime. When they come home they are very likely to complain of the dullness of their life, particularly if they return to quiet country villages. This in most cases will only be a passing phase, but it is very understandable and needs to be met with sympathy.'

Everyday life was one thing to take on board for the returning man but the other was the whole question of children. In 1943, when the peak of mobilization was reached in Britain, 684,334 babies were born of which up to a third had fathers serving in the forces, so by 1945 there would be some quarter of a million two-year-olds who had never met their fathers. Bearing in mind that many men left home well before 1943 returning at best for short leaves, it would be no exaggeration to suggest that upwards of a million children under six had not met their birth fathers by the end of the war.

This did not always make for an easy homecoming for the fathers but it also gave the mothers the problem of juggling the everyday needs and demands of their young families with the often conflicting demands of their husbands who, after years away, understandably wanted a good slice of their wife's attention. It could give rise to jealousy between fathers and children, neither of whom were prepared to give ground, and left the mother torn between her thrill and delight of having her husband home and anxiety about how it would shake domestic stability until normality returned. For some this took days or weeks, for some it took months or years and for others it never happened at all.

There are many tales of the reactions of young children to their fathers coming back. Some hint at the tensions that lay beneath the surface only to bubble up again and again, others convey the bewilderment of children at having a man introduced, often without ceremony or explanation, into their lives or, worse still, into their mother's bed. 'Where is Daddy going to live when he comes home?' asked one six-year-old, who had never seen his father in his living memory. 'Well, he'll be living at home, won't he?' replied his wiser older sister, who had been four years old when her father left. 'But where is he going to sleep?' the younger boy insisted. 'Why in Mummy's bed of course!' his sister said. With this the six-year-old ran out of the room crying loudly, 'But that's where I sleep. I don't <u>want</u> him in my bed.' This little boy was typical of many small children who suddenly found themselves playing second fiddle to their reunited parents.

A four-year-old girl who was taken to the station to meet her father turned to her mother when Daddy was pointed out and said in some dismay, 'That's not my Daddy. He's got legs.' It took her mother a few moments to realize that her daughter had only ever seen the photograph of 'Daddy' on the table in the hall which was a three-quarter portrait showing a man with apparently no legs. When this was explained to her she accepted her father but not without some doubt as to whether she was really seeing the man whose photograph she had kissed every night before she went to bed.

Maggie Lanning had no memories of her father. He had been in India for several years but she recalled his homecoming vividly:

I remember this shadowy figure appeared in our lives one cold, foggy January evening. We knew he was coming and my mother was obviously very excited, but it didn't really spill over to me. I can remember sitting up with my mother at the upstairs window, me ready for bed, and seeing this figure in uniform with a kitbag over his shoulder walking up the slope of the street to the house. And a little later on there was this person saying hello to me, and then Mum tucking me up and sending me off to sleep. The significance didn't really make an impact on me . . .

Maggie's recollection of her childhood was that her younger sister, born in 1947, was much closer to her father. 'She was diabetic from the age of five, and being involved with medical matters in his work, his focus was much more on her – the things he did and the way he acted. I became very much the older sister, having to take more responsibility than I should . . . My mother was a lone mother for four years, it probably made her stronger in some ways and self-sufficient. We were always very close and this continued until she died.'

Maureen Cleaver was seven years old when her father was called up in 1939 so she had memories of him before he went away. She had a younger brother who was just six months old and neither of them saw their father until 1945, when Maureen was thirteen and her brother nearly seven. Before the war the family had lived in Portsmouth but Maureen's father was sufficiently concerned about the risk of the harbour being bombed that he insisted that his family should move into the countryside, and in fact only visited the house once before his departure so it was not surprising he had difficulty in locating them on his return. When he did come home he arrived at the house in the country late at night. The knock on the door came and Maureen's mother asked her to open it: 'There stood Dad. He didn't recognize the thirteen-year-old as his daughter. In his mind I was still a little girl. "Oh, I'm sorry," he said, "I have come to the wrong house" and promptly turned round to leave! Of course he didn't get very far . . .' Maureen's little brother was woken up and brought down to greet his father, a man he knew only from old photographs. 'He was promptly violently sick,' Maureen recalled.

After this inauspicious start things took a little time to settle down. Maureen's mother had to remind her husband on several occasions that the children were not his army recruits. 'It was difficult accepting that this man had the right to correct our behaviour after so many years and I remember my brother saying "I wish you were back in the army – we were happy until you got home." This must have been very hurtful to Dad, though he never showed it.' After a few months, Maureen recalled, they became happy and united. She added:

> Incidentally, Mum and Dad celebrated their seventy-fifth wedding anniversary before dying within six months of each other at the ages of 97 and 95. The hardship and separation of the war years obviously did not affect their lifespan. Judging from the many sad results of the men returning home I feel doubly blessed to have had such a loving family. It is only since I was widowed a few years ago that I [have] realized just how strong, mentally and physically, my mother must have been to have coped single-handed with children, air raids, food rationing, a large garden and no news for months on end from my father.

For Jean Marten, a baby when her father went abroad at the beginning of the war, her father's homecoming was a surprise: 'I do not remember my father until the age of six because he was away in the war from 1939 when I was born. One day as kids, we were sitting on the bridge when suddenly someone said, "Hey Jean! There's your dad in army uniform coming down the brow." That was my first glimpse of my father. Of course this was commonplace during wartime.' She was delighted when he came back. He was practical and she remembered how he made her a sledge with her name on it, of which she was extremely proud. During the war she had lived in a matriarchy in a small village called Haighton, eleven miles north of Blackburn. Hers had been an idyllic childhood barely touched by the war. 'We had lived in the village in complete security. My memories of the war are few. People seemed to talk about the practicalities of everyday living. Nobody in the village had a lot of money but everyone helped everyone else. A lot of fathers were away so it was nothing unusual to have no man in the house. My mother was an amazing person and coped so efficiently while she was on her own.' When Jean's father, Don Allsop, came back from India in 1945 he had a warm welcome in the village. 'Mum still ran the house and Dad was happy for her to carry on like that. It seems to me that my father simply took up where he had left off.' On reflection, though, it seemed that all was not as well with Don Allsop as his young daughter might have believed. He took a job with the War Office when he came home and travelled a great deal, often spending weeks away from home. 'He would go away and when he came back he was often at a tangent for a week or so,' Jean explained. 'Mum was the constant in his life, she was the steady influence. She knew how to deal with his moods. After he died we wished we had understood more about him but things weren't talked about in our house, not things like that. It was a question of the stiff upper lip.'

From the men's perspective there was much to adapt to. Coming back into an all-female household was not easy after years of army life with predominantly male company. For men like Don Allsop who walked back into a warm and welcoming village home it was at once reassuring but also at times claustrophobic. One solution which many resorted to was a garden shed. The sale of sheds escalated after the war and there are countless stories from children recollecting their fathers' private domains, often beautifully ordered. 'I remember my father's shed was so tidy,' said Marion Platt. 'He used to keep his nails, screws, nuts and bolts in bottles, the lids of which were screwed to the wall in neat lines. That way he could see exactly what he had and could put his hand on any tool he needed. In that shed he made all manner of things – things for Mum in the house or toys for me and Betty. The shed was his sanctuary.'

To Ruth Bird, born in 1943, her father was a total stranger. For the first three years of her life, Ruth was brought up by her mother, who was working as a nurse at St Nicholas' Hospital in Plumstead. Her grandmother helped out with caring for Ruth as Bessie's nursing skills were needed throughout the war. When they were evacuated from Woolwich in South London to Bridlington Ruth was placed in a nursery while her mother went out to work. They formed a tight little unit of two and developed a love and respect for each other that lasted for the rest of Bessie's life: 'She was amazing and my best friend – so strong and firm – and only 5 feet tall. I still miss her and she has been gone for 27 years,' Ruth wrote.

In 1946 her father returned from three years away and family life resumed in Woolwich. Although Bessie and Len tried to take up where they had left off many things had changed. For one, there was Ruth to contend with. She was jealous of her mother's attention to her father, this man she recognized only from photographs, and for another her father was a changed man. 'Mum always said he wasn't the same man who went away,' Ruth recalled. When he came back from Burma he had become a heavy smoker and she remembered the smell of his Capstan Full Strength cigarettes and his terrible cough. He also had asthma, allergies and suffered from recurring dysentery that had affected him during the war. And she remembered him screaming in the night, terrified by the nightmares that disturbed his sleep, nightmares of which he never spoke. Bessie, despite her shock at having a stranger in her house, took on the job of nursing him back to physical and mental health. She looked after him, Ruth said, until the day she died and never had a day off from that responsibility. In 1947 a little boy, Norman, was born. 'My father and I never bonded,' Ruth wrote in 2003. 'Perhaps I resented him coming between the close relationship I had with my mother. Throughout my childhood and teenage years arguments were always present. I never had the easy relationship with my father which my brother had. I did not have an unhappy childhood but the regrets are still there, even now. There are many casualties of war.'

Some children born during the war never had to share their mothers afterwards. Their fathers, killed in action, did not come back and the repercussions of this loss were felt well into adult life. Now in her sixties, Christa Laird explained:

> There is no doubt that the death of my father in 1944 before I was born has informed much of my life. I was born three months after he was killed and my mother, who was a wonderful, loving woman, always encouraged me to talk and ask questions about my father. Strangely I seldom wanted to then but now of course I bitterly regret not having asked a thousand questions before she died. I remember being five or six when a friend said to me 'It's all right, you never knew him.' The implication was that you can't miss what you've never had. That remark hit me almost as if it had been a physical blow to my stomach. I still remember that feeling to this day. The fact that I never knew him has given rise, on and off, to a lifetime's search.

Christa's father, Rudolf Julius Falck, was born into a German-Jewish family in 1920. His own father, a distinguished architect in Cologne, was, incidentally, responsible for Germany's first escalator in a department store. As the Nazi Party rose to power the Falck family realized they would have to leave Germany and so they moved to Holland where Rudi's parents and his two sisters remained, under occupation from 1940, for the entire war.

Rudi was sent to Balliol College, Oxford, to read law in 1937 and in 1940 he was interned on the Isle of Man because he was a German. By October of that year, however, he had joined the Auxiliary Military Pioneer Corps, was commissioned in 1942 and in April 1943 married Christa's English mother, Pauline, who was in the ATS. At first Rudi was sent to North Africa and then to Holland with the Parachute Regiment where, being trilingual (he spoke English, German and Dutch), he worked as an interpreter for German prisoners of war during Operation Market Garden at Arnhem. On the night of 25/26 September 1944 he was killed during the retreat down to the river along with a small group of other officers and men.

Pauline did not meet her parents-in-law until after Rudi had died but when they did meet they were warm and welcoming towards her and their granddaughter. Rudi's twin sisters kept up the affectionate family relationship after their parents died and the contact with the Falck family continued to the next generation. 'My mother married again when I was five and had a little boy when I was eight. She asked me several times if I wanted to change my surname but I was always fiercely proud of my father's name and I kept it. The strange thing was that I did not meet another child born posthumously to a man killed in the war until I was twenty-two.'

Although her father had been buried by one of his men, who had been wounded in the attack in which he was killed, his grave was never registered by the army burial parties. His name is therefore recorded on the memorial at Groesbeek, one of over 1,000 names of men whose remains were never identified. All of this detail about Rudi's death came to light long after Pauline died in the 1960s, when Christa had begun to do more research. 'The urgent need to know about what happened to my father comes and goes with no particular warning,' Christa said. 'There is no doubt that my father's influence on me reached into my adult life. I chose to read German at university I suppose, in part, because of my father and my further degree was related to the Third Reich. My family tease me that the three novels I have written all involve children looking for their lost fathers.'

In 1994 and 2004 Christa went to reunions in Holland to mark the fiftieth and sixtieth anniversaries of Operation Market Garden. 'The fiftieth anniversary was a particularly heart-rending experience because my elder son was about to be twenty-four, the age when Rudi was killed. For the first time I think I truly understood how hard it must have been for my grandparents, who had not been able to see Rudi for five years. It affected me very deeply indeed.' In 1994 she stayed with an hospitable Dutch couple who told her how they recalled seeing the sky go dark as Allied aircraft flew over and thought: these gliders are our salvation. 'I know from one of my aunts that my grandparents thought the same thing, little knowing that their son was caught up in the battle. At last, with the kind help of an historian of the Company, John Hamblett, and a description from the very man who had given my father his temporary burial, I almost definitely located the spot where he was killed and was able to lay flowers there both in 1994 and again, with my younger son, in 2004. It felt right to have one of Rudi's two grandsons there.'

Not all children whose fathers were killed had a mother who helped them to feel comfortable about seeking out information on their fathers. Mary-Jane Hoe was born in 1943 while her father was in India. He was killed in 1944 at the age of twenty-four and is commemorated on the Rangoon Memorial. Mary-Jane was brought up by her mother and a very loving stepfather, called Bernard, whom she always knew as 'Daddy'. Of her father she knew nothing at all. On her eighteenth birthday Bernard took her aside and told her something so surprising that it almost caused her to collapse: 'He said to me, "MJ my darling, I have loved you like a daughter ever since I married your mother but I think you ought to know that I am not your real father. He died flying over Burma during the war." Well, I was devastated. My whole world just crumbled around me.' From then, until she was fifty, Mary-Jane stumbled from one disastrous relationship to another. She battled with alcoholism and addiction but finally found help from a divorcee who showed her kindness and under-standing. He encouraged her to visit the memorial in Rangoon and to contact her father's former colleagues. Mary-Jane has now done research into her father's short life and has come to terms with her turbulent past. 'It would be no exaggeration to say that the war had a dramatic impact on my life,' she said grimly. 'I know my parents did what they felt was best for me at the time but I wish so much that I had been able to grow up being proud of my birth father. I would not have loved "Daddy" any less but I feel that I had the right to know. I wonder how many other chil-dren found themselves in my position?' Statistics for such cases do not exist but several thousand people now in their mid-sixties never knew their fathers.

For other girls, older than Christa and Mary-Jane, there were different concerns about their fathers. Diana Turnball was eight-een when hers was reported missing in Italy. Nothing had been heard of him for months but in 1944 came the news that he was alive. The Red Cross informed her mother that he and a party had escaped to Switzerland by walking over the Alps. Diana wrote to a school friend, Emma, about it: 'Dad was older than the others and he's suffered most but they're safe and they're alive and that's the most important thing but it's hard on Mum, believe you me. It's the not knowing that tells on you. We didn't know if he was alive or dead for ages.' A few weeks later John Turnball returned and Diana wrote to Emma about his arrival home: 'I've an enormous piece of news. Daddy is back. Can you believe it? He was smuggled out across the south of France and through Spain. He's so thin and doesn't look like Daddy. I'm a bit frightened of him. He walks about at night dressed in a towel. He can't sleep and has terrible dreams. Mum is wonderful. She never pushes him, just sees to everything he wants. She's so happy to have him home . . . Think of us nursing Dad back to normality.' Several weeks after that Emma visited her friend. She was deeply shaken by John Turnball's appearance: '. . . she led me through to the sitting room. I had to take a deep breath to hide my shock. Mr Turnball had changed from the big physical man he had been to a bent, grey-haired skeleton but the dark eyes were just the same, piercing yet laughing . . . He must have noticed the look on my face because he said, "Don't worry, child, with these two women looking after me, I'll soon be as right as rain." '

More often than not the effects of the war on the mental state of returning men took months and sometimes years to come to the fore. 'Many outstanding soldiers who are at their best in the close-knit society of the army and under the tight code of discipline that governs service existence lacked the self-discipline and control to run their lives effectively post-war,' wrote General Sir Peter de la Billière in his book *Supreme Courage*. 'But what of the women and families of these heroic men who have to put up with anything from drunkenness and violence in the home to anxiety and financial disaster in the work place?' Although the perception of the majority is that there was no help on hand, there were a handful of voluntary organizations that were dedicated to helping men with predominantly mental health problems. One was the Ex-Services Welfare Society, which was formed in 1919 by a group of women who were concerned by the lack of support for their husbands after the First

World War. It catered for men who had been seriously affected by their war service. Many of these men had been committed to asylums after the war. Their womenfolk had been convinced at the time that it was the wrong thing to lock men up who were suffering from shell shock and other related problems. It was in fact not until during the Vietnam War in the 1960s, according to psychiatrist Allan Young, that post-traumatic stress disorder (PTSD) was recognized as a condition.

By 1937 the Society was renamed the Ex-Services Mental Welfare Society, reflecting the nature of their charitable work. After the Second World War their work extended to cover men who returned from theatres of war all over the world and for those men released from prisoner of war camps. It was and still is the only services charity specializing in helping men and women from all ranks of the armed forces and the Merchant Navy suffering from psychological disability as a result of their service. Renamed Combat Stress in recent times, the charity continues to receive requests for help from service personnel who have been affected as a result of more recent conflicts. The society points out that 'it is seldom appreciated that the number of psychiatric casualties of war far exceeds those who are killed or physically disabled'.

Some men suffered such severe mental damage that they did not make the adjustment to civilian life nor did they get the help they clearly needed. Dr W. L. Blakemore was deputy state medical officer for the state of Perak in Malaya. Before the war he had been chief health officer in Singapore and after the fall of Singapore had been compelled by the Japanese to work for them 'under conditions involving great mental strain, after which he was sent into internment'. In July 1947 Blakemore was accused of murdering the wife of a British colleague, Mrs I. T. Dickson. The case was reported in *The Times*:

Eye-witnesses state that last Friday night Dr and Mrs Dickson took Blakemore's wife home after a party attended chiefly by members of the Government medical service. On arriving at Blakemore's house Blakemore rushed from behind the house brandishing a revolver. Dickson grappled with him, but he fired several shots, wounding Mrs Dickson, who died soon afterwards, and wounding Dr Dickson. Blakemore then rushed inside the house and set it on fire with petrol. He was found by the police sitting in the garden semi-conscious. Yesterday Blakemore was charged with murder and attempted murder in Ipoh court, while he himself was unconscious in hospital, but a remand was offered for mental observation. Blakemore died this morning from the effects, the police believe, of a self-administered drug.

This tragedy was put down to the effects of Blakemore's incarceration at the hands of the Japanese and indicates how badly some men were affected by their imprisonment.

This depressing story is an extreme example of maladjustment. Several people said that life after the war had been happy and fulfilling. Jean White's husband, Pat, who had been unrecognizable to his mother on his return, adjusted well once the initial shock of coming home had passed. 'I never treated him differently from anyone else,' Jean explained. 'Pat was very well adjusted and the only lasting effect of the war was that he hated eating rice. He told me he had spent the war planting rice and he never wanted to see it or eat it again. Although he had nightmares he did not suffer from any major health problems and we had a long and happy marriage until Pat died in 1995 at the age of seventy-four.'

George Schramm's older brother, Edward, was part of a unit in Alaska during the latter half of the war. He was, George said, the perfect older brother and proud to serve his country.

The Second World War was a remarkable event but it was only one in a line of conflicts in which our family took part. My father fought in the First World War, my brother in the Second. My brothers and I took part between us in the Korean War and Vietnam. For all of us these were extraordinary emotional experiences and the benefits to us were the camaraderie, the shared feeling of responsibility and the examples of bravery that outweighed the fear of death. Yes, there was sadness when men died but for those who came back there was a feeling of pride and my mother, a very remarkable woman, was amazingly brave. She was the gentle presence that helped us all to adapt when we came home. My brother's girlfriend had not waited after the war but he married two years later and had five children. We don't talk about the wars much now but we have had long and fulfilling lives.

Mrs Topping from Yorkshire wanted to put on record the fact that her marriage to a former prisoner of war of the Japanese was a happy one. 'I am pleased to say that we had a normal married life. We had three sons and two daughters. Although Albert suffered badly with his stomach for years and had malaria twice a year he celebrated his eighty-ninth birthday last year. We have had a very loving and successful marriage.'

Eileen Mottram from Wiltshire described the post-war years as the happiest of her life: 'My husband Allen joined the Forces in 1940 and served all his time in England with the RA Coastal Command. He was discharged in 1946 and although he never went abroad we had not been able to see each other very often so for us his homecoming was a very happy and thankful event.' Having lived for two years with Eileen's parents, they got a two-bedroom house in Manchester and Allen was able to return to his pre-war employer who had held his job open. 'Food was still quite scarce but I had vegetables from my father's allotment, fresh milk delivered daily because I had a little boy and I could get fresh meat from the butcher's so we fed quite well. We had no tele-phone, car or washing machine and the wireless was a great treat but believe me these were the happiest days of my life. Every day one appreciated being able to live and work normally. So many of my friends and relations had sad and worrying times but we were contented and grateful and enjoyed life.'

4

THE FOG OF WAR:
THE MOTHER'S TALE

The death toll in the Second World War was higher than in any war of recorded history. On the day the war ended, the parents, widows, children, families and friends of the dead were those for whom the ending was sad and bitter. These, Paul Fussell has written, were 'the survivors, those whose lives are ruined by their sons', husbands', fathers' sacrifices for ideologies. The men don't feel anything: they're out of it. It's the living who are the casualties.

Martin Gilbert, *The Day the War Ended*

Mothers of men who went off to fight in the 1939–45 war had all lived through the First World War of 1914–18 and knew only too well the desperate sadness felt by a million families who had lost men during those terrible years. For them the worry of watching their sons go to fight in this next war was particularly poignant. Many would have lost fathers, brothers, husbands in the First World War and the memories of twenty years earlier were all too fresh. There is little material telling the mother's side of the story. The focus of the documentation and literature that came after the war was on the younger generation: on the heroes who fought and died, on those who came home as victors and on the young women who waited for them to return. There is no glamour attached to being the mother of a soldier, sailor or airman and over the years they have received woefully little attention. By and large in memoirs they are taken for granted or treated to the odd aside 'For his mother, of course, it was worse because she could remember the time when her two brothers were killed in Flanders' or 'It can't have been easy for my mother-in-law. She knew all too well what it meant to be on the receiving end of a telegram from the War Office to say that her brother was missing.'

Statistics tell us that one in three men of fighting age was married, meaning that there were over a million wives of servicemen in Britain alone. But if 4 million men were mobilized between 1939 and 1945 then there must have been over 2 million mothers who kissed their sons goodbye, not knowing when or if they would see them again. Some of them died, some came back physically or mentally damaged. Almost all of them returned changed. Some mothers paid what must have been the heaviest price conceivable, losing one or more of their sons.

Mary Hamilton (Polly) Cartland was a 62-year-old widow at the outbreak of the Second World War. Born into a wealthy family, she had, in her father's opinion, married 'beneath her' and he made no financial settlement upon her, which was to have serious consequences for her later in life. Her husband, Major James Cartland, was killed in action on 27 May 1918. Not that Polly had known that immediately. He had been posted 'missing' and his body was never found. He is commemorated on the Soissons Memorial, a name among 3,800 who died during the final German offensive that spring. Polly was left virtually penniless to bring up her three children, Barbara, Ronald and Anthony. Despite her difficult circumstances Polly was defiant. 'Poor I may be,' she once said, 'but common I am not.' She was cheerful, strong-willed and fought hard to give her children an upbringing in the style to which she wished them to become accustomed. After her husband's death she moved to South Kensington and opened a shop which sold woollens.

Her daughter wrote of her in 1948: 'My mother, a wonderful person whom we all adored, imbued us with high ideals, the ambition to succeed and the determination never to let poverty stand in the way of opportunity.' At the outbreak of the Second World War Polly could feel justly proud of her children and their achievements. Barbara was already a successful novelist with twenty-one books published by 1940, Ronald had been elected a Tory MP for the King's Norton Division of Birmingham and was held by many in the party to be a rising star, and Tony had joined the army where he was forging a career for himself in the Lincolnshire Regiment and had attained the rank of captain. In September 1939 Tony left Britain for France, and his older brother, Ronald, who joined the 53 Anti-Tank Regiment R.A., followed in January 1940.

Polly by this time was living in Malvern and threw herself into voluntary war work with an energy which, as more than one friend commented, would have been startling for a woman in her forties, let alone a widow in her sixties. She let rooms in her house to billetees, worked in a canteen in the town, for the Red Cross and for the Women's Voluntary Service; she did bookbinding for the troops and sorted and parcelled up books for the Merchant Navy.

Ronald sent home long letters from France expressing his frustration at the unpreparedness for war, the shortage of guns and ammunition and the slow organization in the army. Tony was agitated about lack of action and longed to feel he was doing something useful. In May 1940, just after the German Army had invaded Belgium and Holland and the British Expeditionary Force was called into action, he wrote: 'This is just to send you my love and bless you always. Don't be anxious if there is a long silence from me – the fog of war is pretty impenetrable. We shall win in the end, but there's horror and tribulation ahead of all of us. We can't avoid it. What a waste it all is, but after months of desolation we shall gain and retain what you and I have always understood the meaning of – freedom.'

The silence fell, as Tony had predicted. Barbara wrote:

> I shall remember those hot, dry, sunny days all my life. I was at our cottage in Bedfordshire. The lilac was in bloom, huge bushes of white, purple and mauve; the may trees were crimson, and the blossom was heavy on the cherry trees . . . It seemed to me that a great quiet lay over everything, as if the earth itself held its breath. I walked up and down the garden waiting for the telephone to ring. Darkness fell . . . the telephone did not ring. But to a woman waiting alone, in an empty home, came the tidings that both her sons were 'missing'.

There was every possibility that the brothers had been taken prisoner and it was weeks before anybody knew what had happened to the troops who had not returned from Dunkirk. Polly Cartland clung to the hope that they had been captured.

In January 1941 came the terrible news that Ronald had been killed in action on 30 May 1940. He had been hit in the head by a German bullet and died instantly. The rest of his men had been captured and marched off to imprisonment and his body had been left where he had fallen: 'We had gradually been losing hope of hearing that he was alive – now we knew the truth. My mother was wonderful. "Missing" is the cruellest uncertainty of all, as she well knew, for my father had been missing in 1918; and that ghastly waiting, watching, hoping and praying was hers all over again – not twice, but three times, for Tony was still "missing".' It was several months later that Polly received a letter telling her that Tony too had been killed in France. He had died on 29 May 1940, a day before his brother. A year later she learned that her nephew had been killed when the HMAS *Perth* was torpedoed by the Japanese on 1 March 1942.

Polly Cartland's situation was bleak, her daughter wrote: 'Now that the last hope was gone, the future looked lonely and empty for her.' But she would not be defeated. 'My mother behaved with a courage which equalled that of her sons. "I must work for other people," she said and proceeded with ever-greater energy in her voluntary work while looking after her sister, who had since moved into the house, and caring for her lodgers, for whom she now cleaned and cooked breakfast. She was often overworked to the point of exhaustion but she never gave up and it seems that in her frenetic activity she was able to hide some of the pain and sadness at the loss of her two sons.'

Her anguish was felt by thousands of mothers throughout the world. The reaction of many women was to brace their shoulders and carry on but their sacrifice was a great one. There was nothing they could do to bring their children back and life had to go on: 'Memories, however golden, cannot fill an empty place – a home that is suddenly quiet, a desk at which no one sits, a silence which remains unbroken by a voice.'

All over the country people were trying to find out what had happened to their men and it was not always easy to get the information they wanted. In a queue for the butcher's in Birkenhead Jennifer Hill and her friend B got into a conversation about a missing boy: 'Another lady came up and told us that her sister has been trying for nearly 12 months to find out, through the War Office, etc where her son was killed and where his grave is, in Normandy, but nothing is known. Mrs Clark, whose second son Bill was "missing presumed killed" in Burma was bitter. She said: "I could tear their eyes out for hate. <u>They</u> don't care what's become of the poor lads. Just a body and an army number, among thousands, to them. But it isn't just another body and an army number to the poor mothers at home.'"

For other mothers the agony of waiting was hideously prolonged and in some cases neither the War Office nor the Red Cross were able to supply any information on what had happened to their sons. By the end of the war countless families were still waiting for news. And in their desperation they pursued any avenue in order to glean information. In November 1945 the parents of Lieutenant John Daniel Vincent of the 51 Field Regiment R.A. put a notice in the *Daily Telegraph* to celebrate the safe return of their son from a prison camp in Borneo. The result of this was a bulging postbag of requests for information from families whose sons had also been prisoners of war in that part of Malaya, and of whom nothing was known. Part of the correspondence is stored at the Imperial War Museum and in reading the letters it is possible to get some inkling of the aching pain that the families suffered:

Dear Sir, I am writing to ask you if you can give me any news or information of my son Lt John Lawson – I noticed the announcement of your return from Borneo in the *Telegraph* and wondered if you could have met him. We heard unofficially that he was moved from Malaya to Borneo – so far we have never had a line from him since the fall of Singapore. I shall be most grateful if you can tell me anything. Forgive me for troubling you so soon after your return.

Vincent could tell Constance Lawson nothing of her son's fate. John Lawson had been one of 130,000 prisoners of the Japanese kept in over 1,000 camps throughout South East Asia, and even in Borneo, where Vincent had been imprisoned, there were several camps housing nearly 3,000 men. Later the family discovered he had died on 5 March 1943 and he is commemorated on the Singapore Memorial, meaning that his body was never identified.

Vincent was overwhelmed with letters asking for information: 'If you could tell me <u>anything</u> about him or the movements of him and his company since that date . . .' Mrs Lucy Orchard wrote about her son. 'We thought you might have come across him in Borneo . . .' wrote Dora Burley. '. . . I am another enquirer,' wrote Nancy Graham to Vincent: 'My brother, Richard Sobell Abbott, was interned in Kuching Camp and died of dysentery probably in February 1945. I fully realize it is extremely unlikely that you ever met him but in cases like these one clutches at straws. Also I know you must want to forget about the horrible experiences of the last few years but if you ever did come across Dick I should be more than grateful for some news, however slight.'

Vincent wrote back to all the correspondents who had requested information, clearly trying his best to help wherever he could, but there is a hint of his unease at the scale of his task when Mrs Laing, with whom he had exchanged several letters, wrote to apologize for troubling him: '. . . I am sorry I have asked you so many questions. I never took a thought as to how you would be feeling after the time you have had in Borneo,' she wrote in late November.

In the main he did not know most of the men about whom the mothers, fathers, wives, daughters and brothers wrote to him but one or two had been friends or at least compatriots in Kuching camp. To them he could give a more detailed response but some wrote back, certain that Vincent had made a mistake in suggesting that one or another young man must have died. 'Are you sure this is the same man?' one anxious mother wrote. 'Higgin is spelled without an S, and he was a gunner. Were you in the same regiment? When were you transferred from Singapore? How is it that I have not yet heard from the War Office that he is dead? Please look at the enclosed photograph and tell me if you recognize him?' The agony this woman must have gone through is still achingly real even sixty years on. In her bewilderment she struck out at poor Vincent, only newly returned from an ordeal of his own, and it must have been very troubling for him.

As the army burial parties made their way around South East Asia more information became available to the families of men who had died in the prison camps in the Far East, but it was sometimes years until information could be confirmed. And with the men buried at what was at that time an unimaginable distance it was almost impossible for the families to contemplate visiting the cemeteries and memorials.

Other families were fortunate in that their sons returned after the war but often these men were changed. A perceptive witness was a housewife from Barrow-in-Furness called Nella Last, whose wartime diary became the subject of a successful book and television programme. The Mass Observation Survey, to whom she submitted her diary on a regular basis, was founded in 1937 by three young men, who aimed to create an 'anthropology of ourselves'. They recruited a team of observers and a panel of volunteer writers to study the everyday lives of ordinary people in Britain. People were invited to write diaries and these provide an important historical record of day-to-day life during the Second World War. Nella Last wrote meticulously from August 1939 until February 1966. Much has already been made of her brilliant observations on everyday life during the war years but it is her comments about her younger son, Clifford, that are so fitting in the context of this book: 'How remote the last six years are becoming,' she wrote in August 1945. 'It's odd to realize how Cliff has lost such a slice from his life. Turned from a charming if headstrong boy to a man who shows his oppression of life and having as yet no "stability" of a settled place in the community by moods, and a general look of strain.'

When the Second World War broke out Nella Last was married with two sons and had been a submissive and devoted wife for nearly thirty years. The war changed Nella. She found a focus in joining the WVS (Women's Volunteer Service) and the ATS. She helped to run a canteen and even set up a charity shop to raise money for the Red Cross. She knitted, sewed, cooked, washed, ironed, talked, wrote and often wept her way through the six years of war.

Running through the whole diary was Nella's hatred of war and of the dehumanizing effect it had on people, particularly on the young men who went off to fight. In the very first entry in her diary she referred to 'those boys with their look of "beyond" '. And it was a theme that she came back to again and again. On 15 September 1939, Cliff, then twenty, left home to join the army. The day before he left she wrote: 'He has been so thoughtful and quiet these last few days, and so gentle. I watched his long sensitive fingers as he played with the dog's ears, and saw the look on his face when someone mentioned "bayonet charging". He has never hurt a thing in his life . . . It's dreadful to think of him having to kill boys like himself – to hurt and be hurt. It breaks my heart to think of all the senseless, formless cruelty.'

A month later she realized that the boy she had seen off would come back a stranger: 'I missed Cliff very much from the start,' she wrote, 'but even now get shocks when I realize that my "little boy" went away and will never come back. However, I love the man who will come on Saturday. He will be in some ways a stranger with a very different outlook, and I'm mother enough to mourn my baby.'

The changes she feared did not show themselves on his first visit home, nor on his second. But by February 1941 Nella noticed that Cliff had become restive. On his visits home he was fidgety and nervous, he hated the fact he could not imagine the future. This worried Nella:

> It gives me a fear of the aftermath of things, and a wonder about how all the boys and men that are left will begin again . . . It's the young, raw lads I'm thinking of, who were snatched from trades they had learned but not practised, who had never known the responsibility of a wage to spend, of making do and saving, of a steady courtship and reconciliation of interests with a girl they would have to spend the rest of their lives with. It will be a brave new world all right – but whether, as Huxley calls it, a 'Brave New World' remains to be seen.

Nella's diary was also full of humour. Her new-found confidence and her determination not to take things lying down as she felt she did before the war had unintended consequences at home. She observed that her husband appreciated her meals and paid her more compliments than he had ever done in the past. 'And he notices flowers and best plates and different dishes and table-cloths: he passes nice remarks about them, and says, "By Jove, when I hear some men talking about what they get to eat, I realize how lucky I am." Thirty years of marriage, and two wars, for that remark. Everything evidently does come to them who wait!'

One of Nella's party tricks was to read tarot cards and in May 1942 Cliff persuaded her to read his for him. They turned out to be strangely prophetic:

He got them out and I spread them. He is going on a long journey and the voyage looks dangerous; there are more hardships than
he realizes now, but there will be some honour and advancement.
I'll not see him for a long, long time. He will come back to things
completely changed, and to little that he knows – and I don't think
he will return to this house. Those boys *do* make me laugh. They
say I'm 'imaginative' or else 'no good', but out come the cards
when they come home. They look on it as 'Mom's party-piece'!

Cliff Last sailed towards the end of July 1942. He was heading
for India but was of course not permitted to tell his mother,
although they had arranged a code so that he would at least be
able to hint at where he was being sent. When his next postcard
arrived she noted in her diary: 'Strange, there was always a letter
"I" in his [tea] cup, before India became a war zone, and we used
to wonder if it was Ireland or Iceland.' For eighteen months she
had to rely on postcards and airmail letters that made their erratic
journey from India, the Middle East and finally Italy, where Cliff
was injured in the leg and sent home in November 1944.

The diaries for 1944 were lost but by May 1945, six months
after Cliff came back to Conishead Hospital, some five miles
from Barrow-in-Furness, Nella Last had serious worries about
her 26-year-old son. In the first few weeks after he returned
everything she did seemed to irritate him, if not actually annoy
him. By the spring he was allowed to come home for visits and
her neighbours noticed that he was restless but Nella found him
much improved from the winter. She wrote in her diary on 23
May 1945, two weeks after VE Day: 'For the first time, it seems
he *wants* to begin to build his life, and doesn't talk foolishly of
never settling down again . . . His years abroad and his illness, on
top of having no security, had made him very difficult, both for
himself and for us who love him. I've shuddered at times when

I've thought, "I'm his mother, with memories of a difficult, way-ward little boy – *what* would a young wife have done?" '

Throughout the summer of 1945 Cliff Last worried about what he would do in the future and Nella continued to record her anxiety about her son in her diary. Sometimes she was overwhelmed with fears for his future and at others she worried about the fact that he had 'never yet earned his own living or done "a man's job" in civilian life'. Finally they heard that he was to be demobbed in February 1946 and it was at that moment that Cliff decided he would go to London and do an interior design course. This did not please his mother: 'I find my thoughts so often going to Cliff, often wishing he had been settled in his father's business – for both their sakes – when I see sons eager to come back and settle down in a waiting job. I wonder if Cliff will be successful in his Interior Décor, hearing of many who are taking it up. Knowing how Cliff tires of "failure", knowing how easy things have come to him in the past and how he sees his "luck" to continue.'

On the more personal level she worried about the way he was developing emotionally. She feared he would become like her bachelor brother, selfish and caring only for himself: 'More and more does he seem to live in a world of his own, a kind of egoism grows on him to a degree that gives me a sadness. He is not greedy or "selfish" in that he would share his dinner, his money, clothes or anything "tangible" – but not his time, company or "consideration".'

Cliff Last never came back to live in Barrow-in-Furness.

After demobilization, I lived in London for twelve months trying out a number of work situations. Increasingly I missed the open-air life of my seven years in the army, so decided to try Australia. Immediately on arrival I knew I would settle down with the wel-coming, relaxed Australians, their love of open air, the beaches and the sunshine. In London, I had felt a strong urge to try sculpture and, in Melbourne, took advantage of the rehabilitation scheme for ex-servicemen, working for two years as an art student.

Nella's predictions about her son and his inability to settle to life in Barrow after the war had come true. Clifford remained in Australia and became a successful sculptor. He returned home in 1967 to help look after his parents, who were by then elderly and in the initial stages of senility but he found he could not settle and went back to Melbourne after six months. Nella Last died in 1968 and her son, Cliff, in 1991.

Hazel Watson was just twelve at the outbreak of the Second World War but although she was so young, her story belongs in this chapter because it is really the tale of her mother seen through her daughter's eyes. Hazel, although then still a schoolgirl, had to take responsibility for her parents whose lives crumbled when they learned that their only son, Tony, was reported missing and was later found to be a prisoner of war. She became the figure in the family who held everything together, both for her parents and her brother: a dutiful daughter, a carer, and a kind and understanding sister.

Tony Littler was nineteen when he joined up and twenty-one when he was captured by the Japanese in February 1942. He was taken prisoner in Java and was in Bandoeng camp for a year. In June 1944 the family heard that he had been moved from Java to Osaka in Japan from where he wrote: 'Thanks for your letter July 1942. Here at Osaka Camp, Nippon. I work every day, except Sundays, for which I am paid. My health is good so don't worry. Lots of love and kisses to Maud, yourself, Dad and Hazel, your loving son, Tony'.

The hope he expressed that they would not worry about him would not be fulfilled. Mrs Littler was in her early fifties and

Tony had been the apple of her eye. She was distraught for him when she heard of the fall of Singapore. For months they heard nothing of his fate, a torment for thousands of families all over Britain and Australia. Then came a telegram in July 1943 from the War Office to say that they now knew Tony had been taken prisoner. That was more or less the only official communication they received about him until he was released. The effect on Mrs Littler's mental state was severe. While Hazel continued to bombard the Red Cross, the War Office, their local MP and various other ministries with requests for news about Tony, her mother became ill with anxiety. Hazel took a year off school to stay at home and look after her mother who was unwell for almost the whole time until Tony returned. 'I found I just could not carry on with the pressure of my school work and with looking after my parents. My mother was understandably perpetually anxious while Tony was imprisoned. At times it was worse than others and she struggled to keep going. I always dreaded what might happen if a telegram arrived while I was at school to say that Tony had died.'

When Hazel heard in September 1945 that her brother was safe and that he would soon be coming home she began to concern herself with his rehabilitation. She had a strong feeling that Tony would find readjusting to life after the war difficult but she also knew that he would have a shock when he realized how badly his parents had suffered as a result of worrying about him. It is remarkable, considering how young she was, that she understood this was going to be such a problem. She took the decision to write a summary of her diaries that would trace all aspects of life during the period of his captivity, explaining local, national and international events to him, letting him know the fate in the war of his friends from Staffordshire of whom, she knew, he would have heard nothing in the Far East.

Shortly before her eighteenth birthday in October 1945 Hazel wrote Tony an enthusiastic letter in which she spoke of her intense excitement at the thought of having him back home:

My dear Tony,

. . . You just can't imagine what a difference the last three weeks have meant to us. It's just like a Nirvana after all the long time of wondering & waiting – however – more about that when we see you!

We were overjoyed to receive your 3 letters sent from Manila. Mum just cried when she saw the first. During the whole of the time you were a POW we only received 2 cards and 2 letters. The first 15 months after you were taken prisoner we heard absolutely nothing, though we wrote many letters.

Quite honestly, I never thought the time would come when I could go out without fearing there'd be bad news when I got in. As for Mum & Dad they felt it even worse, naturally. I may as well warn you in advance that neither of them look the same as when you went away – the strain has been awful – thank goodness it's all over.

As for you, you old rascal, I might have guessed you'd pull through alright! I wonder if I shall recognize you – I'm darned certain you won't know me! I'm much taller than Mum or Dad – quite the giantess of the family.

When the 'old rascal' returned in November 1945 he was far from all right. His parents were overjoyed to see him but Hazel felt in her bones that it wouldn't work out. 'I lost my innate optimism and feared that it was not going to be the wonderful homecoming that I had looked forward to. I realized that everyone's expectations were too high.'

Tony talked about his worst experiences, mainly to Hazel. She used to sit by his bed as he poured out the awful times he had been through and the terrible things he had endured as a prisoner. He told of a massacre of Ambonese that he and other POWs had been made to watch, of being threatened with execution for stealing food from the docks: 'You can see why I was resigned to whatever happened after that,' he told Hazel. He felt his survival was partly due to his compact physique and his ability to be part of a group: 'You worked out the optimum for being a survivor. It was no good being a loner. 3 men were too few, 5 in a group was optimal. We could lay aside a bit of food for one another if one was ill and could not work.'

Once he had unburdened himself to Hazel he never spoke of his experiences again and he did not mention them to his mother. Hazel remembered her mother being upset by Tony's behaviour. He could never walk into a room without looking behind the door and he was restive at home, unable to settle down.

Not long after his return two things happened that seriously affected his life. Before the war he had been in love with a girl called Maud and the thought of marrying her after the war had kept him going in the prison camps. He wrote to his mother on his release telling her of his intentions: 'As you can guess Mum I shall want to get married to Maud as soon as I can, but please don't think you will be losing me by this. I've altered a lot since you last knew me. I know I have enough love to keep you both near me. This is my only worry that I can do right by both of you, so please Mum help me, will you, as you have always done?'

Maud and Tony were engaged soon after he returned but in April 1946 she went away for the weekend and wrote him a letter to say that she had come to the conclusion that she had to break off their engagement. It was a disaster for Tony. One of the main props of his world had collapsed and he felt the rejection very bitterly.

At about that time he bought a motorbike. He had an accident shortly afterwards and broke his leg badly, so that he was at home in plaster for several weeks. The fraught atmosphere combined with his devastation at Maud's rejection brought him very low. It was then that he met a girl who became his wife. 'She was older than Tony and had no idea of what he had been through. I felt they got married far too quickly,' Hazel said. There was a great deal of jealousy between Tony's wife and his mother, particularly when the two little boys came along. Mrs Littler was very fond of her grandsons and loved to give them presents but these were not welcome and Hazel remembered the friction between the two women went on and on for years. It cannot have been easy marrying a former Far Eastern POW, Hazel conceded, but unfortunately Tony's wife seemed unable to understand his physical problems and particularly his stomach troubles that plagued him in the post-war years. 'When the anniversary of his being taken prisoner came round each year he would become depressed but he never had any psychiatric treatment and these problems were never discussed. Tony's wife would complain about him to my mother, which was sad as Tony was still her "boy".' Family relations between Tony's wife and mother deteriorated further and during the last nine years of his mother's life from 1975 to 1984 when she was in a home Tony did not visit, which was a great sadness to her.

Hazel, who had been the linchpin of the family both during the war and its immediate aftermath had less and less contact with her brother as the years went by. In her thirties she married Bernard Watson, an ex-RAF officer. They had no family of their own but they lived a full life in London interspersed with visits to Staffordshire to visit her parents, cope with their problems and at times stay and look after them. 'My husband was a saint as far as my family was concerned,' Hazel said. 'He put up with all my going to and fro to Staffordshire; he made financial sacrifices for my parents and he never complained that my brother and his wife should be doing more. After my mother died I drew a line under that part of my life, out of consideration for Bernard.' Tony Littler died in 1998 at the age of seventy-eight. When his son rang to tell her that her brother had died Hazel said that she was sorry, given all he had been through in the war, that he had been ill for a long period before he died. It was only during the brief telephone conversation that she realized that the boys had not understood how much their father had suffered as a POW. 'By then I was a widow and I didn't want to have to go over the whole story of why our family had collapsed in the way it did. When my father died and the house was cleared in 1975 I discovered that all the letters and documents about Tony's captivity were still together. I kept them until 2004 and then decided to place them in the Imperial War Museum, which seemed to be the best place for them.'

5

IN THE EVENT OF DEATH:
THE WIDOW'S TALE

I tried to feel him near me, to pierce the barriers which divided us, to be convinced that he was there. That is, I believe, the real hindrance, our desire to be convinced logically, to know in a physical sense that those whom we cannot see are close. We strain and strive and listen and grasp at them with our bodily senses.

Dame Barbara Cartland, 1948

Over sixty years after the end of the Second World War it is all too easy to think of widows as mature or elderly ladies, dressed in black, heads bowed at the Remembrance Day services every November. However, in 1945 a very large number of widows were in their twenties and some even in their teens. For them the grief at losing their beloved husband, in most cases a man they had been married to for only a short time, was immediate and bitter. Their lives were altered by the course of events way beyond their control and all too often they had had little preparation for coping with the future. Many were unqualified and woke up to the shock that with just over a £1.00 a week pension (the equivalent in 2006 would be £30.00) they would have to seek work to make ends meet.

The story of Emma White, a wartime teenage bride, who was widowed before her twenty-first birthday, is a poignant reminder that widowhood was often a young woman's plight during the Second World War.

'Damn this bloody war for making life so urgent and difficult,' wrote Emma in her wartime memoir. She was writing of the moment she had to make the decision to leave her parents in India and travel to Britain where she was to be married to her fiancé, Peter White, in early 1944. She was nineteen years old and events were buffeting her like a leaf in the wind. Every decision she had to make seemed to her to be critical and there was no time to wait and reflect on what might be the best course of action. The war moved so quickly and life seemed at once so precious and precarious that she felt she could not afford to hesitate.

Emma had been born in India but had grown up and been educated in England, living near London with an aunt. When war broke out her parents asked her to come out and join them. She was fifteen and had only seen her father for a total of four months since she was four. For two and a half years she lived with her parents in their mountain lodge high up above the Shillong plain, working in various war-related posts with mixed success until she met Peter, a 27-year-old career soldier. They fell deeply, madly in love and after only three days together Peter asked Emma to marry him. His life was a whirl of activity and she was swept up by the extraordinary energy of his personality. He wanted them to marry immediately; he wanted to talk about plans for his future, after the war, when he would work to help people who were less fortunate than he was. He insisted, however, that he had a role to fulfil as a soldier and she would have to accept that he needed to go and fight. He was impatient and she was frightened. A few weeks later, he persuaded her to let him ask her father whether they might be married forthwith. Her parents refused, saying that she should wait a year. Peter was bitterly disappointed and Emma was confused. In the event she remained in India and fell seriously ill with malaria.

Peter was posted back to Britain to join his regiment in Scotland and Emma was left trying to decide whether to follow his urgent calls to join him or to listen to her parents who were cautioning her to wait a while. Peter wrote long letters trying to persuade her to take the leap, to jump, as he put it, her own 'Beecher's Brook'. When she recovered from the fever she decided to follow her instincts and go to join him. Eventually her father helped her to get a position as a nanny for a wealthy family on a ship and she sailed in February 1944. She arrived in Britain four weeks later and found herself alone in Liverpool with no one to meet her. The next day she caught a train to London where she was met by her mother-in-law to be. So much of what Emma encountered in London was unfamiliar that she seemed to be in a state of permanent mild shock. The war had wrought so much damage at close quarters that she was forced to face its immediate horrors that had seemed so remote in Shillong. Rationing was rife, buildings and homes were wrecked, families shaken up by evacuation, death and destruction, loss. Everything seemed unfamiliar.

Ten days after her arrival, dressed in a new suit, she took a train to Edinburgh to meet Peter for the first time in nine months. She was bursting with excitement and looked so radiant that an elderly woman in her carriage could not help but comment on her appearance: '"You've got such a light in your eyes," she said. "I'm just so happy," I told her. "I'm going to meet the man I'm going to marry and I haven't seen him for ages." "What a lovely story. You make the most of every good minute while you have them. Sometimes they don't last that long." I realized then that she was in black. "Yes, my dear. I'm wearing black in honour of my three boys. I lost them all within a year but seeing you looking so happy has made me realize that there is a glimpse of hope in the world." I wished that my precious moments hadn't been shattered by the sadness of this elderly lady. Did happiness always run in tandem with sadness?'

Emma and Peter were married on 28 April 1944 at Crieff and spent a blissful week in a hotel on the edge of a large loch. 'Peter's enthusiasm for everything infected me. We walked across hills. We fished in the loch. We looked for young grouse. Peter seemed to be part of this world. He was a country boy at heart and he was content to watch the journey of an ant or to lie on his stomach to tickle trout. There was nothing to mar our first week together.' But even as the idyllic honeymoon came to an end, Peter began to talk of what might come: 'I'm a soldier and I've got to face the war,' he told Emma. 'You've known that from the beginning. I'll be as careful as I can especially now that I have you to come home to . . . No tears, no looking back, no regrets should I end up as some soldiers do.'

A few weeks later he was ordered to leave Scotland and head for the south coast of England where he and his regiment were to await embarkation orders. Emma was sick with worry for his safety. She had got a job working as a nurse in a hospital in Edinburgh and had seen wounded men coming back from the front. Peter was in France in September 1944 when Emma was called into the matron's room. Matron was holding a telegram which she read out to Emma: 'War Office regrets to inform you Major White slightly wounded on September 25. stop. He will be returned to UK soonest. stop. Will notify you details of hospital. stop.' Peter had been hit in the thigh, a bullet had gone clean through the muscles and although he had lost a lot of blood he was expected to make a full recovery. He was sent to a hospital in Derby and for six weeks after his release Emma was able to nurse him at his parents' home. But as he got stronger he became impatient to return to his men. Eventually he succeeded in persuading the doctor to pass him as fit. Emma was furious. She wrote: 'I halted in my tracks and looked out to sea, my voice angry: "Why do you have to be so urgent to get back? Why do you still have to prove your worth? Why can't you realize that you are not indispensable?"' Peter would not be dissuaded. He returned to France before Christmas and Emma went back to work.

In February 1945 she received another call to see Matron. A further telegram had arrived informing her that Major White had been slightly wounded and would be coming back to Britain. She was half-horrified and half-relieved, remembering how quickly Peter had recovered the last time. A week passed and still no telegram arrived to say which hospital he had been sent to. Another week went by, and then another. Emma became anxious and agitated. She had packed and unpacked her suitcase a hundred times, ready to jump on the first train to wherever he was. Then Matron called her in again. She had a telegram in her hand: 'You must sit and be very brave,' she told Emma. 'It reads like this: "War Office regret to inform you Major Peter White killed in action on 15 February 1945. Previous telegram sent in error. Major P White of the Canadian Forces was slightly wounded. Please accept apologies. Further information to follow."'

'There were no tears, no drama, just dull hurting pain. I heard Peter's voice saying that I was to be brave, not to cry . . . All of a sudden I felt exhaustion and despair sweep over me like the rough waves on a beach, pounding and retreating, pounding and retreating.'

Emma was a twenty-year-old widow. With Peter dead and her family thousands of miles away in India she felt marooned in a strange country with her distraught parents-in-law. 'All I knew was I'd got to face this damn world squarely with only Peter's memory to help. The greeting from his parents at Nairn was sombre but loving. Sir Aubrey found it hard to control his tears. Lady Olivia walked about as if in a trance. Movement and activity helped to swamp the pain, but at night it returned, worse than ever. I slept in the bed that we had shared and wept silently into the pillow.'

The shock that followed Peter's death left Emma unable to make any decisions about what to do next. She felt, she said, like a flat fish. When her mother wrote and suggested she go back to India she thought dully that she really did not want to go back to Shillong and become 'a little girl all over again'. But it was the only sensible suggestion and her father-in-law felt it was right that she should go home. So, in May 1945 she found herself in London saying goodbye to her aunt. '"Leave a little room in your heart for me," said the old lady. "I wish I could carry some of your pain." She tucked my hands into her old gnarled ones and carried them to her lips. She turned away without kissing me. I paused and looked at the little house, hoping for some comfort but there was none.'

Emma sailed on a Dutch-owned ship. 'I tried hard to join in with the talking, the drinking, the general bonhomie but I spent much of my time on the upper deck leaning against the rails. I had sailed for England with so much hope. I was returning with nothing.' As the end of the war was announced the ship's company erupted into a huge party. Champagne and wine flowed in the dining room but Emma just felt numb. For her the war had not ended soon enough.

She was one of over 300,000 women who were widowed by the Second World War, most of them young women, some with small children, whose lives had been dramatically changed by the course of history. 'It was easy to pick out the bereaved: the sad eyes above the smiling mouths,' wrote Mrs E. Knowles in her memoirs. For those who were widowed there was little to console them in the first few years after the war.

When a young man dies in the prime of his life it is often the sense of a lost future which is bitterly mourned. They died as heroes in the eyes of their families and the construction of an image of what the young men had been and what they might have become sometimes took on almost mythical proportions. 'The fantasy of perfection remains like a persistent shadow in the narratives of those women who lost their husbands during wartime,' wrote the historian and expert on widowhood Professor Joy Damousi of the University of Melbourne. She has done extensive research into war widowhood and has recorded some remarkable first-hand testimonies of life for such women after the trauma of losing their husbands.

In researching her book *Living with the Aftermath*, Professor Damousi interviewed a large number of war widows. One woman, Jean Fry, whose husband left Australia in 1942 when she was seven months pregnant and who died serving with the Royal Australian Air Force in June 1944, was emphatic in defining two types of war widows. There were those women, she insisted, who lost their husbands during the war and those whose husbands died after coming home, sometimes years later. There is no differentiation between the two different types of widowhood in the eyes of the governments of Australia and Britain and yet Jean Fry felt strongly that there was a fundamental difference. She told Damousi: 'Just imagine the difference between [that and] what we real war widows went through. The trauma of your husband never coming home. Never seeing their child and you being left with less than a living allowance and the other ones who had joy of their husband . . . there would be some relationship between you left, and also they had the joy of seeing their children.'

Jean's frustration was directed also at women who complained that their men were different on their return from the men they had known in the pre-war times. 'I know they probably had a difficult time with the men when they first came home, but they *came* home and that was the man of their choice that they had married and here he was home.'

She felt that creating an umbrella organization to encompass all war widows diminished the status of all those women whose husbands were killed in action. 'It makes nonsense of all the effort we've put in for the last fifty years which doesn't compare with them having their husbands for twenty, thirty, forty or fifty years. Having their husbands to help pay the house off. I've paid this [house] off myself. Having to rear the children, educate the children, buy cars.'

All these practical considerations were very real for newly widowed women and in the first instance after the war there was not a lot of help, support or understanding for their predicament. Once the initial shock of widowhood had passed, and this often understandably took time, there were the practical matters of how to deal with life without a husband, almost always the main wage earner, and how to bring up children without a father.

In Australia things moved more swiftly than in Britain for war widows. In February 1946 an energetic woman called Jessie Vasey, wife of General George Vasey, set up the War Widows Guild. 'Her endeavour to assist widows became a life-long crusade and she demanded the rights to a certain measure of comfort and dignity not merely a pension sufficient to keep their heads just above water.' She set up branches of the War Widows Guild throughout Australia and drummed her message home to the authorities that the war widows had not only to survive on their own account but that they had a duty of care towards their children. Their role was not just to bring up their children but 'to make up to our children, as far as humanly possible, the very terrible lack in their lives which the loss of their fathers had caused'. Certainly the financial situation for the Australian war widows was bleak in the late 1940s. Their pension was less than half the amount of the basic wage and many families struggled just to survive.

In Britain things took a great deal longer to get sorted out and there was no organization to take up the fight on behalf of the women. The War Widows Association was formed in 1972, nearly thirty years after the end of the Second World War. And it was formed as a result of one widow's battle with the Inland Revenue. Laura Connelly returned to Britain from Australia to find herself facing bankruptcy proceedings by the Inland Revenue. In Australia a war widow's pension was paid tax free. In Britain, however, this was not the case and when Mrs Connelly refused to pay tax on her pension she found herself in trouble. Her plight came to the notice of a Sunday newspaper in 1971 and an article appeared about 'Britain's Forgotten Women'. Fourteen women wrote in support of Laura Connelly and they met up in London to discuss what was to be done. At their first meeting they decided to form an association 'to fight for the removal of the burden of tax from the pension'. Constituted the following year, the association, under its first chairman, Jill Gee, fought to get the government to reconsider the whole question of taxing war widows' pensions. They achieved partial success in 1976 when 50 per cent of the tax was removed and full success in 1979 when the remaining 50 per cent was removed. Why, one wonders, had it taken almost thirty years for British war widows to have their own representative association when the Australians had managed to establish their own guild just eight months after the end of the Second World War?

For the women who had suffered loss the greatest difficulty by far was in coming to terms with life without their husbands. Some women in Joy Damousi's study, such as Mary Ellen Simpson, accepted widowhood in a fatalistic way, believing that 'it was meant to be'. It seems an almost romantic way to accept the death of a much-loved husband and yet this was a view that was prevalent all over. Perhaps it had to do with the belief that the war was fought in a just cause and that sacrifices had to be made in order for the war to be won. And yet, Mary Ellen Simpson admitted, she was never really prepared to accept that her young husband, William, was dead: 'I used to dream, you know, of meeting him at Spencer Street station, what I would wear and what I would put on Alan. I could see him running to meet his father but it just wasn't meant to be. I think life's planned out for everybody. We all have a tick beside it but you're going quicker during wartime.' When the telegram arrived at her door telling her that William was missing over France she declared to herself there and then that she would never remarry. Her husband was idealized in her mind and she could never find someone else to match up to his memory. 'I had many an opportunity but nobody ever . . . came up to him.'

Mary Ellen found it hard to endure the sights of returning men, welcomed into the arms of their wives and sweethearts. The reminder of all that she had lost was overpowering and the pain she felt never really went away. Fifty years later she felt her love for William Simpson was undiminished. 'I always say in life you'll fall in love and your first love is your only love.' One of her greatest regrets was that William's body was never recovered so that she had no grave to visit, no certainty about where his remains lay, although it is most probable that they were lost at sea. Warrant Officer William Alfred Simpson of the Royal Australian Air Force, who died on 5 January 1945 aged twenty-seven, is commemorated on panel 284 on the Runnymede Memorial overlooking the River Thames on Cooper's Hill at Englefield Green, four miles from Windsor and over 12,000 miles from his home in Ararat, in the Australian state of Victoria.

Eve Harris lost her husband, Albert, in 1943 when his plane was shot down over Germany. He too is commemorated at Runnymede. 'We were only married for six years . . . I suppose time dims everything. I love him more now than I ever did . . . I realize his worth . . . he was [an] honourable, decent human being.'

Some young widows did remarry after the war. There was tremendous pressure to have a husband to help care and provide for them but these marriages were not always successful. Joyce Tilley had married Arthur Thornton in 1942, when he was just twenty-two. The two of them had met in 1936 when they were both working for a department store in their teens. Arthur and Joyce spent barely six weeks of married life together before he was sent abroad by the air force. He died on 10 April 1944 but the circumstances of his death were never known and she spent most of the rest of her life wondering how and where he had died. It was much later that she heard that Arthur was buried in Denmark, at Esbjerg (Fourfelt) Cemetery. She was never able to visit the grave and his memory remained 'an obsession with her even when she remarried'.

In what now must seem a cold attempt to help her daughter forget her first husband and make the most of her second marriage, Joyce's mother destroyed all the letters, photographs and telegrams that she had ever received from Arthur. Her friends also 'helped' Joyce to forget Arthur. Her new husband too was in the air force but was never sent overseas as he had contracted polio while in an air-force hospital. The couple had two children but the marriage was unhappy and Joyce took responsibility for a part of this because, she said, she was consumed with memories of Arthur in her 'inner life' although they had made a pact not to talk about him. Particularly difficult for her was the fact that the date of Arthur's death fell on the same day as her new husband's birthday. When her second husband died of cancer she was consumed with sadness for the death of her first husband: 'How can I say this without making myself a monster? A certain amount of relief and yet sadness for a wasted 50 odd years. Regret that he hadn't turned out better. Regret that it could've been my fault. A lot of regret. And then I started to think more about Arthur that had been more or less put into the back of [my] mind through the years . . .'

The events surrounding Arthur Thornton's death continued to obsess her and in her interview with Joy Damousi she spoke of the questions that went round and round in her head: 'I don't know how he died. I'd love to know how he died.' She was haunted by worries that he had suffered before he died and thought endlessly of what might have been had he returned home safely: '. . . the dreadful part about it is that I think far more of Arthur than I do of Larry in my thoughts in the last five years. It was like I suppressed it and they just flooded out when he died. So I'm mourning for my first husband again.'

Shortly before her fifth wedding anniversary in September 1944 Ena Mitchell received a letter from the War Office. She was with a cousin at home when the post arrived. She saw the letter and assumed it was from Bill as he always sent her something to mark their anniversary. She opened the rest of the post and then turned to the envelope on the side. The letter began with the words: 'I regret to inform you . . .' For a moment Ena could not believe her eyes. Surely there was some mistake. The rank was wrong. They'd got him mixed up. It must be someone else. Sadly it was not. Bill Mitchell had been killed in Belgium on 9 September 1944 when a Bren-gun carrier he was travelling on blew up. He had not stood a chance. A company quartermaster sergeant with the East Yorkshire Regiment, he had been in France since D-Day. Now he was dead at the age of thirty-three and Ena was a widow at under twenty-five.

The great irony was that Bill had done twelve years in the army before the war, nine and a half of which he had spent in India, and had left to take up a post in the civil service. Then the war came and Bill felt he had to go back to the army. He had four brothers and just could not bear the thought of seeing them fight while he stayed behind in a safe, comfortable job. So off he went and signed up again with the East Yorkshire Regiment. The other four boys came back after the war. Only he did not.

For the next four years Bill was posted all over the country and spent his leaves with Ena who was living with her parents in the village of Kingsley near Bordon in Hampshire, about ten miles south-west of Aldershot. They had married in 1939 and their daughter, Anne, was born in 1942. When Bill left for the last time in July 1944 she was two years old. Ena recalled: 'I remember him saying to me as he left the lane that this would be the last time, the very last time, that he would ever have to go away from us. I had cried so many tears on the many occasions that he went away and little did I think that this would be the last time I ever saw him.'

The day after the letter arrived from the War Office to say that Henry William Cecil Mitchell had died Ena got a letter from him to say that he was to be moved from the East Yorkshire Regiment to the Durham Light Infantry 'as so many of our friends have been killed'. At that stage she did not know how Bill had died nor indeed exactly where he had died but a friend of her mother's who was a chaplain offered to try and find out more. It brought a little comfort to know that he was buried at Leopoldsburg War Cemetery and in the ensuing years she and Anne visited the cemetery to put flowers on his grave. Ena said:

> I never received any help, any counselling, any communication at all in fact after that initial letter from the War Office. Just information to tell me that I was entitled to the war widow's pension which was 26s a week. Bill had had life insurance but that didn't pay out in the event of death in war so we just received the premiums he had paid in. Nothing else. There was no hope of me getting any work where my parents lived because there were only two buses a day from the village and the first left at 10 am which was no use. I was determined that Anne should receive a good education. Her cousins would and I didn't want her to get left behind. So that became the main focus of my life.

They moved to Abingdon in Oxfordshire and there Ena began her new life as a young widow with no prospects and little but her wits to live on. The problem in Abingdon after the war was that many people who worked at the nuclear site at Harwell were looking for accommodation and Ena was competing with them to try to find cheap digs. Her pension amounted to a shilling a week was less than the cost of the rent she would have to pay for a room so she was on the back foot from the word go. What she did not know, and no one told her, was that she was entitled to help with her rent because she was a widow with a child. Furthermore the civil service would have been willing to assist with Anne's school fees. Eventually this latter help came through but not for years. 'When we moved to Abingdon and I realized how difficult it would be to find somewhere to live I sat in the park and wept. It was all so hard.'

At first she lived in a small room with no heating. It was so cold that she used to offer herself as an overnight babysitter so that she and Anne could at least sit in a room with a fire of an evening. Then she placed an advertisement in the local paper to say that she was seeking a room and would not only pay rent but would also do housework. She was offered a room in a house belonging to a man who claimed to be a teacher. 'In fact he was no such thing. He taught beekeeping. I hated living there and was always frightened that he would try and get into my room at night. So I used to pull the chest of drawers in front of my bedroom door to prevent him.' What Ena did not realize was that in Abingdon, as a newcomer, she was regarded with suspicion and it was widely believed that she was a single mother with an illegitimate daughter. Years later people who became friends said they would have liked to have helped her back then but had not understood her situation. It must have felt at times as if the whole world was against her.

Nevertheless Ena was a fighter and a survivor. Her focus remained Anne's education and she did all manner of odd jobs to keep little bits of money coming in so that the two of them could live and she could pay the school fees. 'I became the first traffic warden in Abingdon,' she said proudly.

I didn't have a uniform but the police were very friendly and taught me all about traffic control. Then I got in touch with the British Legion. That was when I began to get a little support. They told me of a family who lived in a big three-storey house where the top floor could be a self-contained flat. The mother had died of cancer and the father was living there with his two children, a boy of fourteen and a little baby girl of two. We moved in with the widower and I looked after his two children who were lovely.

Although Ena's circumstances were poor she had a great deal of emotional support from her family. 'My brother was wonderful. Even though he was so weak he could not walk up the path to his house without a puffer, so badly had his lungs been damaged in the Great War, he always stood by me and I adored him. Bill's brothers were also very kind to me. Anne and I often spent our holidays with my brother-in-law and I became very fond of my nephew, who has remained a loyal friend.'

Sometime in the 1950s the civil service got in touch with Ena to tell her they were making a book of remembrance for all the men and women who had been in the service and who had lost their lives in the war. She had a visit from a representative who told her that if she were ever in 'dire straits' she should let them know. She did not realize that this extended to help with Anne but when that became clear and the service contributed towards the school fees life became a little less hand-to-mouth.

In 1971 Ena heard from a friend in Oxford that a group of war widows had met in London and had decided to set up an association to represent them. She became one of its first members. It proved to be one of the most rewarding things she ever did in her life. She soon became a regional officer for Oxfordshire and Berkshire and found that she and others benefited enormously from the mutual support they could offer one another.

We all have each other's phone numbers and can ring each other up to chat about things. At the beginning all the talk was about our pensions. That was the big issue at that time. Now we talk about our medication! The time I really needed help was just after the war and that's when I didn't get it. I don't want to give the impression that people didn't want to help us – our local war hero and MP, Airey Neave, was aware of our plight and tried hard to help us but there was little he could do. The government was not interested in the war widows. So when the War Widows Association started it was a godsend. I've met such wonderful people through it over the years and I've been to some amazing places. I had tea with Prince Charles at Highgrove and I've sat on a sofa in number 10 Downing Street. I just hope the young war widows of today will want to join the association. It is a great comfort in times of loneliness. And believe me it is still lonely sometimes, even after all this time.

Ena also said:

Most people would never understand me if they heard me say this but I was so pleased that Bill died when he did. He was such a fit and sporty young man that I am certain he would never have coped with being blind or permanently injured. He would have hated that. But I missed him dreadfully. I did have other opportunities to marry but I was focused on Anne and her education. And, anyway, I had so much hassle and humiliation being a widow in the early years. I'd never have believed it. No one else understands us. We had such a very hard time after the war but we coped. I never had a penny of debt all my life.

With a daughter to care for Ena had had no option after Bill died but to look forward and to make plans for the future. Although her life had been completely shattered in the immediate aftermath of his death, and life, for the first few years at least, was a constant effort to keep things ticking over, she did not have the time to reflect on the sad situation she found herself in. Alice Hill did. She said she never fully recovered from the traumatic experience of being widowed in her twenties and it took years for her to rebuild her life after her husband was killed. Now in her eighties, almost blind and deaf, Alice spoke about her lifelong quest to understand what had happened to her husband in the last few weeks of his life.

Alice's father, who had been in the Royal Marines for twenty years, moved to Castleford in Yorkshire in 1930 to work as a PE teacher at a local school. Arthur had been a pupil at the school and was working as an apprentice to a local blacksmith when he met Alice. She was four years younger than he was. 'We met in 1935 when I was fifteen,' she said. 'We were engaged when I was twenty, married when I was twenty-one and I was widowed at twenty-four. That's the bare bones of my life to be frank. The world left me behind after that.' Alice's story is one of a woman desperately trying to come to terms with what happened to her husband in 1944 and understanding the fateful final weeks of his life. It took her over sixty years to pull the pieces of the puzzle together but she succeeded to her own satisfaction and in 2003 she made her final visit to his grave in Normandy which she had first visited in the summer of 1946.

In 1939 Alice's father, George, was called up by the navy. As he was not yet fifty he knew he would have to serve again if a war came. He left home in August and did not return, other than occasionally for leave, until 1945. Arthur was called up in April 1940, two months after the couple had announced their engagement. Alice had always known that he would be, because, as she explained, having been in a family with three generations of men in the services, she was used to the idea that if war came men had to leave to fight. 'However, Arthur and I believed the war would be over quickly and then we could marry and get on with our lives. We were both desperate for a family.' Arthur was drafted into the Royal Artillery and spent the first four years of the war stationed in the UK. Every three months he would come home for a week's leave to see Alice and his family: 'Subsequently I was very grateful for those weeks we had together. I was luckier than some women whose men went away at the start of the war and didn't come back for six years or, worse still, didn't come back at all. At least I saw a bit of Arthur after he was called up.' In 1941 conscription of women began. 'That focused our minds,' she explained, 'I knew that if I didn't volunteer to go and work in the local munitions factory I would be told to join one of the women's services. That would have been awful because I might have been posted somewhere and missed Arthur's leaves. As it was I was keen to be around whenever he had time off, even if it was a special unannounced twenty-four hours. That's why I went to work at the factory. I hated the work but it did give me the freedom I wanted.'

Arthur and Alice were married on 22 February 1941, the day after her twenty-first birthday. 'He only had a week's leave for our wedding but I managed to get a room in a B&B close to his barracks in Aldershot for the following week so that we could spend the evenings and nights together. It was a lovely time, it really was. When we weren't together Arthur used to write to me every day. He numbered his letters so that I would know if any went missing. Sometimes I would get two or three in one day but it was very rare for two days to go by without my hearing from him.'

In the summer of 1944 her father-in-law became gravely ill and Arthur asked her to contact the War Office and obtain a special leave form to which service personnel were entitled if they needed compassionate leave. At the same time Arthur was moved to the south coast and all he could tell her in his letters was that they were holding out, awaiting instructions. She hadn't seen him for three months and his leave was due in July. 'I knew it was all very hush-hush because I suddenly started getting censored letters without an address. I don't think he knew very much more than we did because all the planning around D-Day was kept so secret.' Alice heard about the D-Day landings on the BBC and she knew that he had not gone over to France in the first wave because two days later she received a letter from him saying: 'Well you will know the news now that the balloon has gone up. You can see I was not in the first lot.' There was a delay in his letters which she had not been used to but in his next one, dated 25 June 1944, she was able to work out that he was somewhere in France. That was the extent of her knowledge. On 2 July he wrote to tell her that he was at Bayeux and a week later she got another letter to say he was resting behind the lines. The letters were sparse and she could glean little. On 18 July she got a letter from him dated three days earlier thanking her for the parcel she had sent him, which, she remembered, had contained crisps, cubes of Oxo and some jam her mother had made from the wild strawberries in the hedgerows. Then there was silence. For a week she heard nothing. For a second week there was still no word from him but she refused to believe that anything bad had happened to Arthur. She presumed he had been injured and was being sent back to a UK hospital for treatment.

I hadn't got a place of my own as my mother had said it made no sense for me to live alone while the two of us were without our men so I stayed with her. There was a post-office on the road where my parents lived and I often used to drop in on my way back from work to pick up any mail that might have come in the second delivery. I was always keen to see if there was a letter from Arthur. So the post-office staff knew me quite well. This particular morning I bumped into the postman and he said to me: 'I've got a letter for you.' 'Oh good,' I replied, 'is it on HM Service?' 'Yes,' he said. Well I was delighted because I thought it was probably the application form for compassionate leave. When I ripped open the envelope I read: 'The War Office regrets to inform you . . .' I can't remember what it said after that, I just passed out. Someone got me home I think. It was the first day of August, I remember that because the new issue of clothing coupons came out that day. Later, much later, the postman's wife told me that he came home in a terrible state and said: 'I would have given anything not to have been the postman today.'

Arthur had been killed by a blast from a mortar shell on 16 July 1944. For months that was all Alice knew. Then she received a letter from the army chaplain to tell her that he had buried Arthur in a military cemetery along with a number of other men from their regiment on 18 July.

That was so sad for me. I had had a letter that day thanking me for my package and all the while I had been imagining him eating the little bits we had sent him from home he was being buried in France. For a long time this was a part of my husband's life I knew nothing about. He had been picked up and taken away from me and killed. I felt this huge need to find out more about what had happened to him and to try to understand where he had been, what he had seen and above all, how he had died.

When Alice's father returned to Castleford in the late summer of 1945 he was deeply shocked by the state of his grief-stricken daughter. He promised her there and then that he would spend his gratuity that he had received from the navy to take her, her mother and her younger sister to France to see Arthur's grave. This he did the following summer. The family spent a week in a *pension* near Bayeux so that Alice could visit the war cemetery every day.

One day I was there on my own in the evening when a little girl came over to speak to me. I had only schoolgirl French and she spoke no English but we understood one another. She, it transpired, had been part of a local scheme run in French schools to adopt a soldier's grave and she had chosen Arthur's. I don't know who was more astonished, she or I, but it was a wonderful moment for me when I realized that he would never be forgotten and even if I couldn't get to see his grave as often as I would have wanted, there would be somebody local to put flowers on it for his birthday or our anniversary. And so began a friendship with the Oilly family that has gone on for sixty years and more.

Alice's quest to find out about the last three weeks of her husband's life became an obsession. She discovered from the padre that he had been buried with the little silver chain she had bought him for his dog tag the summer before his death. 'That meant so much to me to know that little detail,' she said, 'to know that he has got a bit of our life together buried with him.' She wrote letters to Arthur's commanding officer and to members of the regiment who were able to give her little bits of information that helped her to build up her picture. 'Anything to do with my husband I wanted to be involved in. I needed to be involved, in fact.' She read books about the war and visited Normandy as often as she could. She talked to the French villagers who had witnessed the landings and gradually, over the years, she met other women who had lost men on 16 July 1944. The one thing she could not bring herself to do was to visit the place where he had died.

At home her life was in tatters. 'What I would have done without my parents I shall never know,' Alice said, 'I was so depressed and miserable I think I would have disappeared completely. They were marvellous to me and looked after me so well.'

Thirteen weeks after Arthur was reported killed Alice stopped getting his pay and began to get her widow's pension.

When it first came I was so shocked I thought there must be some mistake. It was £1 1s 8d. That was it and it remained at that level until my fortieth birthday. Had I had children I would have been paid at the same level as the forty-year-old widows but as I had not, it was considered that I would be able to go out to work and earn my own living. Well, I hadn't planned it like that. I had wanted to get married, have a family and live at home. I had no training for work at all. It will seem strange to younger people reading this but that was my expectation. I wanted to stay at home, be a housewife and bring up our children.

For the first four years after the war Alice lived at home and felt very sorry for herself. 'I was pretty bad for a long time,' she admitted, 'I knew I'd never have children and that was a great sadness to me. I'd lost my stake in the future. I felt as if the world was going on without me and what's more, it really didn't matter to me.' Behind the scenes Alice's mother was talking to various people in the town about what her daughter might do and how they could help her to find something that would give her some sense of self-worth.

Eventually, after a lot of resistance on my part, I was persuaded to help out with the local girl guides. At first I hated it so much I would come home in floods of tears. It broke my heart every time I saw a little blonde girl that could have been mine. But the guide captain persisted and she encouraged me, little by little, to take on more responsibility. Well, all I can say is that it became my life. Working with young people was so rewarding and so wonderful. I feel now that even if I didn't have my own family I did manage to have a stake in other children's lives and I never thought I would hear myself saying that.

Alice continued to live with her parents until her mother died in 1983 and her father ten years later at the age of ninety-eight. After his death she inherited the little bungalow where they had lived since 1960. 'It's funny to think of it now, but I've still got wedding presents I've never used. I'd just gone on using my mother's things all my life.'

In 2003 Alice made her final visit to Normandy. How could she be so sure it would be her last visit?

I realized that I knew everything I was ever going to know about the last three weeks of Arthur's life. I had seen the hills that he had seen. I'd seen the war devastation in Caen in 1946 that he would have seen two years earlier. I'd heard the birds singing in the hedgerows and watched the clouds scudding across the sky. On my final visit to his grave I felt absolutely and completely at peace. I don't need to go back there again. No, not now, and not in the future, because I know I've done everything I can for my Arthur.

She still wears the locket Arthur gave her in 1943 and her sitting room is full of photographs and memorabilia about his short life. There is a sense of sadness at what might have been had he come home alive but Alice is also proud of what she has achieved in her life, both professionally and on a personal level. 'The war cost me a normal life,' she concluded, 'I would so have loved to have had a family but my work has brought me many rewards.'

6

THAT DISTANT LOOK:
THE WIFE'S TALE

It is sad to say that only those of us who experienced this deprivation and degradation will ever realize our desperate plight. Mothers and wives were very understanding but really did not know the full flourish to this day.

Edward R. McDaniel

Nothing in Kitty Sitwell's background prepared her for life during the Second World War. She had been brought up to curtsey to the Queen and to take her place in upper-class society. By the middle of the 1940s she was being taught how to cook by her daughter, Mollie.

Kitty was born Catherine Florence Parke Olive on 7 January 1896, a twin daughter, and was brought up in Leamington Spa. Her upbringing was quiet, as was typical of the period. She was very beautiful and very naive. When she married Degge Sitwell in 1919 it was considered that he had been fortunate to find himself such an attractive wife. Kitty, in her daughter's own words: '. . . had had a tremendously sheltered childhood. She had a very limited education and I always felt she was a bit adrift intellectually as a result, but women of her standing grew up like that. She had absolutely no experience of the real world. In Edwardian days women in the "upper classes" were supposed to be beautiful and helpless.'

Degge Sitwell was educated at Wellington College and at the Royal Military Academy, Woolwich. He served in the First World War with the Royal Artillery from 1914 to 1918 and won the Military Cross in 1917, emerging from the war as a captain. He also fought in the first Battle of the Somme in 1916 at the age of nineteen.

He returned after the Armistice and married Kitty almost immediately, in January 1919. Their only child, Mollie, was born in 1920 and when she was six years old Degge and Kitty went to India for six years leaving Mollie to be brought up by her grandparents. By the time Mollie left school war was looming so she remained in England and married a young officer, Frederick Charles Wolseley 'Tim' Timmins, in her father's regiment.

Kitty Sitwell had been married for twenty years by the outbreak of the Second World War. 'Theirs was a very happy marriage,' Mollie said, 'but it was not a marriage of equals. My mother never made any decisions about anything of importance. She was good at running the house and deciding on what flowers to have and she was much loved by the servants. However, on all decisions to do with matters outside the home she deferred to my father, who was a very strong man with great leadership qualities.' Degge Sitwell was promoted to lieutenant colonel in 1939 and to brigadier in 1941. He left England that same year and was sent out to the Far East where he was GOC British Troops in Java.

He was not to return to England until September 1945 and for just over a year Kitty had no knowledge of her husband's whereabouts, nor whether he was alive or dead. In fact he was captured in Java by the Japanese in 1942 having been promoted in the field to major general by General Wavell, who instructed him to fight a rearguard action against the Japanese. On 4 March 1942 he wrote to Kitty from British HQ on Java: 'I'm afraid it can only end one way as the odds are too great, we are putting in companies where we ought to put in divisions.' After his capture he was sent to Formosa (Taiwan) with other senior British, Australian and Dutch officers. 'My mother only learned later in the war that he had been taken prisoner.' Mollie explained, 'I always felt she had every bit as bad a war as my father. She was completely alone and nothing in her upbringing had prepared her for having to cope with life without her husband.' Mollie had to take the lead in everything. Kitty's sheltered life had meant that she had never learned to stand on her own two feet, Mollie said. 'But I admired her tremendously for the way she learned to cope with life during the war,' she added.

Four days before the evacuation at Dunkirk Mollie was married, so Tim missed that debacle but he was sent back to France as a gunnery instructor. For the next four years he had occasional leave to visit his family. Mollie gave birth to their first daughter in 1942 and their second in 1944. Tim came back to see his second daughter that summer and returned to France after a short leave.

Mollie was living in a small furnished cottage at Ferndown, six miles inland from Bournemouth and close to her Sitwell grandparents. After Degge left Britain, Kitty moved in with her and they settled down to an uneasy existence, neither knowing what was to become of their respective husbands. 'My mother had no experience of small children as she and my father had gone to

India when I was nearly six and I was brought up by my grand-parents, and nanny of course, until I was twelve. She wanted to have nothing to do with my daughters' upbringing and she never interfered with that. In fact her presence was entirely beneficial to Anne and Jill. They always adored her and continued to do so after the war.' Nevertheless it was hard work for Mollie and this, combined with the very real anxiety Kitty felt about the disappearance of her husband, put a strain on life in the cottage. Kitty wrote to him once a week until he was set free. But letters were so hopelessly delayed that it was difficult for him to keep up to date with the news from home.

The worst possible news came for Mollie in 1944. Tim was reported to have been killed in action on 1 October, three months after his last leave. He was just twenty-seven when he died and Mollie was a widow at twenty-four. Tim was buried in Bergen-op-Zoom War Cemetery in the Netherlands, one of nearly 1,200 men buried in that cemetery, but it was years before Mollie got to visit his grave. Suddenly she was faced with a yet more uncertain future with two small girls, no financial security and a mother who had no idea how to cook. There was no way that Mollie could afford to go to pieces after Tim's death: 'One had to learn to cope with it because you knew it happened all around you. It happened to people you knew, to friends and relatives. It happened to countless people you didn't know and they all had to cope too. It was much more difficult for my mother-in-law. She was devastated by Tim's death. He was her son, after all. But I had my babies and my own mother to look after. I just had to get on with life. No choice.'

The Pacific war came to its abrupt end on 15 August 1945. Degge Sitwell was moved to Manchuria and from there was released by the Russians. On his release he received several long letters from Kitty and Mollie updating him on life over the last three and a half years. He wrote his first long letter as a free man to Kitty:

17 August 1945 – a wonderful day. I shall keep it as an anniversary for the rest of my life. . . . First of all, bar the fact that I am very weak & thin through 3½ years of starvation I am <u>absolutely well</u> physically, and none the worse for the purgatory we have been through. Mentally I'm not so certain, and won't be able to tell till we get out, but I now understand what they mean in the Bible about 'the iron entering into the soul', having been kept in manacles for a month at one time, as I will tell you about later. Some of us here are definitely odd and I think all will want a considerable rest before we are fit for anything again.

In the same letter he explained how he had refused to order his men to go on a death march and was punished by the Japanese: 'I was stood up against a wall faced with a firing party and kept in handcuffs for 3 weeks of which 10 days were behind my back; it was absolute agony: in addition I was beaten a good deal and generally pretty badly manhandled. They gave me up after a month as a bad job.' He concluded that he was not sure if he would get another job 'as I am a bit mental'.

Given his high military status he was flown home to Britain at the beginning of September, one of the first Far Eastern POWs to return, rather than having to travel back by sea as the majority of the others did. He arrived in Poole harbour in a seaplane just twenty-four hours after Kitty had heard that he was due to come home. It was a great shock for them both. 'My mother said it was so awful when she met him in Southampton. She barely recognized him and he seemed to her to be almost a complete stranger, certainly not the man who had left her four years earlier.' When he left in 1941 he had weighed sixteen stone. On his return he weighed under ten stone and had shrunk by three inches in height. A photograph of him taken shortly after his arrival shows a shadow of a man with a big frame in a baggy suit and a faraway look in his eyes, so typical of many returned prisoners of war. 'I always felt his return was too quick, far too quick,' Mollie said. 'He was of course anxious to get home and take up where he had left off but there was no preparation, no advice. He was just flown in and left to get on with life on leave until the army called him up again. And the doctors had no idea how to help him to get back on his feet. They just said he was hungry because he had been starved but once he regained his weight he would be fine.'

Degge Sitwell spoke little to his wife and daughter about his captivity on Java but Mollie knew that he used to replay the mental cruelty the Japanese had subjected them to in his mind. She said:

> He was bitter about the callous attitude of the Japanese towards the prisoners but my father was very strong mentally, so he managed to stand up to the treatment the Japanese used to mete out to him and the other officers. The guards used to line up his soldiers and threaten to shoot them one by one if he did not tell them what they wanted to know. He never spoke of the physical torture he received but he had two big lumps on his head from 'bashings' that were still there when he died. I think he felt guilty that he had survived when so many others hadn't and he felt guilty that he had not been able to save more men.

Immediately upon his return Degge and Kitty Sitwell moved in with his parents. It was a strained homecoming and he found it hard to come to terms with the normality of life around him and to the attentions of his anxious wife. He was also perplexed by everything that had gone on in his absence. 'I know my father was upset that he knew little of how the family had got on while he was away. He felt things had been beyond his control during the war and he had not been able to protect his family as he would have liked.' His doctor advised Kitty to feed him up. This, of course, could have proved disastrous had Mollie not been able to intervene and stop her mother and aunt giving him bacon, butter and rich foods they had saved up for his return but which upset his delicate and damaged digestive system. 'When I saw him three days after he got home his body could not even digest bread,' she recalled.

The whirl of activity on his return sent him into a form of shock and Mollie worried that neither he nor her mother had had any time to come to terms with their being reunited before he was scooped up by the army and prepared for service overseas again. He had little time to digest the news that his father had died while he was in captivity, that his son-in-law had been killed in action and that he was now a grandfather of two little girls. Kitty Sitwell expected her husband to be retired. He had been given a general's pension on which they could live comfortably. All he really wanted, he told her, was to have a flat in Chelsea and to get some new golf clubs as the Japanese had taken his away when he was captured. However this was not to be. He was only forty-nine and the army decided to give him another command, sending him out to the Middle East in early 1946. He was a district commander in the Canal North District in Egypt from 1946 to 1949. This was good for him, Mollie said, because he was forced to take up the career he had so enjoyed before the war but it was very tough on Kitty who found life in the Middle East trying. Following that spell he came back to Britain and took over as a deputy district commander, East Anglia District, from 1949 to 1951.

He eventually retired in 1951 and was made a member of the Royal Household with the job of Keeper of the Jewel House in HM Tower of London in 1952, a position he held until 1968. This was much more to Kitty's liking. 'They had a beautiful flat in the Tower and my father could indulge his interest in the history of the Crown Jewels, publishing, as he did, two books on the subject: *The Crown Jewels* in 1953 and *The English Regalia* in 1973.'

Kitty's biggest concern about her husband was his nervous state. The doctors told her that he should not be allowed to do anything that would exacerbate his anxiety. There was a particularly difficult period in 1953 when he was in the final stages of writing his first book. The deadline put him under great pressure and he became a little unbalanced, which frightened Kitty. 'I know my mother felt she was letting my father down because she couldn't cope when he became anxious. She simply didn't know how to help him. She always tried to do everything she could for him but psychological problems were too difficult for her to deal with.' One physical manifestation of his anxiety was that he developed a then little understood condition called oesophageal achalasia which was difficult to diagnose and deal with. The fundamental symptom is an inability to swallow food and is the result of a neuromuscular failure of relaxation at the lower end of the oesophagus. This used to occur when he was in social situations, such as eating out, and caused Kitty unease and embarrassment. She was always fearful that he would suffer when they were at some grand dinner and she never felt entirely able to relax over meals, even at home.

Like so many others', Kitty Sitwell's life was utterly changed by the Second World War. Although Mollie believes that her parents' marriage was happy, she has no doubt that the terrible privations of the prisoner-of-war camp resulted in problems for her father that only her mother would ever have to deal with.

'She would have felt, I am sure, that this was something she had to cope with. It was simply her role to support my father regardless of what came her way. It was her Victorian upbringing that prevented her from discussing any concerns she might have had about my father even with her own doctor.'

After the war Mollie had to take stock of her own situation. After years of focusing on getting by and making do she had to consider her own future as a young widow with two little children, no income beyond her widow's pension and nowhere to live. 'I was offered a great-aunt's house in Stratford at a reduced price but I couldn't afford it. Anyway, I got a bit of help from the family and managed to buy it in the end. My parents lived with me for a while there until they left for the Middle East.' Not long after the war had ended Mollie met Bill Lodder, a solicitor and landowner in Henley-in-Arden, not far from Stratford. She and Bill were married in 1947. 'We had an idyllic marriage that lasted thirty-eight years,' Mollie said with pride. 'And we had four more children.' The war was a brief and disturbing interlude in her long life, which spans seven generations. She remembered visiting her great-grandmother when she was a little girl and now has fourteen great-grandchildren of her own. 'One thing the war taught me was that you have to learn to cope with whatever comes your way. I have always said, and have always believed, that my mother's experience of the war years, although completely different from my father's, was equally difficult and self-destroying in its mental anxiety over his time as a Japanese POW and certainly at the time as anguishing as my own experience when Tim was killed.'

In April 1945 Frances Campbell-Preston received a telephone call from her husband, Patrick, to say that he would be back the following day. It would be the first time she had seen him in five years.

She and Patrick had married in 1939: 'That year was to be the last year of normal life as I had known it. As a blissful newly-wed it had a soufflé quality. It is difficult to define our state of mind – or states of mind. In a consciously suppressed state, the war was inevitable, yet there were waves of hope.' Patrick was an officer with the Black Watch and was stationed at Dover Castle and the two of them lived in a small flat on the front at Dover. Immediately after war was declared the Black Watch was moved to Aldershot where they were to be amongst the first troops to go to France with the British Expeditionary Force. Frances remembers them both realizing it was the end of an idyllic time. They wept as they packed up their flat and went their separate ways into an unknown future. 'To talk of the future was theoretical to the point of fantasy,' she wrote, 'the past disappeared . . . Patrick left for war. We had one last sight of each other when his embarkation was delayed and I join him in Aldershot. At the end of the week the Battalion marched through Aldershot and I found myself lining the street to wave goodbye, just like the women pictured in all wars.'

By the time Patrick left England Frances was expecting a baby. Their daughter, Mary Ann, was born on 15 February 1940. Patrick came home on leave shortly after the birth and found the change from troops preparing for war to life with a small baby a shock. Having not been through the pregnancy with Frances he found an apparently invalid wife and a bundled-up baby daughter a surprise. The leave was not a great success and he returned to France after ten days. That was the last time Frances and Patrick were to see each other until the end of the war.

Frances moved between her parents' house in London and her mother-in-law Molly's remote home in Scotland, a former priory, called Ardchattan, thirteen and a half miles from Oban on the northern shore of Loch Etive. Molly had two sons in the BEF and her fears were heightened because she had lost three brothers in the First World War and knew only too well the horrible toll that had taken on her family. Life at Ardchattan was light years away from London in every sense. They slept peacefully at night and had no air-raid sirens to worry them. The only restriction they felt was on coal, which meant that the bedrooms could have no fires. They moved into the sitting room, which also served as a dining room, and waited. Letters from Patrick continued to arrive in a trickle during June 1940. He vacillated between sounding cheerful and deeply gloomy about the war. Frances was convinced he would survive but she had no knowledge of his whereabouts. 'I did not get the standard War Office telegram reporting him missing until August. As far as I was concerned, this merely stated the obvious, but for Molly it was more chilling. In the 1914–18 war this was invariably followed by a "Killed in Action" notification. Molly never voiced her fears or misgivings to me. Her courage and support was of rock-like quality and she kept me as sane as she could.'

Finally, in the autumn of 1940 she received her first letter from Patrick since his captivity. It had the chilling address of his camp in German, *Oflag VIIC*. 'Our ration today is coffee, cabbage soup, 10 potatoes and 2 inches of bread,' he wrote. 'Life palls here at times, however we might be worse. David Walker and I Highland dance and now we get some exercise playing basketball. But I can see no end to this rot.'

In October 1942 Patrick and two others escaped. They spent five days on the run before they were recaptured by the Germans: 'Unfortunately the plan failed so here we are shut up in a couple of cells, well treated and in good form if a little downhearted. You must not worry; there was no risk. I can't tell you anything about it except that I had a beautiful beard after five days. Although restricted in space I have never felt better in all my life.'

Patrick escaped for a second time from a camp in Warburg and was once again caught. This time he was sent to Oflag IVC, better known as Colditz, from where there would be no escape. Frances and Patrick continued to correspond throughout the remainder of his captivity but although this was a great comfort to them both, Frances admitted that 'we were never able to express deep feelings in our correspondence, and took the view that it would be unkind to give vent to feelings of sadness and depression, which could easily be long over by the time the other read about them, letters taking so long to arrive. So our understanding of what either of us had gone through was necessarily limited.' On one occasion she heard a chilling account that some of the prisoners in Colditz had been shackled by the guards but Patrick never mentioned the episode. He described it later as a minor incident but at the time she found it frightening.

By the spring of 1945 we knew that at last the war was ending. Excitement mounted, but I was afraid. The month before Patrick got back was the most gruelling. The Allied armies were advancing across Europe but my eyes were fixed on a tiny spot, and anxious about the fate of one individual caught up in this huge drama. To my fevered imagination the armies appeared to zig-zag all over the place, which army, which General would reach Colditz first – mad rumours circulated. The Germans in a final gesture might shoot everyone? Russians might get there first and everyone disappear into a rambling mess? The prisoners might break out and stream home on their own.

In the middle of all this worry came the news that Patrick was to be liberated. Frances's sister Laura described the atmosphere in the house in London at the time: 'Poor old Fuff was wonderful while she was waiting, but every telephone call was a torture to her, and it never stops ringing in this house! She listened to every news bulletin in every language, of course the midnight bulletin that gave the news that the camp had been released caught me asleep, and I thought the house had had a direct hit when Frances let out a bellow like a mad bull. Then for a week, nothing. The only night F stomped off to bed before 1 am of course the telephone rang at 1 am and there Patrick was.' Frances had refused to believe he was safe until she heard his voice. Eventually she listened to him telling her that he had flown into an aerodrome at Beaconsfield and hoped to be home that afternoon. He arrived at 12:30 when Frances was out. Her father wrote of his son-in-law's return: 'Patrick has just walked in – he looks very well, a bit thinner which makes him very handsome – he is really very good looking – now and then like most men who have been through a great trial, a distant look comes into his eyes.' A few days later he revised his opinion of Patrick: 'The more one sees of Patrick the more one realizes he has suffered very much and been through a tremendous ordeal. One's first impressions were that he looked thinner . . . but fairly well. But on second and third interviews one realized that he was not too strong and he is sure to have a reaction and will, I believe, require quite a period of rest, but provided he takes things quietly he will very soon be himself again.'

Another prisoner of the Germans summed up how it felt to be freed after five years in captivity:

When I came out [of hospital] on May 14, life was just marvellous. I found, however, that the comforts and conveniences of normal life, so eagerly awaited for 4 or 5 years, quickly began to pall. I now realize that the Frenchman who said: 'One is never so happy or so unhappy as one thinks' was right. It's an awful thing to say but I believe we were often happier than we thought behind barbed-wire. One adjusted oneself in some curious way and made the best of it. When one came back to normal life, one had to adjust oneself once again, and the process was apt to be upsetting. I wouldn't indulge in this introspection only I believe this feeling of 'anti-climax' has been shared by a lot of returned prisoners of war. It made one moody, I found, and one or two of my friends had the same experience.

The first thing that Frances and Patrick did was to make for their cottage with their now five-year-old daughter, Mary Ann.

The first days were a rush of talk. This was the only time Patrick ever talked of his experiences. After that he never referred to them again. It was like lancing a colossal boil, after which the wound was sealed and healed. I got the impression that the last two years had been the worst. When escape was impossible, when one or two friends had nervous breakdowns, Patrick worried that the younger officers captured at nineteen might find the constant disappointments almost too hard. (One of them had as good as committed suicide trying to make an impossible escape, and had been shot by the guards.) He suffered from the lack of news from home and the sense of being cut off from all our feelings, not only individually but nationally.

Patrick's arrival home was a great surprise to Mary Ann who, faced by a proper father rather than a virtual one, had to readjust. Frances wrote to her sister Vera and described her reaction: 'Mary Ann is a bit astounded at her father. She took him on at once and behaved as if he'd never left the house but on second thoughts she finds he occasionally gets in the way and has a habit of meaning "no" when he says "no". She doesn't approve of him sleeping with her Mamma and has said several times that to her mind it would be far more practical if he slept with Minnie [the nanny], and she and I slept together.' There were changes all around, which Patrick found disorientating. When he had last seen his mother in 1940 she was running a house with twelve indoor servants. On his return she had just one cook and a daily help. 'The social market baffled him,' Frances wrote, 'in quest of bedroom slippers, we went to Fortnum and Masons only to find they were out of stock. Patrick told them somewhat abruptly that if they continued to fail to sell him bedroom slippers he would remove his custom elsewhere. Embarrassed I led him out, all too aware of the sniggers behind us.'

The greatest difficulty, Frances admitted, was that neither of them really understood what the other had been through during their five years of separation. How could she really have any knowledge of what it must have been like to be locked up in a German prisoner of war camp with hundreds of other men, crammed together with almost no privacy and little space for physical activity? He, in turn, she believed, had no comprehension of what she had been through during those five years. He had no knowledge of the Wrens or the WVS (Women's Voluntary Service) – what was all that about? he wondered. And she came to realize that this gulf of understanding could not be crossed. 'Lots of people had been separated during the war,' she said, 'so one didn't make a fuss but it would have been helpful to have counselling immediately post-war for basic things, like advice on how to settle down together.'

Frances wanted to move on and build a new life with Patrick away from the family. She was tired after the war, emotionally drained, and thought that that reflected how many people in England felt at the time. 'There was a general fatigue and a lack of creative spirit,' she recalled. But she was unable to fulfil her wishes and they moved up to Ardchattan.

Patrick began to put on weight and look better. Mary Ann adjusted to finding a strange man in her mother's bed and was delighted by the acquisition of a father. Frances overheard her asking nanny Minnie if she was pleased to see her father back. When Minnie replied yes, Mary Ann responded: 'Well, why don't you kiss him all the time like Mummy does?' Although Patrick never mentioned his experiences again after the first outburst when he returned home, Frances was aware that they were never far from the surface. 'Even when he got together with others who had been in the prison camps with him they didn't really speak about it. I was amazed there wasn't more animosity between the former prisoners after the war, after having been cooped up together for all that time. But occasionally he would spot someone walking down the street and he would cross the road to avoid him. I had the impression that there were a few men that Patrick <u>really</u> did not want to see again. Ever.'

Frances realized that Patrick was desperate to pick up the threads of his army career. He had to re-establish his self-esteem and she knew that it was instinctive for him to do this but they would almost certainly be separated again in the near future. Sure enough Patrick was posted to Greece with the Black Watch: 'I was shattered and felt quite unequal to a prolongation of our separation,' she wrote. He went in August 1945 leaving her aghast and totally miserable. At first she cried a lot, she said, and got the frustration out of her system. So desperate was she not to be separated from him for any length of time that she undertook a journey to Greece on her own to volunteer as a member of the YWCA. She sailed to Cairo in a troopship before trying to get a passage to Athens. After a month in Cairo she learned that Patrick had been posted to staff college in Camberley and would be leaving Greece shortly. She then undertook an eventful voyage home, arriving in England two days before Patrick.

For six months they enjoyed a blissful life in Camberley without fear of imminent separation and then were posted to Perth where they were able to celebrate their 'first' wedding anniversary together after seven years of marriage. After a bitterly cold winter, during which they were snowed in for over a month, their son Robert was born on the newly formed National Health Service and life continued peacefully. In 1948 Patrick was posted to Duisburg and this time he had married quarters so Frances could go with him. At first it was a shock for her to consider going to Germany. After all, this was the country where her husband had been imprisoned for five years. 'I couldn't summon up the energy to hate the Germans,' she said later, and found that to her surprise she was happy with their new life in Duisburg.

While they were there the Russians challenged the right of the Allies to remain in Berlin and they watched the extraordinary efforts of the Berlin Airlift from close quarters. Immediately after the airlift ended the Black Watch was moved to Berlin and soon after Patrick took over command after its previous commander, who coincidentally became Frances's brother-in-law, collapsed with a heart attack. Command of the Black Watch was the fulfilment of Patrick's highest ambition and he was blissfully happy.

Sadly the happiness was short-lived. Patrick became breathless and suffered extreme tiredness. Frances knew his condition was serious and was shocked but not surprised when a cardiologist diagnosed a serious heart condition. It was a bitter blow to them both and spelled the end not only of Patrick's military career but of active life for him. 'In fact,' she wrote, 'when he had his army check-up before being discharged, he was classified as P.8, which meant that technically he was dead.' Although they were determined to start afresh for a second time since the end of the war,

Frances had constant worries over Patrick's health after his discharge from the army in 1952 and in February 1953 he suffered a thrombosis. Over the next six years his health was up and down. Two more children were born, one in 1955 and another in 1958. Patrick was unable to accept that he was dying and Frances tried not to either but his health deteriorated in 1959 and following a head-on car crash, in which he was badly hurt and from which he never fully recovered, he died in March 1960 leaving her with four children.

Five years after Patrick's death a friend from Colditz, Martin Gilliat, invited Frances to a drinks party at his apartment at St James's Palace. 'Before I could quite take in what was happening, I had been offered the job of lady-in-waiting to the Queen Mother. It was like a bombshell and I was left gasping.' For the next thirty-seven years Frances had a full and busy life as part of the royal household. At times it was a struggle to juggle the demands of her job with her young family but she is now able to enjoy watching her grandchildren and great-grandchildren growing up around her.

Frances was in no doubt that the effect of five years of imprisonment not only affected her husband's health, leading to his premature death, but it also ruined his career. She said:

It is impossible to understand what it must have done to a man to be imprisoned for five years. It is one thing if you have hit someone on the head and you go to prison for it. But quite another if you were taken prisoner of war and especially as a professional soldier. It is a matter of great shame to be taken prisoner and it certainly affected Patrick both at the time and after the war. It's not something that is easy to get over. It was not something we discussed and I discovered after I'd published my own book in 2006 that it was something I had hardly ever talked about to the children. It was only after they read the book that they really understood what their father had been through in the war.

For other women separation was shorter and the effects of the war less detrimental to their husbands' health and careers but the impact of those years was still felt. Barbara Lewis, a widow in her eighties, described her husband as being 'like the curate's egg: good in parts'. She was born in 1920 in London, a proper 'Cockney lass' with a good sense of fun and humour. At the age of eighteen she applied for a job as a typist at the solicitors Frere Cholmeley where she met William George Lewis, fifteen years older, who worked as a managing clerk. He was known all his life as Bob. From Frere Cholmeley she went to work at the *Sunday Pictorial* but stopped work when she and Bob married in 1940. Soon after that he joined the Territorial Army and moved to Trowbridge for training. Their daughter Anne was born in 1942 and Bob was moved to Bridlington, seventeen miles south of Scarborough. She and Anne could not stay in Bob's quarters but a kindly woman who lived next door to his office offered to take them in.

Bob Lewis achieved the rank of captain quartermaster and saw active service in France when he was sent abroad in 1944, winning a Military Cross and being mentioned in dispatches. The experience of the army unsettled him, however, and on his return to London he felt dislocated and out of place. He was demobilized quickly after VE Day because of his age. Barbara and Anne were already in London sharing a house with her sister. 'I remember that I was out when he came home. I knew he was coming but not exactly when or on which day. He had to climb in through a bathroom window! Not the best welcome home.' In the first instance Bob went back to his old job at Frere Cholmeley but found that he could not stand the hierarchy of the solicitors' office. 'There was a huge gulf between the articled solicitors and the clerks,' Barbara explained. 'He had been an officer in the services and had been used to being referred to as "sir" and being looked up to. Now he was back in a civilian situation and found he hated being talked down to by the senior partners and addressed by his surname. It was too much a case of "them and us".'

Bob was offered a salaried partnership at the company but he told Barbara he was too old to start studying again and so one day in the summer of 1945 he came home and announced that he couldn't take it any more and that he intended to throw in the towel and buy a pub. 'The war changed Bob only in as far as he had got used to giving orders and he no longer liked to be bossed around. But this had a major impact on our lives because suddenly we became publicans with all the long hours and different way of life that that entails.' So Barbara, Bob and Anne, now three, moved out of London to take over the Hare and Hounds at Ledburn, just outside Leighton Buzzard. Barbara explained:

It was a man's world back then. I never had any say in what we did. Bob was quite Victorian in that respect. He made the big decisions in our lives and I just went along with it. I regret that now. I was so much younger than Bob that I felt he treated me like one of the children. Except in bed. I used to get very cross with him but he never listened, he would just put me down when I became argumentative. But he was very funny and entertaining. I think I spent most of that part of my marriage either laughing or crying. Although our marriage was a partnership, it was never a partnership of equals. How much of his character was shaped by the war I don't know because he was already in his thirties when he joined the TA but the decision to leave Frere Cholmeley and run pubs certainly was a direct result of his life in the army and that shaped all of our lives forever.

Not all servicemen were sent abroad during the war but separation was still an issue for those women whose husbands had military responsibilities at home. Doris Cole's grandson, Andy, wrote in July 2007: 'My Grandmother, Doris, is 95 years old and in a nursing home. She is fully lucid but alas her physical condition is letting her down. The girls at the nursing home are fascinated by her as they feel that she comes from a different world. It will be people like yourself that will enable people like my Gran to have stories preserved for the future.' I interviewed Doris in the nursing home three weeks later. She was amused by the interest that my visit caused and told me that she would not tell the nurses why I had come. 'I'd like to leave them guessing a bit. They might think you are someone important.' Sitting in a wheelchair in her room with a view over the Hertfordshire countryside she looked frail but her mind was sharp and she spoke for over two hours about her memories of a time she described as 'extraordinary but interesting'.

Doris's father told her to sit down when she was told that her young husband, Charles, had been called up to join Fighter Command in 1939. A veteran of the First World War he knew what Charles might have to face over the coming years. Doris's strongest recollection of the First World War was at the age of five seeing her father off at the station as he went back to the front after leave. There was an emptiness in his eyes as he left even though he could not know, she said, that he was going to a worse place than he had been before. This thought came back to her in 1939, twenty years after her father's safe return from Passchendaele, that place in Belgium whose name is synonymous with death on an unimaginable scale and in unthinkable conditions. Her father had never spoken about his experiences there but she knew instinctively not to ask him about what he had been through.

Doris and Charles had married in the mid-1930s and she had given birth to their son in 1937. They were living in London but the majority of her family were still living in Lincolnshire where she had grown up. In 1939 they were in the process of buying their first family home in Hendon. Charles was called up at the end of August and Doris followed her father's advice and took her son Michael to live on her brother's farm in Spilsby, twelve miles inland from Skegness, making occasional forays back to Hendon to collect her valuables in case the house was bombed. Michael was disappointed to be separated from his father and initially he was not very happy to be in Spilsby but Doris's father, who was working in Lincolnshire as an ambulance driver, was insistent. He knew that London would be targeted by the Germans and he did not wish to have any members of the family living close to danger. 'It was a blow when Charles was called up,' Doris recalled, 'I knew he would have to go but I didn't realize the war was so close. I packed all my valuables into a box and moved up to stay with my brother on his farm.'

Charles Cole worked for Fighter Command throughout the war planning missions. He was also responsible for RAF stations all along the east coast. One of his jobs was to board a destroyer at Chatham and sail up the coast to near Berwick and travel on to the base at Rosyth and back again to see whether there were enough planes to cover convoys. He was allowed to send Doris a telegram when he left Chatham to say he was going on tour and another when he returned safely but was not allowed to contact her during the voyages, something that left her burning with anxiety for his safety. Although he was not involved directly in the fighting his role was a risky one and Doris was never convinced that he was out of danger until she heard he was safely back in port. For the first two years of the war he was able to make frequent visits to see her and Michael but later on he was unable to take as much leave and they went sometimes for months without seeing one another. Their relationship was kept alive by their correspondence. Doris would write to him daily, telling him about Michael's progress, about the goings-on at her civil service job as a counter clerk in the post office and about life in Lincolnshire.

Doris lived initially with her brother and sister-in-law on their farm but soon she felt the need to be a little more independent and took a signalman's cottage four miles from Spilsby at Firsby station at the bottom of an air-force runway where she and Michael lived for the rest of the war. Each day she would take her bicycle and pedal four miles to the post office where she worked, past the airfield which was on her father's ambulance patch. She got into the habit of counting the bombers out as they left each evening and counting them back as they returned in the morning. It was always a sad day when the numbers did not tally. On one terrible morning there was a crash at the airfield. Her father, as foreman at the ambulance station at Firsby, was on duty and she remembers him ordering a dozen coffins for the crew who died in the crash. It was his job to arrange transport for the bodies from the base station to their eventual resting places. 'He was never the same again after that. He was always wary of the bombers coming home after that terrible experience when he witnessed the crash. They were all such young men. It really affected him deeply. It must have brought back terrible memories of the Western Front in 1917 but he never mentioned that.'

Life during the war was busy and eventful for Doris and on the whole free from danger, if not from worry about Charles: 'I wouldn't want to go through it again. I was running two homes, I had a job, a child and my parents to worry about as well as Charles out on convoys. But it just happened and you got on with it at the time,' she said. When the war was finally over Charles joined Doris and Michael in Skegness and took the holiday that he was supposed to have been entitled to when war broke out in 1939. 'He came back to us for that holiday and we realized we would all have to get used to each other again. Michael was by now eight years old and although Charles had been kept up to date by my letters and Michael had been kept up to date about his father through my telling him stories, there was a period of adjustment for the two of them before they could get back on an even keel.'

Doris, Charles and Michael moved back to Hendon in the summer of 1945 and opened up the house properly for the first time in five years and Michael was enrolled at the local school. There were lots of children in the neighbourhood so that he quickly made friends and had plenty of playmates. For Doris and Charles this period was more difficult. He used to go up to Stanmore regularly to keep up with the air force and he often chose to go and eat in the officers' mess rather than at home. This she found very difficult to accept. 'I suppose with hindsight he had got so used to male company and to the camaraderie of eating with the officers that he found it difficult to give that up. He had had plenty of contact with women of course, because he had 87 WAAFs directly under his command. In fact, three or four of them borrowed my wedding dress and veil to get married in after the war. But it was the fact that he seemed to prefer the all-male environment that was difficult for me.' Eventually Doris felt she had to put her foot down: 'I told him "It is time you saw more of Michael. If you don't want us I can go and get a job in Skegness." That brought him up short.'

What Charles needed, Doris soon understood, was time to himself and a space of his own. She came up with the idea of getting him an allotment. It was a brilliant scheme and it worked like a charm, she said. Very soon he acquired a second patch and then a third. He grew flowers and vegetables and in the end became a horticultural judge. When rationing tightened in 1946 twenty of them on the allotment joined together to form the Pig Club. They would buy twenty piglets from a farm in Cuffley and feed them at the allotments until they were big enough to slaughter, then they would sell them to Walls, who had a factory not far away. If there was a special occasion such as Christmas they would keep one pig back and have it butchered for their own consumption. But Doris drew the line at eating her own pigs: 'They were so sweet and trusting. It made me sad and I never ate pork after that, or lamb for the same reason.'

'In the end I was married for sixty-one years,' Doris said. 'We didn't argue much once things had settled down after the war. If we did I would go for a walk and calm down. Charles was a placid sort of man and that suited my temperament. I have had a lovely, varied life. It's interesting to talk about it now but it wasn't interesting then. I hated the war. But we were lucky. We had no money worries and in the end it all worked out well.'

Reflections on the war, even from the perspective of sixty years, often make people realize that the events that shaped their lives are still clear in their minds. Some women, such as Amy Clifford, have made a point of recording their memories for posterity but, as she explained, it was the pre- and immediate post-war periods that remained more sharply in her mind than the war years themselves. 'Thinking about the events of 1946 is raising such feelings in me, remembering the seeming hopelessness of my situation,' Amy wrote in 2007. Born in 1918 in Thornbury in Wiltshire, Amy grew up in Malvern, the place she liked to think of as her real home. In 1935 she moved to London and went into service in Muswell Hill. She was not happy in the job so moved to a job in the West End where, she said,

I worked very, very hard. They were such long hours – six o'clock in the morning to nine o'clock at night with just Tuesday afternoons off and every other Sunday afternoon from lunch until ten o'clock. There was no time to meet anybody really but my sister had a pen friend living in London and through her I met my husband, William Henry Clifford, who was this pen friend's brother. He was twenty-one and had never had a girlfriend before. He only had one friend, actually, and he used to do everything with his sisters. Well, he was absolutely smitten with me and I couldn't shake him off.

William and Amy were married on 13 July 1940. 'William was called up six weeks before the wedding so he only got forty-eight hours off to get married. We didn't know anything about birth control in those days so the next year I had my first baby, a little girl.' A second daughter followed in 1944. 'Both the girls were born in Malvern. The local midwife delivered them. I remembered her because she was the nurse who used to come around the school checking heads for nits. She was one of the first people I knew who had a car, a little Austin 7. There were few telephones about in those days and if a telegram arrived the post-mistress, who lived in the village a mile and a half away, would have to get on her bike and deliver it.'

Amy spent the war looking after the girls, living alternately with her parents in Malvern and with her parents-in-law in North London. 'As soon as the war ended I moved to London full-time and lived with William's parents, his three unmarried sisters and a lodger called Martha.' The house was full to bursting and Amy used to do a lot of the housework because the sisters had to help their parents who were caretakers of the Presbyterian Church at Haverstock Hill. 'From the moment I moved back to London I longed and longed for a place of my own where the children and I could live as a family.'

William Clifford was demobbed in 1946 and came home to live with his wife, daughters and parents in the overcrowded house. Their oldest daughter, Judy, was five years old and had to share a bed with one of her maiden aunts, which Amy found most unsatisfactory. There was almost no quiet space for them and Amy found herself longing to have the privacy to start their married life properly. 'William had been all over Italy, in that country full of treasures, but he never wrote about them to me. He never wrote to say he loved me and complained in his few letters that he had nothing to tell me. I used to tell him all about the girls and their goings on. My husband seemed to be a different man when he came home. "Where was the love?" I asked myself. Whatever he had felt for me when we first met he had got over by the time he came home five years later.' It did not seem to bother him that they were living with his parents, on the contrary he seemed to relish the security of his old family life.

Amy would walk the streets looking and hoping that they might soon find somewhere to settle down. 'I haunted St Pancras Housing Office for nearly a year hoping they would find somewhere for us. In those days you could buy a house for £2000 but we did not have that kind of money.' However, they were frugal, saving up his demobilization allowance so that they could buy furniture and furnishings when they were eventually rehoused. Finally, in December 1946 the council allotted them a tiny little prefabricated house in North London. Amy was delighted.

I loved that little house in Dartmouth Park Hill. It wasn't quite finished when we moved in but St Pancras was so anxious to house young people like ourselves that we had to make do with whatever we could get. The bathroom and kitchen were still all in one room with a bath one end and a sink the other but I had an electric fridge. It was all electric, it was absolutely lovely and it was our own place. We had a nice big garden near the reservoir and we were very happy there for eleven years although that first winter was very, very cold.

In fact 1947 was the severest and above all snowiest winter since 1814. Every day from 22 January to 17 March snow fell somewhere in the United Kingdom and as the temperature seldom rose more than a degree or two above freezing the snow accumulated.

It kept on snowing and freezing until March. The house only had one little fireplace and we were terribly cold. We were only entitled to one hundredweight of coal a week but because we had the two children we were allowed to go to the doctor and get a certificate so that we could get another hundredweight. That is how we survived until the thaw came. But I was happy. I had my own lovely little home to look after and life became more stable once we were settled in and the weather got warmer.

William had been working for Shell before the war and his job had been held open for him. He used to earn £7.00 a week, Amy remembered, and one week he was late giving her money for the rent on the pre-fab. When she asked him about it he accused her of nagging him. 'Well, when he came home I hit him over the head with a frying pan. He never made me wait for my rental money again!' As soon as their younger daughter was at school Amy went back to work and with two incomes life settled down.

After eleven years the council announced that the pre-fabs would be pulled down and the family was moved to Langley in Hertfordshire. In their later life William and Amy developed a passion for travelling. They bought a Morris Minor and drove all over the country, discovering new places: 'It opens up the world when you have a car,' she said. Looking back on her marriage Amy was philosophical. 'He was madly in love when we met but it all wore off when he was away at the war. But he stuck at it, he was one of those. And you rub along, you make the best of it and get on with life. You have to. I'm a cheerful person, always have been.'

For women who worked during the war readjustment to life in the post-war era was difficult. New-found independence, both financial and emotional, had an impact on relationships and created expectations on both sides that could not always be fulfilled. Thousands of women became wives of men who, damaged by their experiences, needed attention and patience for years after the war. For these women the war did not end in 1945. For some it only ended with the death of the man in their care.

Monica Littleboy came from a family of dental surgeons in Norfolk who were proud to claim they could trace their roots back to William the Conqueror. After leaving school she tried a domestic science course but that did not suit her so soon afterwards she left home and went to London to do a beauty course, living in digs in Earls Court. This was more to her liking. She found the big city exciting.

Not long after arriving in London she met a handsome, dark-haired young man called George Symington. He worked as a financial journalist and lived in the house opposite. She noticed once or twice that his curtains twitched as if he were watching her from behind them. She had had a few friendships with boys before but this one was different. 'I liked his spirit among the hustle of commuters. One morning he asked me if I would go for a drink. I shall never forget that first meeting. The charm and courtesy of this young man swept into my heart. It was my first experience of deep feeling. And London that spring seemed a place of beauty overflowing, full of colour and elegance. Our young lives were as yet untouched by the bad news of the war clouds gathering over Europe.' When the war broke out George told Monica he would have to leave London and head up to Scotland to join the Gordon Highlanders. His grandfather had been a colonel in the regiment so there was no question in George's mind but that he would follow in his footsteps. Monica was dismayed: 'When he left for Scotland it was as if one more light had gone out of my life. London now seemed empty. I decided to go home to Norwich to face up to the reality of war.'

After a spell in the Land Army and the WAAF Monica became an ambulance driver, joining the FANY (First Aid Nursing Yeomanry). Once settled she continued to serve as a driver for the rest of the war. The work exhausted her and put her in danger but she loved the camaraderie with the paramedics and was humbled by the intense gratitude of the patients she was able to help. 'I covered every conceivable case you could think of, motor crashes, plane crashes, bombings, mine accidents, gun accidents, dysentery, pneumonia, appendicitis, paralysis, broken limbs, infectious diseases, burns, VD, wasp stings and coping with the drunks.'

At the end of May 1944 she was sent to the Isle of Wight and shuttled between there and Portsmouth over the D-Day landings, dealing with some shocking sights of men badly burned and injured as they were brought back to Britain. 'Many planes crashed on the island at that time,' she wrote, 'and not many of the pilots survived. Only too often no one could tell who the charred remains belonged to and one would think of someone waiting anxiously of news of someone who never returned.'

When peace came Monica went back to London. She had heard almost nothing about George Symington and had moved on since 1939 so that he did not really feature in her life any more. 'By now the Japanese war was over, and we knew that many POWs were being released, some in a terrible state. Camp after camp was freed, with gruesome tales to be told. No news yet of my boyfriend, and I didn't seriously think he would ever come back.' She joined the BBC as a recorded programme assistant and settled down in digs to her new life in London. It was lonely in comparison to life in the FANY but she enjoyed the work and there was plenty to do in London to keep her occupied.

George had sailed for the Far East in 1941 to join the Gordon Highlanders in Malaya, where the regiment had been since 1937. His mother had been able to inform her at some stage that he had been captured on Singapore but after that Monica moved around so much that there was no way Mrs Symington could keep up with her movements. Monica, meantime, had had a series of boyfriends, one of whom, an older officer, had been very serious about marrying her but he too had been posted abroad. This had saddened her greatly so she kept her friendships with young men superficial and, by her own admission, fast moving.

In the autumn of 1945 Monica got a considerable shock:

Out of the blue there was a telephone call at my digs. I was off shift. The call was from the docks at Southampton. It was George Symington. I could hardly believe it and was not a little perturbed, for I was rather involved with my present boyfriend and angry to be involved in something I had not bargained for.

Of course I said he should come round. What else could I do? He was insistent and I had to see. I was puzzled. So long ago, another life, not mine. A voice from the past, not mine. A POW voice. I was not the same nor ever could be. That life was different and gone.

George arrived at her door in a taxi, complete with kitbag. He had come straight from the boat and it was clear that Monica was his first port of call. She wrote:

I felt vulnerable, not in command of the situation. He stood there. I couldn't believe my eyes. This was not the young man I had known. I was stunned. Misshapen, pitted, scarred. Only the eyes were the same. I could have wept. So while we had been fighting, that is what this poor wretch had been turned into. I thought of the handsome boyfriend I was to meet next weekend – dark, tall, in command of every situation. I looked at this hulk of humanity and my heart bled.

That evening George invited her to go along to dinner with him at the flat of a friend. She agreed but found it a terrible experience. She was trapped by the powerful pity she felt for the wreck that her former boyfriend had become and repulsed by him at the same time. That night he took the train up to Scotland to visit his parents: 'My heart did not go with him but my pity did,' she wrote.

While George was back in Scotland with his parents, Monica had to take compassionate leave from the BBC to look after her mother who had fallen ill. She spent several weeks in Norfolk on convalescent duty and all that time she was troubled by the images she had in her head of the young man who had so abruptly walked back into her life. 'I tried to think. I couldn't stop thinking about the shock of it all and the ghastly humiliations he must have suffered. It was as if all that was left of my youth was gone in the moment I saw him. He was part of the glamorous pages of my past and now it was there no longer and never would be again.'

There is a sense throughout Monica's memoir that she had no option but to be a part of George's life. Every fibre in her body, she wrote, railed against this man, who was not the man she had known in 1939, but refuse him she could not. When she was in Norfolk George phoned her and wrote to her, eventually asking her to meet him in London: 'I had to go. I could not say no to him. The sound of his voice crying in the wilderness of his life was too much.'

When they met in London he was clearly ill and sure enough came down with a severe bout of malaria that left him almost in a coma for two days. Monica had had the sense to take him in a taxi to her sister's house in Wimbledon where he shivered and perspired for two days. George recovered and went back to Scotland. The meeting had not been a great success. Before he became ill they sparred like cat and dog, Monica recalled. A few days later he came back down to London to take her home to meet his parents.

Once there she found herself in a difficult situation. His mother liked her well enough but she was jealous of her son's obvious passion for Monica. 'His father was withdrawn. For him the war might not have happened,' Monica said. All the time she was there people turned up with presents and warm good wishes for George's recovery. 'Presents of food and wine overwhelmed us and all the time I kept thinking that I could not marry him as he was.'

Then, on a visit to see an old cousin of George's in Edinburgh, Monica suddenly realized:

Here was the challenge given to me for peacetime. Could I meet it? London and the BBC were empty after my wartime activities. Could I keep this man alive and help him to get back into life again? I loved the spirit of the man, but could love nothing else. I had to do it. There was no other way. The toughness I had acquired would be all his, the humanity he had so lacked in the war I had in full measure . . . So, crying to say no, I said 'Yes.' Looking back now, I am reminded of the title of Françoise Sagan's remarkable first post-war novel: *Bonjour Tristesse*, adieu jeunesse.

Their decision to marry was greeted with dismay by his parents. They put up every conceivable obstacle, so desperately concerned was George's mother about her son and his obvious dire mental state. Her own parents were relieved that she would at last be settling down with a husband and 'that my long line of boyfriends would at last cease!' They had no financial security and no prospect of any in the immediate future so they decided to spend the weeks before their wedding helping George to find himself a position so that he could take up a job when they got back from their honeymoon. He was fortunate to get a job with British Petroleum and they were happy to wait until the spring of 1946 to take him on full-time.

George and Monica were married less than two months after his return from the war in a brief service in St Peter's, Eaton Square. Monica wore a simple suit bought with coupons, a hat and veil made by her mother, shoes from her uncle who ran a shoe factory and underwear made out of parachute silk. 'The simplicity of the service after the tumultuous war years was very moving. It started our healing process.'

In the comfortable knowledge that George had a job to come back to, the couple took a three-month honeymoon using his demob money. She wrote:

I shall never forget our honeymoon, but not for the usual reasons. My husband was mentally sick as well as physically. I was shocked at what I had done. He could not eat what he wanted after being starved for so long. He could not play games without dizziness, nor drive a car. He wept when he went to the cinema. . . . all his mental scars would come out all the time. I was horrified. The war had been hard. But here I was faced with a social and love life in chaos, a sick ill-looking man who required my attention every moment of the day. My mind kept returning to my handsome, healthy boyfriends whom I had left behind.

And yet, after three months Monica could see a glimpse of the warmth that she had known before the war and when they finished their honeymoon in Scotland his mother was astounded at the change in her son: 'She seemed to realize that I had already miraculously brought something out in him which had been dead.'

Monica and George went back to London and began their married life. It was, from the start, not going to be a settled one as BP had told George that they needed him to work abroad. His first task was to enrol at the School of Oriental and Eastern Languages to learn Persian. Monica, meantime, was setting about trying to make a home of the one-room flat they had rented from friends in Radcliffe Square. 'It was a soothing atmosphere, since the friends' house where our flat was had the sound of music filling it with Chopin and Fauré. There was an opera singer and a cellist in another room. All this gave us a good start.'

After six months George was posted abroad and Monica was due to follow him once he had found accommodation and settled down. They both expected this to happen within a few short months but letter after letter from George made no reference to her moving out to join him. George's letters spoke of his repeated bouts of illness in hospital, he was suffering in the heat and he was desperately unhappy. It was agreed that George should come home, regardless of the consequences for his career. The next few years were very up and down. When he was in good shape physically and mentally they greatly enjoyed each other's company and Monica could feel positive about the future. But there were dark times too when George would slip into a state of depression and anxiety.

All the time Monica had been convinced that her best approach to George was one of gentle and understanding sympathy. She had received no advice on how to deal with a returned prisoner of war and her instinct told her that he needed to be handled with great kindness. However, by the end of the 1940s this approach was no longer working:

> The more I gave him the more I was rejected. One evening I knelt beside his chair and put my arms around him. I was told to get away and leave him alone. This was such a shock, and went so deep that life was never the same again; and what a good thing. For a week I wept with lost pride and humiliation. Then my wonderful inner strength pulled me up. I knew I had to get on and take the lead. I knew that George was suffering in a much bigger way, with his ghastly entry into an unknown life, that I must be caring but strong. I resolved to start a family. What better way of going forward?

Monica was unsure about how George's captivity would affect their ability to have a baby and, if they did succeed in conceiving a child, how it would be affected in its lifetime by the legacy of his war experiences. She fell pregnant but lost her first baby and became despondent about her prospects of having a healthy child. But 'after much medical help and many injections we managed another . . . Alexandra was born on August 17, 1951. She was a good baby and gave us no trouble. But George was a worry, as was the shortage of money.'

Monica's life became a roller-coaster ride of house moves, life with a small child and marriage to a man with repeated bouts of physical and mental illness. 'He was no companion and difficult to handle,' Monica wrote, 'quiet, morose and joyless. His work drained him and left nothing for anyone or anything else. Alexandra suffered from this and was thrown more onto my company because of it. George gave this impression of unapproachability to people. He frightened them.'

After George retired they decided to travel: 'We were determined to go while we could still enjoy it and went to many places worldwide. We flew to Singapore where George seemed pleased to be back and to be showing me round. Trouble really surfaced though for George when we went to the little chapel at Changi and the nearby museum. One look and he broke down. A kind Australian comforted him, a gesture I shall never forget, and we thought the upset would pass.'

Unfortunately it did not and George collapsed in Perth. Monica managed to get him back to the hotel but he spent the next two days lying on his bed weeping uncontrollably. Although they continued with their travels across Australia and home via California, George was far from well. When they got back to England he was just as he had been when he originally returned from Borneo, completely introverted, difficult and silent. 'I consulted our doctor but he didn't know what to do, never having seen that sort of thing before. At last the grandchildren came to stay and it was they who pulled him out of himself. They made him play games, draughts, chess, all the board games.'

For the last year of his life George was supported by carers who were at a loss as to how to handle him. One of them told Monica that she thought George was 'dead inside' and she put Monica in contact with a doctor who worked as a volunteer for the Medical Foundation for the care of victims of torture (The Helen Bamber Association).

Dr Gwen Parr told Monica that there was no quick-fix solution to George's mental torment: 'The first thing is to get him to talk,' she explained to her. 'It will take unhurried time. Ex-POWs, especially [those imprisoned by the] Japanese, will seldom talk but if they can it helps to resolve things in their minds and to relax.'

George was at first indignant at Dr Parr's questions and assured her that he was not mental as he had been able to hold down a good job. But gradually he admitted that there had always been something wrong and that this was something that had affected his mind. Dr Parr convinced George that if he would talk to her it would help her to assess his experiences and in turn to help other people. This had a gradual reassuring effect and George began to talk to her about things that he had never mentioned to anyone else since his release. She explained to Monica that the reason why George had reacted so badly on his return to Singapore nearly forty years after the end of the war was because of a sense of guilt that he had survived while so many of his men had perished. This, she said, was a common feeling among these men and it was something that never left them, the fact that they had come home and others had not. 'This is the tragic thing: Japanese prisoners of war cannot speak of what happened to them. They will tell something of the camps and such, but never anything deeper. It is as if the mind has a deep wound, much as if they have been wounded by a sword thrust in the body.'

George died in September 2000. In a moving conclusion Monica Symington wrote:

Looking back over the years I realize that the young man I knew in that marvellous year before the war never came back after it. I fell out of love with him because he could not form a relationship. His emotions were killed inside. All I had left was a deep feeling of compassion, to help him survive . . . I often look back now and think of George's sojourn in a Jap POW camp as if he had had both legs amputated and so could not run away. Only it was his mind which he could not run away from. To come back into the world after such an experience, no one could ever be normal again. The eyes that so haunted me when George asked me to marry him in 1945 were still there when he died. I have to live with the thought that I don't know whether I did anything for him, as I could not remove this feeling of haunting. For a long time I wrapped myself in a cocoon so as not to hurt anyone or to be hurt myself. By doing so I was able, as a carer, to look after him right to the end. Now the burden which was with me for so many years has been lifted. I have felt the most enormous sense of freedom. I am now freed from that sense of not being able to help him.

7

LOVE AND SEX IN TIMES OF WAR

I want to say this and to say it after six years' experience
of Welfare work: there has been a lot of nonsense talked
about the immorality of service women and the number of
illegitimate children born to them. I think it was absolutely
amazing how few unwanted babies there were – only an
infinitesimal percentage of the women serving. After all, if
you put men and women together in close proximity in a
danger shared, a mutual attraction is not only the inevitable
result, it is what we should expect, and we should be very
surprised and perturbed from a national point of view if it
wasn't.

Dame Barbara Cartland

The war disrupted family life in so many different ways but it was
the role of sexual freedom with all its repercussions that had one
of the greatest impacts on family life. From today's perspective
it is difficult to imagine or understand the stigma caused by extra-
marital affairs and, if they came, illegitimate children. For both

men and women during the war there was a sense that living for today was fine because tomorrow you might die and this spilled over into behaviour which to some, most especially the Church, seemed reprehensible but which to others was inevitable and not even particularly surprising.

'"War aphrodisia", as it has been called, had been traditionally ascribed to men in battle. In total war, however, a related hedonistic impulse reaches many other segments of society.' John Costello, in his 1985 book *Love, Sex and War 1939–45*, looked at the changing attitude towards sex during the Second World War, charting its beginnings in the First World War when the emancipation of women began its twentieth-century journey. Thousands of women had left their traditional place in the home to do men's jobs, many serving in uniform for the first time. This gave millions of women a freedom and independence they had not had before and it was certainly a contributory factor to their gaining the vote. 'Women celebrated their new freedom with liberated fashions and liberal behaviour. They bobbed their hair, donned short skirts, smoked in public and wore the heavy make-up which had formerly been the attribute of the harlot.' This liberation was short-lived in Britain as the Depression of the 1920s bit at all levels of society. 'Divorce rates had plunged with the collapse of the stock market. Significantly they reached a post-war low – 40 per cent below the 1928 level – in 1933, the year that the dole queues were longest. The number of weddings also fell as hard times caused many couples to postpone marriage.'

Nevertheless the seeds of emancipation had been sown and the flame was fanned hardest in the USA where the combination of a buoyant stock market, bootleg gin and the racy novels of Scott Fitzgerald fuelled the frenetic pace of the social revolution. Hollywood played its part, producing erotic films for a mass audience and elevating the leading stars to almost legendary status.

Audiences flocked to films such as *Alimony*, which promised 'brilliant men, beautiful jazz babies, champagne baths, midnight revels, petting parties in the purple dawn, all ending in one terrifying climax that makes you gasp'.

It is no coincidence that military triumphs in the Second World War led to an increase in the birth rate. Between 1939 and 1941 the birth rate in Britain declined, despite the increase in the number of marriages. In 1938 there were 621,204 births recorded in Britain and in 1941 that figure had dropped to 579,091. By contrast, as the war turned in Britain's favour and the Allied victories of the second half of the war filtered through the birth rate rose to a high of 751,478 in 1944, an increase of almost 200,000 on the low point of 1941.

Historically in Britain an unmarried mother had been viewed as a disgrace and at best she was able to seek help from voluntary organizations such as the Salvation Army. Babies born to married women were regarded as legitimate unless registered otherwise. Children who were fathered by another man were often not declared illegitimate and did not appear in illegitimacy statistics. Some municipal authorities, such as Birmingham, did carry out research into this nebulous area and discovered that by 1945 the number of confessed illegitimate children born to married women had trebled since the beginning of the war. 'Illegitimacy rates were highest among the young wives of servicemen, suggesting that their work in war production encouraged an independence that often snapped the bonds of marital fidelity already strained by the extended absence of their husbands.' The Office of National Statistics recorded a rise in the number of illegitimate births from 43.4 in 1000 in 1939 rising steadily through the war until it reached 93.3 in 1000 in 1945, a figure that remained a high-water mark until 1978, by which time society's attitudes had changed. The increase in figures can be explained in part by the fact that pre-war there were couples who succeeded in making it to the altar once a pregnancy had been detected whereas during the war the man might be abroad and therefore not around to legitimize the birth, even if that had been the couple's intention. But there can be no doubt that the increase in illegitimate births was as a direct result of wartime affairs. That so many married women gave birth to children whose fathers were not their husbands is perhaps not widely known but it gave rise to considerable difficulties for returning men after the war had ended.

A moving account of how this situation played out was described by a survivor of a wartime liaison in 1984. She and her twin brother were adopted soon after they were born: 'I only knew and loved one of my three fathers. When my mother's husband arrived home from overseas he was devastated to find her "with child", or, as Father would have it, "with children". My twin brother and I were born in the summer of 1945.' She went on:

> They were lonely days for the little wife left behind working in the factory so my mother sought comfort in the arms of another military gentleman (home on leave, I presume). My brother and I were the result of that war-confused union. Divorce was not a consideration in 1945, single mums were not in fashion, and a war-weary, unskilled man did not feel able to support alien twins. Though I have the documents and certificates to prove my origins and true parentage, I have never met either my genetic father or my mother's husband. Indeed the saddest aspect of this triangle is that I have never met my birth mother. Something I would have dearly wished for, if only to have been able to say 'Thank you' for placing me, through adoption, with the most wonderful and loving parents any child could have wished for. My brother and I have been most fortunate.

During the war welfare officers found that a considerable portion of their time was taken up dealing with the question of unwanted pregnancies. Barbara Cartland, in her role as a welfare officer, had a great deal of experience of all different types of relationship problems: 'Men [who] came home and found their wives had been unfaithful; women who wanted a divorce after a few months of marriage; girls who were pregnant; soldiers who arrived home to find their wives ill and no one to look after their children; children with a bad mother and a father overseas – there was no end to them.'

As a counsellor Cartland was warm and generous and people responded to her: 'No one has ever minded when I have talked to them, and I've been both personal and intrusive. Being a novelist helps. I don't know why, but people always want to confide in novelists, and the other thing which I believe makes everything alright is the fact that I am sincere. I do believe what I say.' She found it impossible to condemn girls for succumbing to the temptations of wartime promiscuity, and admitted that where she could she tried to encourage young women to give their husbands a chance, especially when there were complaints about sexual incompatibility, which she explained might well be down to wartime anxiety. But she was even-handed, and counselled men too, admiring those who were shaken by their wives' wartime infidelities and subsequent pregnancies but who came round to the view that it was not the child's fault. She wrote: 'At first they swore that as soon as it was born it would have to be adopted – then sometimes they would say, half-shamefacedly at their own generosity, "The poor little devil can't help itself, and after all it's one of hers, isn't it?" '

One story that illustrated this was that of Lilian James. She was married in 1939 and had a baby girl, Muriel, the following year. There was great rejoicing in the family as the first grandchild was born fit and healthy. Three months after Muriel's birth Lilian's husband, Greg, was called up to join the army. Sent first to India, he spent in total three and a half years away from home, ending up in Burma where he fought the Japanese during the bloody battle of Kohima. He was wounded in the leg and spent the last three months of the war in hospital in Calcutta. All the time he was away he wrote to his wife and his sister in Plymouth. They were a close-knit family and the letters the women wrote back, he said later, sustained him in the very worst times in Burma and he was always glad to read about the day-to-day activities of life at home. Lilian sent him a photograph of Muriel on her first birthday, which he kept throughout the war, punching two holes in it and tying it with a string so that he could hang it around his neck. The photograph came back to Britain with him.

In 1942 Lilian gave birth to a little boy, Johnnie. He was dark haired and beautiful but as both Lilian and Greg were blond there was some doubt as to his parentage. Eyebrows were raised. Jean, Greg's sister, decided that she would have to write to her brother and explain that he had become a father again, although he had not seen his wife for over ten months. At first Greg was shocked but when Jean assured him that the family had rallied round and accepted Johnnie as part of the family he came to terms with it. If one were sufficiently vague about when he had gone away, Jean suggested, then people could talk all they liked but it was not a clear-cut case. And, anyway, there was little he could do from India. Greg accepted his sister's wisdom and over the next few letters he began to ask Lilian to tell him in her letters about the baby's progress.

Then in 1944 Lilian had a less discreet affair with an American GI. People began to gossip. She was by no means the only woman to have her head turned by the handsome American soldiers with their wide smiles and easy manner but within her community she was the only one who was already married. In early 1945 another baby appeared. This time there could be no mistake. The new baby was the result of an affair and the chattering voices were louder and less kindly. It was decided that she should move to a smaller community closer to her own family where she would get the support she needed to bring up her three children, all under five years old. Again Jean acted as the go-between. She wrote to Greg and once again, after the initial shock and indignation, he was stoical.

When he finally returned to his home in October 1945 he found a ready-made family of his little girl and two small strangers, Johnnie and Adam. Lilian was understandably unsure of how her husband would react to her when they met face to face but he had reassured her in his letters that the war had thrown people into strange situations where they did not know from one day to the next what might happen. He was magnanimous and Jean was proud of her noble brother. She knew that Greg had been to hell and back while he was in hospital and it had been her good counsel and generosity towards Lilian that had convinced him that he could have been far worse off.

He told his sister later that he had come to terms with Lilian's infidelities by convincing himself that she had found herself in an extraordinary situation during the war, working in a service canteen in Plymouth, surrounded by temptation, and he had decided he would treat the two boys as if they were his own. Jean, he always maintained, had been the voice of reason and sanity and he was indebted to her for handling a delicate situation so gently and not allowing him to follow his first instinct, which was to turn his back on his wife and demand a divorce. 'Greg was a lovely man, a really lovely, gentle man,' one of his nieces explained. 'He loved Aunt Lilian and spoiled her terribly. He completely forgave her. I will always remember him playing with the boys and joking with them in his gentle voice, teasing them but with great kindness. They returned his love and trusted him instinctively.'

A fourth child was born in 1947, another boy, William. 'He was the spitting image of his older sister and looked as unlike his brothers as it was possible to imagine. But we never really knew for certain what had happened during the war. As we got older we realized something "funny" must have gone on but Uncle Greg was such a gentleman and such a brilliant father that no one ever dared to ask too many questions.' It was only after both Greg and Lilian had died that the true story of the wartime increase in the size of the family came out. Jean told her daughter all about it. She was unemotional but it was clear that she was proud of her role and even more proud of her brother. 'Your Uncle Greg was a man with a huge heart,' she concluded.

The arrival of 1.5 million American servicemen in Britain by 1944, prior to the D-Day invasion of France, brought a flash of excitement to British women, tired of three years of blackouts, Blitz and rationing. It seemed to many that these strapping, well-fed and confident young men had stepped straight out of a Hollywood film. 'Suddenly the GIs were there,' recalled a Derby woman. 'If they'd dropped from Mars we couldn't have been more surprised.' A teenage girl from Birmingham was enthusiastic: 'We were half starved and drably clothed, but the GIs said we looked good anyway. A lot was said about them being over-sexed, overpaid and over here; maybe it applied to a few, but it was mainly a myth. It was just the case that the British women and the American GIs were in the same place at the same time – it was rather pleasant, really!'

The GIs were indeed different from the British servicemen. Their uniforms were smarter and cut from a better cloth. They were generous and outgoing and above all they were fresh and not war weary, which so many of their British counterparts had become after three years of war. On the whole their overtures were very friendly and the great gift of nylons, an unknown luxury for women who could not afford silk stockings, was something that thousands of women were thrilled about.

Some husbands seemed to be happy with their womenfolk flirting with the GIs, some actively encouraged it, one writing to his wife to say he was having a good time with pretty girls and that she should have fun too. But not all men were happy with the situation. One GI died in Norfolk when the husband returned home to find his wife in bed with an intruder. There was a violent struggle and the husband flung the GI to his death through the bedroom window.

Although many of the wartime affairs between GIs and their British girlfriends were essentially temporary, 20,000 women applied to become American wives after the war and the US Army postal service noticed that in the first month after D-Day a quarter of all the mail sent was to British addresses.

The circumstances of total war changed both attitudes and opportunities: 'We were not really immoral, there was a war on,' explained one British housewife. The 'what the heck I could be dead tomorrow' attitude of some of the fighter pilots, for example, brought many couples together, and hastily arranged marriages, with often only forty-eight hours to spend together, were not uncommon. Few couples could consider what would happen after the war, when life might return to normal. They lived for that day and perhaps the next. 'They were loved and beloved, and by this stage in the war love was about the only thing left unrationed.'

'It is very easy to say what a woman should do or should not do when she hasn't seen her husband for four years . . .' Cartland wrote. 'They were young, their husbands were not fluent letter-writers – they started by not meaning any harm, just desiring a little change from the monotony of looking after the children, queuing for food, and cleaning the house with no man to appreciate them or their cooking.' Written in 1948 this counters the dim and prim view taken of extramarital affairs conducted during the war – often, as she pointed out, by women who had been separated from their husbands for anything up to four years and in the first place may only have been married for a matter of weeks. She went on, warming to the romance of her subject: 'He is lonely, she is lonely, he smiles at her, she smiles back, and it's an introduction. It is bad luck that she is married, but he means no harm, nor does it cross her mind at first that she could ever be unfaithful to Bill overseas. When human nature takes its course and they fall in love, the home is broken up and maybe another baby is on the way, there are plenty of people ready to say it's disgusting and disgraceful. But they hadn't meant it to be like that, they hadn't really.' Quite apart from being able to see that the war would provide Dame Barbara with a bottomless pool of experiences sufficient to fill hundreds of romantic novels, the point is that often these wartime relationships had begun as nothing more than a little flirtation.

Some were honest enough to talk about their extramarital relationships after the war: 'The most wonderful days of my life,' one woman said. 'Those days were dreams, every day exciting whether it was good or bad excitement,' recalled another. 'I would not have missed my experiences during the war.' At twenty-four and with an eighteen-month-old baby in tow, with a husband in the RAF where life expectancy was short, Mary Thomas was intensely lonely. Her loneliness was compounded by a real fear of being bombed, as she very nearly was one night in Manchester. She explained what happened next:

When 1942 came in with the hit-and-run air raids, I began to despair that the war was ever going to end. It was in this frame of mind that fate took a hand in my affairs.

The Yanks arrived and set up camps near Manchester, bringing a wave of glamour, romance, and excitement that has never been experienced before or since. They were not welcomed by the British men, but to the English girls they were wonderful. All I knew about Americans was what I'd seen in the films, but Fields Hotel, within walking distance from my home, became the meeting place where GIs danced under soft lights. Eating in secluded corners with their girlfriends, the GIs were able to forget the war for a few hours.

Mary found one young army captain particularly charming. They danced cheek to cheek and later he walked her home but did not, to her surprise, kiss her goodnight. A short time later he called to say he wanted to drop by and arrived with a haversack full of goodies including butter, sugar, sweets, coffee and the all-desirable nylons. He had also brought two buckets of coal, for which she was grateful, as were her neighbours with whom she shared her bounty:

So began another part of my life on the home front. It took a couple of weeks before Rick got around to kissing me goodnight. He asked me a lot of questions about my husband and married life, which I had to admit was a very happy one. I did, however, write and tell my husband about Rick. He was delighted that I'd found someone to give me a break and that Rick seemed a really decent chap.

With my mind free of guilt, I began to come alive again. It would be foolish of me to say that physical attraction never entered our lives: it did. With Rick, I knew it was love, but for me it was

attraction and the need to hold on to someone. So it happened that
we finally made love.

There was nothing cheap about our affair, and if Rick had my
body, my heart was with my husband and somehow I didn't feel
that I was doing anything wrong.

Mary and Rick spent two happy years together until he received
orders to leave for Rome. It had never occurred to Mary that she
would leave her husband although she knew full well that Rick would
have liked her to. When her husband returned in 1945 they tried to
resume their married life together. She found it difficult to forget
her American captain so her husband suggested she make a post-
war visit to America to see him. As she sailed back to Britain after
the visit she realized that, sadly, her great wartime romance was over.

With the increase in the divorce rate in 1945 the Church
became the loudest critic of the decline in moral standards,
urging people to look to the future and not act irresponsibly. 'The
post-war moral crusade intensified after the wild abandon of the
peace celebrations. Sober Victorian principles were offered as
the panacea which would repair the damage that the war had
wrought on the family and married life.' It was not just in Britain
that these concerns were raised but in the USA where President
Hoover*, as early as 1944, had warned that: 'the moral life of
America is in danger . . . We must accept the fact that total war
relaxes moral standards on the home front and that this imperils the whole front of human decency.'

But once social taboos have been broken and the moral fabric
of society changed so dramatically for such a sustained period it
takes more than brave words from figures in authority to reset the
moral clock.

*(1929–1933)

The brutalizing and dislocating effects of war had left many individuals reacting to the cessation of hostilities as another interruption in the transient pattern of existence to which they had become accustomed. Millions of demobilized servicemen had grown used to an adventurous existence which did not reach beyond tomorrow. It took months and even years for many of them to accustom themselves again to a routine of civilian existence. The transition was especially hard for those who had entered the services straight from school and to whom the mundane world of everyday work was as great a shock as joining the army had been.

There was disillusionment too with hasty wartime marriages, resulting in 34,000 divorces in the UK alone in 1945–6, but some had decided to learn by their mistake and make the most of what was to come. One woman wrote:

When my husband finally came home we discovered we were two different people, so much had happened in those years apart. My husband, older than myself, was time-conscious, critical, and came back with the attitude of a regimental sergeant major; it was as if he expected me to jump up and salute when he entered a room. We had to take it that the men were faithful while away, but my in-laws were very quick to tell tales of my friendships with the opposite sex. My husband later threw this at me when I complained of the years I had spent alone. I realized that settling down was going to be hard, but by this time I had had two babies, quickly, and I was stuck in a strange area, strange faces and for hours on my own. He was finding it hard to get a civilian job and having to take orders after having had some measure of authority. I missed going to work and the companionship and intelligent conversation. After a while we settled to some sort of married life, but there were times when I thought that if there was a hell on earth, I was living it. I did not want a divorce, I could never have left the children.

In 1999, Janice Taylor asked her father, Albert Griffiths, what he had done in the war. He replied that if he were going to tell her anything he would have to write it down. And he would have to think about it for a while. Janice knew only that he had been in the army for six years, that he had been an engineer and he was brilliant with maps. She knew nothing more and nor did her siblings. 'Do you want me to tell you the whole story?' he asked her before he started writing. 'Warts and all,' she replied, without really knowing what to expect. When Albert finished he handed over a beautifully presented document complete with maps of all the areas he had been to and stories that Janice could not even have dreamed of. It was, he said, the story of an ordinary soldier but the revelations about his and his wife's past were new to the family. He concluded in the memoir:

Looking back on my 6 years and 115 days of active service, I am convinced that the army life contributed greatly to the building of my character and ability to cope with the family life to follow. I am grateful for the many wonderful friendships it brought me. Conversely I think that no person should have such a long period of his or her life compulsorily interrupted. The personal infidelities, of both sides, were I believe the result of the forced separation of two highly sexed partners.

This, Janice explained, had come as a complete surprise to her whole family. They had known relatively little about their parents' early lives and had certainly never thought to ask too much. When he was seventeen Albert Griffiths met Edna Meehan, the oldest daughter of a family of ten children, four of whom died in infancy after Edna was born. When Edna left school she found a job at a local factory but her freedom was short-lived as soon after she began work she fell down a stone stairwell and fractured her coccyx. At about this time Albert Griffiths appeared in her life. Educated at the local grammar school until he was fifteen but still from a working-class background, Albert was different from other boys she had known at school. His grandmother, Kate, lived in the same street as the Meehans and Albert would pay a weekly visit to drop off and collect his mother's washing. One day Kate asked Albert if he would give Edna a ride on his motorbike. Edna was slightly puzzled by Albert, who was quiet and unassuming. 'She was a party girl,' her daughter Barbara explained, 'and she loved the razzamatazz of Hollywood that she saw at the pictures. She learned to play the piano by ear and was often invited to play at dances and clubs, which she loved to do.'

Edna had known almost no kindness in her life. When once Albert gave her a watch as a birthday present she wept with tears of gratitude. It was the first birthday present she had ever received in her life. When war became inevitable Albert volunteered for the army, joining the RAOC (Royal Army Ordnance Corps). In the autumn of 1939 Edna fell pregnant and Albert's mother, Elsie, quickly had to organize for them to marry while he was on leave. They married on 23 December 1939 and had six days of married life together before Albert had to go back to barracks.

The separation caused by the war threatened to take away everything Edna thought she had ever wanted: a kind husband, security and a future. Albert rented a house for his new wife five doors away from his mother and Edna was able to live at home and give up her work. She lived on Albert's staff sergeant's salary and waited for the baby to come. But she was lonely and found her mother-in-law intimidating so she spent much of her time travelling to see her mother, Eva, who was also pregnant, expecting her tenth child. Edna's baby was born in June, a little boy they called David, ten days after her mother's son Geoffrey came into the world. The two women supported each other during the first few months of their new babies' lives and Edna was able to help her increasingly disabled mother to cope. The following year Albert was fortunate to have seven weeks' leave while he awaited a posting. In fact he was lucky in being able to get Christmas leave for three years running in 1940, 1941 and 1942 but from 1943 he did not return to his home until 1946.

In Aldershot in 1943 Albert received a letter from his mother Elsie saying that:

Edna had become a talking point by the neighbours, about her brazen conduct with the eager Americans. Specifically that she had changed her name to Jean, had been seen very late at night, lying on a neighbour's garden wall, with an American hand exploring her anatomy beneath her underclothes. On another occasion an American had been seen leaving my house, in the early morning. Finally that she had been seen consorting with a civilian.

He was given compassionate leave and went home to confront Edna 'and leave her in no doubt as to what would become of her if she stepped out of line again. Composing this story in 1999,' he went on, 'I am aware that in 1943 I was very naive and unworldly wise. In the meantime, by experience I realize that Edna has always been inherently highly sexed, particularly from her father, and thus highly subject to deviational temptation. Had I been aware of this in 1943 I might have been able somehow to offset the situation.'

In September of that year Edna had another baby, Barbara.

Albert was granted a three-day leave pass, and travelled overnight, arriving home early the next morning to see his little girl. It was the last time he saw her until he returned home for good. In 1944 Albert took part in the D-Day landings, fighting on Sword Beach and then moving on to Holland and Germany, where he spent the remainder of the war. He became part of the occupational army of Germany and at some stage met a Dutch girl with green eyes called Christine with whom he fell deeply and passionately in love. The situation was complicated. Both were married and had children but Christine's husband was a POW in America and Edna was on the other side of the channel looking after two small children. Their relationship blossomed. Albert wrote in 1999: 'I have, as far as memory will allow, tried to record my feelings as they were in 1945. They may or may not have changed since then, but I say confidently, this was no sordid affair, this was real.'

What was also very real was Edna's rage when Albert confessed to her, on a short leave in September 1945, that he was in love with another woman. She was beside herself with fury and determined to make as big a fuss as she possibly could: 'She later searched my uniform and discovered a photograph of Christine. On return to my unit I was bombarded with warning letters from parents, ministers, the local MP. Letters also to my Commanding Officer.'

Forced by circumstances, as well as Edna's indignation, to make a decision about his future, Albert decided to leave Christine and return to Birmingham to be with his wife and children. 'It is extraordinary to think that my parents had been married for nearly seven years by the time my father came back and yet they had never spent more than a few weeks together. They can hardly have known one another,' Janice said. Barbara recalled his homecoming, which to her was something of a surprise. 'I have two strong memories from my early childhood,' she said. 'The main one was going to the station to meet my father on the day he was demobbed. Mum took David and me on the bus to Snow Hill railway station. I had my favourite Teddy Bear with me and somewhere along the way he lost a glass eye, which made me very sad. My father had missed the train so we had to go home again.' When Albert finally arrived at the house later that night the children were asleep. Barbara remembered feeling very worried about meeting her father for the first time in her memory. She felt afraid of him but he was not a frightening man and she soon grew to love and trust him deeply. In 1946 the first of Albert and Edna's post-war family was born. Tony was followed in 1949 by Linda and in 1954 by Janice.

Albert had been a radio engineer during the war but as television was in its infancy and the emerging technology fascinated him, he switched to TV and soon became a branch manager of Radio Rentals in Birmingham as well as running a repair business from his shed, answering on-call enquiries about broken sets and repairing them either on site or at home. He needed the two jobs to fund his and Edna's lifestyle, and in particular his taste in fast cars. He wanted to be able to have a new car every year and give Edna everything she wanted. Janice said that her mother was never completely content with everything Albert gave her. 'Her possessions were her suit of armour,' she explained, 'everyone could see how well she had done by these tangible things. My father understood that and always bought her the best of anything he could afford but it was not always enough for her.'

After Edna's death, Albert would sometimes talk about the war but it was only after he wrote his memoirs that his children could piece together the story of his life. It was extraordinary, Janice and Barbara concluded, that Albert had kept all this history alive in his mind for years but never talked about it. 'My only fear in the war was that if I was "got" I wanted to be killed outright, not wounded and have to come home disabled. I'm not afraid of death, having seen everything I did in France and Germany. Don't worry about me. I'm not afraid of dying.' At the time Janice and Barbara remembered thinking how brave their father was. Albert died peacefully in 2006. Janice said afterwards: 'You always want to believe your father is a good man. We are just incredibly lucky that we genuinely had a good man as a father.'

It was one thing to find out about parents' wartime romances from memoirs, even fifty-five years after the event, but it was quite another and different thing to discover that a romance had led to a family secret involving an illegitimate child that was not revealed for decades.

Valerie Walker first met her half-sister, Melanie, when she was sixty. 'All my life,' she said, 'I felt that something was hidden from me, that something was not quite right. I had always wanted a sister but I didn't find out until my fiftieth birthday that I actually had a half-sister and she had been born just eighteen months after my birth.' Valerie's mother, Stella, knew about Melanie, as did her two older brothers and her father James's brother but no one else was aware, at least no one of Valerie's generation or younger. The story came out after Valerie's fiftieth birthday. She had turned to her cousin and said: 'I always wish I'd had a sister. My cousin felt it was time I knew the truth so she told my mother to explain the background or she would. So my mother told me the truth about my half-sister. I wasn't shocked. I wasn't even surprised when I found out. It was as if I already knew about her even though I had not actually known she existed.'

However it was to be ten years before the two women met for the first time. Valerie's brother found Melanie's details on a website and urged his sister to get in contact. 'It was not at all straightforward,' Valerie explained. 'I thought about it for a long time because I had the thought in the back of my mind that Melanie might not want to be in touch with us, that she might have built her own life and the revelation she had a whole large family might not be a welcome one. But my brother persuaded me to draft an email which he would send off to see what happened.'

Melanie's own recollection of the event chimed with Valerie's. She had written a piece for Friends Reunited some years back, before she even had her own computer, and it was through this medium that Valerie's brother had got her details. When the email from Valerie arrived Melanie was absolutely stunned:

Valerie wrote such a lovely email, explaining that if I didn't feel like getting in touch that was fine by them and I wasn't to feel any pressure. I immediately rang my best friend who warned me it could be a scam but I was convinced it was not. So a couple of days later I replied. I know now that Valerie had promised her mother she would not try to get in touch with me so that makes it even more remarkable. It was quite a while before we met up but when we did photos came out and lots of stories. It was strange to discover I had a family with cousins and nieces and nephews. And it was interesting to hear about Valerie's life and her side of my father's story.

Stella and James Walker were born in 1907 and had met in 1914 when they were at school. James was the son of an army officer and had been born in India, although he grew up in the United Kingdom. They married in 1935 and two boys were born before Valerie arrived in November 1942. James was a regular soldier and had risen to the rank of captain quartermaster by the outbreak of the Second World War. He travelled all over the world during the war and was in France with the British Expeditionary

Force at Dunkirk, in Albania, in Italy and in the Orkneys. On one of his postings he met a young servicewoman called Elizabeth. Elizabeth had also been born in India but had grown up in the UK. In 1939 she had joined the ATS and worked throughout the war as a driver. 'She was quite mechanical and could fix cars as well as drive them, which was strange because after the war she didn't have a car and I did not realize she was mechanically minded,' Melanie explained. Elizabeth and James had an affair and a little girl was born in July 1944. 'I don't think my father's affair was anything other than companionship,' Valerie hastened to say. 'He was not a womanizer. The two of them must have been thrown together in the extreme situation of the war and turned to each other for comfort. My father had very high moral standards. We were not allowed to swear, we had to go to school on time and there was no messing around as children. We were brought up rather on military lines.' Melanie agreed, 'My mother also had high moral standards and my cousin once said to me that it was out of character for her to have an illegitimate child. I think it was that she sought comfort and love during the war and James was able to offer her that.'

After the war James Walker returned to Stella and his family in London and remained in the army until he was discharged in 1948 at the age of forty-one. Valerie said: 'He was a changed man after the war. He was quiet, a bit of a loner really. He spoke very little of his family and I had no idea he had cousins as he only spoke infrequently of his siblings. He certainly never spoke of Elizabeth and her baby. I believe he was more outgoing before the war because his brother was a bit of a lad, but the war affected him. Things between him and my mother had been fine before the war but afterwards it was not so easy.' After James left the army he had difficulty finding work and although he was promised many jobs over the years he never found a trade so ended up doing odd jobs here and there. 'Obviously my mother never discussed my father with me,' Valerie said. 'She was the type of person who just got on with things and accepted her lot in life. I think she saw him only infrequently during the war and I imagine she accepted his affair with Elizabeth as just part of what happened when people were separated for a long time. She had her own children and home to worry about and she accepted him back in 1945 so I think she must have decided she just had to get on with life.'

Stella and James settled in Chingford and just over a mile away Melanie lived with Elizabeth and her aunt, although Valerie was completely unaware of this. Melanie's surname was changed to Walker by deed poll when she was six years old and although both girls were brought up Catholic, they did not attend the same Catholic school so they never met. Valerie remembered, however, one occasion when she was on a bus with her mother and a woman and child got on. Instantly Stella said they must get off the bus as she had developed a migraine. 'I don't think I thought anything of it at the time as my mother used to get migraines,' Valerie said, 'but now I think about it I am sure it was because Melanie and Elizabeth had got on the bus.'

Melanie lived with her mother, her aunt and uncle and a step-daughter who was about the same age as her mother.

Auntie Mary was about fifteen years older than my mother. She helped to bring me up and I had no knowledge of my unusual situation. She had always wanted children so she took care of me when my mother went out to work. She defended me, I see now. On one occasion I remember when I was about five, a visiting child asked where my father was and my aunt replied 'Oh, he was killed in the war.' I recall thinking that was strange as he had been at the house only the week before but it was not until I was in my teens that my mother explained the whole thing to me. My father was not a regular visitor but he used to come round to the house and he was always generous with presents. I remember he once brought me a bike and he used to help my mother out financially. I was happy at home so I never asked any questions about my father and I never guessed the truth behind my story, which is perhaps strange as I was an inquisitive child.

In retrospect Melanie had great respect for her mother's brave decision not to offer her up for adoption at birth but to keep her at a time when illegitimacy was severely frowned upon. She had no recollection of her mother having other men in her life and she knew that James never stayed over when he visited. 'My mother wore a wedding ring and she changed our name to Walker because I think she was worried that I would be stigmatized.' The relationship between James and Elizabeth, she was convinced, was born out of the madness of the war years. Both were attractive people, both were probably lonely and away from their families. They had much in common in their backgrounds and the attraction was understandable but it was not, she maintained, a reckless love affair nor was it ever going break up James's first marriage and his family.

When Melanie and Valerie finally met they discovered they had so much in common. Both had wished they had had a sister and both their mothers died in the same year, 1997. 'Melanie told me she always had a feeling she had a sister but she knew nothing about her half-brothers. My father had never lived with her and her mother but he had provided for her throughout her childhood. On one occasion my mother threw him out and we wondered later whether he had gone to live with Melanie's mother, but he had not.'

'I knew that my father had a family but for some reason I thought I had three half-sisters, not two half-brothers and Valerie. It shows how little information they were prepared to give away about each other,' Melanie said.

Although Valerie and Melanie were cautious about meeting up after sixty years the reunion was a success. 'Melanie looks very like my father, which I do not. I think she is delighted with her "new" family.' Melanie now spends Christmas with Valerie and her family and both are happy that they have finally met the half-sister they both wished they had had as children.

8

STRANGER IN THE HOUSE:
THE DAUGHTER'S TALE

The sense of my father being a stranger persisted through the
rest of my childhood and adolescence. After he died and I
heard people talking about him, I realized that I had never
really got to know him.

Muriel Woodhead

When men went off to war and wives were left alone, sometimes
with small children, a natural reaction was to move back to the
family home and wait out the next few years. The security and
company of three generations of women in one house is something that many never forgot. But it also had the effect of
narrowing the horizons of young wives at a time when their
husbands were being exposed to new and often exciting experiences, as well as attendant danger.

In the autumn of 1939 Anne Stamper's parents moved from
Hertfordshire, where she had been born four and a half years

earlier, to Nottingham where her father, a textile chemist, could take up a new job. Anne attended the local primary school and although she did not see a lot of her father because he worked long hours, she remembered him checking her spellings and times tables: 'He was very strict but very fair, and ambitious for me,' she recalled.

> When war was declared there was an initial panic that schools would be bombed and so, for about six months, all the schools were closed. My mother agreed to our house being used to teach about ten children every morning, and a teacher came to our house and then in the afternoon we went to another house. The schools were not attacked and we all went back, though there was an air-raid shelter in the school playground, and we had air-raid practices, rather like fire drills. We also had to carry gas masks with us in cases to and from school. The only air raids I remember however were at night; then, when the sirens went, my parents brought me downstairs wrapped in an eiderdown, and I slept on the sofa turned against the wall. My father was an air-raid warden and did fire watch duty. I watched him go off carrying his tin helmet. I did not realize then that he would have to join the army and our cosy family life would be so disrupted.

This eventually happened in 1943 when men of her father's age were called up. Her parents had made plans for this happening but had not, of course, involved Anne in their discussions. Everything that happened next was a surprise. When her father left the house to join the army she saw her mother with red eyes from crying. It shocked her. It was the first time she had ever seen a grown-up cry. The next thing that happened was that Anne and her mother moved from Nottingham to Rochdale where her maternal grandmother lived.

This was a total change in life-style, it was like going back fifty years. I just accepted it as part of life and in some ways found it quite interesting. We moved from an ordinary but modern suburban semi to Granny's little cottage which had no bathroom and only an outside loo. It only had two bedrooms and I had a bed in the corner of the room where Granny slept, quite a change from my own bedroom with my toys (no room for my dolls' house now). There was no hot water, just a cold tap in the kitchen and we had to boil water on the kitchen range. My mother and I used to go for a bath once a week at the house of a friend of my mother. My parents' furniture had all been put in store as the house in Nottingham was rented, there was just room for one or two of our family pieces.

Anne knew her grandmother well. She had been a widow for years, her husband having died when Anne's mother, Ethyl, was seven years old, and every year she had spent several months with the family in Hertfordshire and then Nottingham, so she was very much part of Anne's young life: 'She was quite a dominant character and my mother had always been the "dutiful daughter".' Anne remembered her mother being very happy to be back in Rochdale amongst her old friends, having found it a wrench to leave to get married at the age of twenty-six. So the relationship between mother and daughter slipped back into how it had always been in the past. 'My grandmother continued her own social life with her life-long friends and went on holiday with Auntie Nellie as she had always done. However she must have found it a bit crowded in her little cottage with us there and I don't suppose she much liked having to share her bedroom with me.' There were no complaints, though, because this was wartime and compromises had to be made in many families, so Anne just got on with life in Rochdale. The biggest shock for her was

Barbara Cartland in her ATS Uniform, 1941. Cartland was a Welfare Officer throughout the war and a brilliant observer of family matters and issues for returning men.

Leonora Eyles, novelist and agony aunt for *Woman's Own*. Her advice to women about how to handle their returning men was kind and refreshingly straightforward.

Mary 'Polly' Cartland with Barbara and Ronald. She lost both her sons a day apart in May 1940. For the mothers of fighting soldiers there was the agony of the loss of their children but they have been largely overlooked by history.

Nella Last with her younger son Cliff in 1939. Although he came back home in 1944 he was a stranger in the house and soon after the war he emigrated to Australia dashing his mother's hopes that he might work with his father in Barrow-in-Furness.

Ena Mitchell with her daughter, Anne, and her mother-in-law at Leopoldsburg War Cemetery visiting Bill Mitchell's grave. He was killed in 1944. Ena never married again.

Charles Steel with his wife, Louise, and their daughter, Margaret, at Broadstairs in 1950. Charles wrote 182 letters which he kept for Louise to give her a picture of his life as a POW.

Above left: Frances and Patrick Campbell-Preston in Scotland after the war. They were separated for five years, most of which time Patrick spent incarcerated in Colditz.

Above right: Charles and Doris Cole in 1934. Doris described the war as an interesting episode in her long life but she hated the effect it had on people and her relationship with Charles took some time to settle down after their six years of separation.

Left: Albert and Edna Griffiths on their wedding Day, 23 December 1939. Both had extra-marital affairs during the war but came back together in 1945 and were married for 50 years.

Anne Stamper with her parents in the early 1940s. Anne and her mother went to live with her maternal grandmother while her father left Britain and spent three years in India.

Anne Stamper in 2008. Her father's return was in the end a very happy one but India had changed his outlook and she remembers him being a stranger when he first came home.

To BETTY e MARION WITH LOTS OF LOVE FROM DADDY XXXX

Jen Howe in Malaya in the late 1940s, soon after her family was reunited. This enchanting photograph was taken just before the monkey disgraced itself and ruined her dress forever.

Bill Hillman c. 1941. He and his wife Nora kept their relationship alive via correspondence so that on his return in 1946 he could pick up where he left off with his wife and two little girls.

Nora Hillman with Betty (5) and Marion (3) wearing ribbons sent from Italy.

Jean Hammond with her two grandmothers, c. 1942. For Jean the comfortable matriarchy in which she lived during the war was changed by her father returning from a German prisoner of war camp in 1945.

Jean Roberts eventually began to talk to her father about his past shortly before he died. She has made several visits to Thailand to try better to understand how his captivity affected his whole life after the war.

Mary Rockcliffe with her four children (Stephen on the left) in Sheffield, 1955. 'Women like my mum were part of a story that I feel is only just beginning to be understood.'

Stephen Rockcliffe spent years coming to terms with his father's past. 'It is a sad fact that Dad, like so many others, never fully reclaimed his life after the war.'

Frank Percival with his son, Martin, in 1963. Frank spoke mainly of the positive sides of his time as a Japanese prisoner of war and Martin grew up not knowing that his father was the exception rather than the rule in the way he readjusted to life post-war.

Juliet Curry with her mother, Ruth, on the beach at Bournemouth in the late 1940s. Juliet was dunked in the sea daily as a supposed cure for rickets from which she had suffered as a result of malnutrition shortly after her birth.

Chris Best with her father, Malcolm, in 1950. Malcolm Ingelby-Scott suffered from anxiety and depression after the war and died suddenly in 1959. It was not until forty years later that Chris began to learn more about her father's past.

Carol Cooper with her late father's diary, which appeared at auction fifty years after his death. She eventually acquired the diary in 1996 and began a new adventure to find out more about the father she never knew.

Atholl and Elizabeth Duncan in the late 1940s. Their daughter Meg said: 'My mother's need to make my father's life better after the war dominated her own.'

Stephanie Hess and her brothers with 'Gran'pa' in 1978, two years before his death. His stories opened Stephanie's eyes to a world that no longer exists but which created a vital link to the past.

Stephanie Hess with her daughter, Alicky, January 2008. Gran'pa's stories live on through his granddaughter and great-granddaughter for future generations.

Ken Rose with his wife, Elizabeth and daughter, Pam in 1950. Ken's war shaped all three of their lives and robbed Pam of a normal childhood.

the school she had to attend for one term before she could go to Bury Grammar School, her father's old school. It was the one time in her life when she was very unhappy at school. The children (usually boys), she recalled, got caned at assembly in front of the whole school. 'In our classroom we sat in rows on benches and desks; we were put in order of merit each week, and as a new girl I was put at the bottom of the class. After an enlightened schooling this was awful, and on top of that I was bullied because of my "posh" accent.'

Not long before Anne's father was posted abroad she contracted pneumonia following a tonsillectomy. She was very ill and remembers her father coming home on compassionate leave. He sat by her bed making a model out of a 'Bako' building set she had been lent. 'I thought this was very good and kept it after he had gone back, I think I was proud of him although he was a rather distant, rather authoritarian figure.'

Anne's father had joined the Royal Army Ordnance Corps and was due to be sent to the Far East on a convoy that had to go round Africa and then to India.

By chance someone learned during that voyage that in civilian life he was a textile chemist. When they reached India he was given a commission and transferred to the Indian Army to work on fabrics. It was a great stroke of luck. His experiences in India, apart from being interesting (he travelled all over the subcontinent), also kept him up to date with his work – nylon was just being used for the first time. It also meant that he was 'safe' so my family did not have to worry in the way those who had fathers in active service must have worried. My mother's cousin was killed in the RAF.

Life in India was a great deal more exotic than life in the cottage in Rochdale and Anne remembered her mother reading out the two or three airmail letters that she received from him each week. He sent photographs and presents, including a huge tin of Darjeeling tea which the grown-ups all appreciated. Anne was far more impressed by the lovely pictures decorating the sides of the tin. 'I don't remember missing my father particularly, my great-uncle who lived nearby used to play with me a bit and lift me up and have what my mother called a "rough five minutes" which I suppose was the sort of thing my father might have done had he been there.'

Stanley Howarth returned home in 1946. 'He was a stranger to me,' Anne recalled. 'I remember watching him, a slim sun-burned figure, getting out of the taxi with my mother who had met him at the station. I felt very awkward going up and saying "Hello Daddy". We went away on holiday together and I began to get to know him, and found that we did different things now that he was with us, but it took quite a time to accommodate having him in our lives again.'

The comfortable matriarchy into which she had been plunged in the early 1940s was broken up and she now thinks how difficult it must have been for her grandmother to be separated from her daughter and granddaughter after three years of living on top of one another in the cottage. There was further dislocation for the first few months after the war as the family could not properly be reunited. Stanley returned to his job in Nottingham and her parents bought a house. However, it was still being built so Ethyl continued to live with her mother in Rochdale and her father had lodgings close to his work. Anne had been offered a place at Nottingham Girls' High School and as both her parents were ambitious for her to do well they felt it was important that she should begin the academic year of 1946 in the new school. The school had a boarding house and she stayed there for the first term, which she really enjoyed. Her father used to visit her on

Thursday evenings and they would sit in the office provided by one of the staff. 'These were really difficult times,' she wrote. 'He did not know what to say to me or me to him. After he had asked about my school work we ran out of conversation.'

In January 1947 the family moved into the new house and life could begin properly. The furniture was brought out of store and Anne once again had her own bedroom with, she remembered, new 'utility' furniture. 'The only things that now reminded us of the years of separation were the things that my father had brought back from India – carpets, a desk, which I still have, along with the two small elephants he gave me.' She goes on:

> I think that my mother was truly happy to have my father home again and it was exciting to move into a new house and have the furniture out of store and start again as a family. However there was some adapting required. Being a textile chemist he was interested in fabrics and colour, so he had the say on the decoration of the house. I remember my mother saying that, since he had returned from India, he liked much stronger colours, and the carpet he bought for our living room was a strong rusty red with embossed flowers at the corners. She just accepted his choice. My mother had spent four years back in her childhood home; my father had had his horizons widened by his experiences. I remember he told me years later that, had he not had a wife and child at home, he might well have stayed and gone into partnership with a Swiss chap he met in Kashmir.

Anne remembered from a very early age feeling it was her responsibility to look after her mother and no more so than when, at the age of thirteen, she learned that her mother was expecting a baby. Anne was somewhat taken aback and never knew whether this was, as she put it, an attempt by her parents to make up for lost time or whether it was a mistake. Either way she was very concerned about Ethyl:

My mother was rhesus negative – before anyone understood the condition. I was her first child, and thus I was OK, but she had had two other babies before the war, both of whom had died within a few days of being born. I knew this and was duly concerned about my mother. However by this time the condition was better understood and the doctors at the hospital were prepared. I went in the taxi with her when she went into hospital to have the baby, as my father was at work and we did not have either a car or a telephone in those days so he could not get home quickly enough. The baby – a girl – Jennifer, had a complete blood transfusion at birth, but sadly it did not successfully deal with the problem. She lived until she was eighteen months old. The death of my sister made a deep impact on me – as did the time afterwards when my mother became ill with depression. My teenage years were quiet serious years. I wonder how much, if any, of this can be seen as a result of the war, I had never considered this before.

In the end this story was a happy one. 'During my teenage years I became much closer to my father, I suspect he never was very good with small children whereas my mother was. Nevertheless the war deprived me of having a father for those four years, and I did have to get reacquainted with "the stranger in the house".'

Jen Howe's childhood was dominated by distance. Distance from her parents both physically and, in a sense, from her father emotionally as well. Jen was five when her father came back from the war. He had been a prisoner of the Japanese and Jen and her mother had spent the war in Australia. John Godber had worked on a rubber plantation in Malaya before the war and had married Thyra, the daughter of another rubber plantation manager. Jen was born in 1940. When war broke out in the Far East, John and Thyra were on leave in Australia. John immediately sailed for Singapore to join his Armoured Car Company in the FMSVF (Federated Malay States Volunteer Force). Thyra and Jen remained behind in Australia.

'For the first five years of my life, it was just Mum and me, living in a tiny cottage on a sheep station, not far from Sydney,' Jen wrote. 'We lived, slept, ate and played together. There were dogs, horses, a few cows and masses of sheep; I have no memories of anyone else in my life. Neither do I recollect my father's eventual return in October 1945, after his release, although I do remember a tall dark man, who turned out to be my grandfather.'

Thyra Godber's memory of her husband's homecoming was one of great happiness, tinged with the sadness of the loss of her brother and mother, both of whom died in the war. She felt, nevertheless, that she was one of the lucky ones, with a family life on which to build once her husband came home. She and other women in Sydney expecting returning men were warned that their men would need a great deal of support and careful handling. 'But my husband had something to come back to. At thirty-five he just wanted to get back to work and get on with life. One thing I do remember, however, was how much he smoked. He smoked whenever he could.' By November 1945 the family was living in England but Thyra and John found it a depressing place. There had been no rationing in Australia and it was a shock to be confronted by the combination of war-torn Britain and the coupon culture.

In early 1946 John Godber, Thyra and Jen returned to Malaya, where John resumed the life of a rubber plantation manager on an estate in Kedah, in the most northerly and remote part of the Malay peninsula. There were no other Europeans for miles around. It was a tough and lonely life for women and children.

Thyra's sister, June, meanwhile, had married her boyfriend, David Rintoul, and was living in Kuala Lumpur, where David worked as an industrial chemist for ICI. Thyra and John Godber's post-war life was not easy for several reasons. Having adjusted to being together again after the years of separation they were living in an isolated spot with only one another and Jen for company:

> Here conditions were primitive and our only form of transportation was two motorbikes – a small ex-army dispatch rider's bike for Mum and a larger, more powerful model for my father. Occasionally, the three of us would set off on the motorbikes to visit friends on distant estates – me riding in front of Dad, small legs astride the petrol tank. And in fact, this is my first memory of him – two disembodied, hairy arms against my bare shoulders; two large, hairy hands on the handlebars in front of me.

John Godber's health had suffered in the POW camps and he had recurrent attacks of malaria and dysentery throughout his life. He scarcely ever spoke to his wife about his experiences, nor indeed to Jen, until she was a young woman. The only time he talked in depth was when he was with the other ex-POWs. He had however given Thyra his diary, in the form of an open letter that he had written to her during his long captivity, so that she knew quite a lot of detail, unusually, about what he had been through although it was never discussed. 'On my second birthday – October 6, 1942 – my father wrote in his POW diary: "Jen's birthday. . . . and no doubt you will be having a party for her . . . I shall try and imagine it but it's very difficult to think of her as being any different from when I left. I hope you will give her a present from me, I'm sure you will and perhaps you will explain who I am from a photograph . . ."'

Jen had to learn to fit into the new regime, finding her place as the child of a couple rather than the younger companion of a woman rendered lonely by the war. June remembers her niece as a sensitive child who found readjustment to the post-war situation difficult. Jen understood nothing of her father's POW experiences and it led, as it did in many families, to some scenes which grew out of complete misunderstanding:

> At some point, my father decided to raise Muscovy ducks, so that we could have fresh eggs and meat (commodities that were still difficult to come by in upcountry Malaya). The ducklings were adorable and I loved them. They were my playmates. Every afternoon, while my parents were having their siesta, I would go down to the enclosure and teach the ducklings to fly. One by one the ducklings died, until there were only two remaining. One afternoon, my father glanced out of the window and saw me tossing a duckling skywards. That was a spanking I will never forget.

It was only years later that she realized that the outburst had less to do with the ducklings and everything to do with what John would have perceived as a squandering of food. Their food on the rubber estate consisted of dried meat, potatoes and onions supplied by rail in kerosene cans. This was supplemented later on with vegetables they grew in their garden and the occasional scrawny chicken from the far-off village.

> An ex-POW friend once said of him: '. . . He didn't know me and yet he did something that no one else did – he gave me food. Extra food like that was the difference between life and death. I never forgot it and I never knew anyone like him.' But I remember him as swift to annoy. I remember those spurts of anger that would come quite unexpectedly. I regret that many of my early childhood memories of my father are of my fear of him. I'm sure that there were lots

of good times, but my overwhelming sense is that I was in awe of him and he seemed distant and unapproachable. Now I realize that the POW days left their mark on both of us; he must have been pre-occupied with rebuilding his life. I was probably resentful of this strange man who had stolen my mother. Photographs of that time show a rather withdrawn, often sulky little girl.

It is only now, sixty years later, that Jen can understand better what her father had been through and how this goes some way to explain the, to her, incomprehensible flashes of anger. 'The dif-ficult times came and went, but they were frightening to a small child,' she said. June understood that life was hard for her niece. 'She didn't really know her father and she probably resented him coming back and taking over her mother's affections. She felt she was different and despite Thyra and John's best efforts she found it difficult to accept the new situation. John and Thyra needed to spend time sorting out their own problems. They all had to learn how to get on anew.'

In 1948 came the Malayan Emergency and the Godbers decided that it would be better to send Jen to boarding school where she would be safer. 'I became an "orphan" of the Raj,' she said. But it was nothing unusual. Thyra too had been brought up in Malaya and sent to boarding school in England and she had seen her parents only once every three years. At the beginning of the Emergency, Jen became a yearly boarder at St Hilda's School in Perth, Western Australia, returning each Christmas for a five-week holiday in Malaya –

often to a different house from the one I had left, for my father was constantly on the move between estates. Twice, I came home to find a new baby in the house. Never having seen the burgeoning belly or learnt the facts of life, I concluded that the babies must have been a gift from the government – perhaps given as a reward for being married! In any case, I resented those babies – they were my parents' 'second family' and I always felt that I was the outsider; but now, having emigrated to Canada in the early sixties, I find myself wishing I knew that second family better. Boarding school allows for a special camaraderie and a very real sense of family. Back then, it seemed to me that my real home and my real family were in Western Australia – St Hilda's School and its denizens became the constant in my life.

Australia was ingrained in her and, although the annual parting from her mother was always a terrible wrench, she used to enjoy the week-long voyage on the specially chartered ship that took her and other children from Malaya back to Australia for a new school year. The trips were fun and she remembers being highly delighted by the gangs of girls and boys who would chase each other around the ship.

In 1955 life changed again for Jen when, aged nearly fifteen, she was sent for in the middle of the school year to come 'home'. She resented this and never really understood why she had to leave St Hilda's – 'I was a naughty girl, paying frequent visits to the Head Mistress' study, and until quite recently, I had always assumed that I must have been expelled from St Hilda's.' Back in Singapore where her parents now lived she took the entrance exam for Bedford High School as it was planned that John would take early retirement and move back to England. In the event she failed the exam as the Australian school system was about a year behind the English system, so she completed her education in a local convent school.

At that time the divisions of race were still keenly felt in Singapore. The only European girl in my class, I felt large, pink and clumsy beside my tiny Asian schoolmates, who used to tease me gently about my big feet. Although I had friends at this school, the divisions in Singapore society were still so great that I couldn't have asked Mulan, Kamalan, Poh Tin or Chandra to any of the European social gathering places. In a hazy way, I knew this, while never completely comprehending the social and racial intricacies. Within the school compound, we were a happy group, but I did not form the close, intimate friendships that I had at St Hilda's. Other European kids went to the military school or to Tanglin. I remember thinking: 'Why did I always have to be different?'

John Godber had always been a distant figure for Jen but now she was back in Singapore, living at home, she began to get to know him:

It was here, during my teens, that my father suddenly popped into focus for me. He seemed enormously handsome, clever and powerful, yet at the same time often austere and unapproachable; and I was still essentially fearful of him for he set very high standards, he didn't suffer fools gladly and, while I adored him, I almost always felt inept in his company. Even so, it was to him that we children invariably turned when we needed *obut* [healing ointment] for small ailments, or even words of encouragement when we were down; and he could be great fun. There were the times when he would wrestle and have water fights with us on the lawn, taking on the whole bunch of us. My friends thought he was marvellous and wonderfully dashing. I remember that he teased me a lot and this was something that for the most part, I enjoyed, but not always. He was never a demonstrative man and looking back on it, I guess that the teasing was the only way he was able to make contact with me – a sort of towel-flicking, 'hands-off' love.

In her absence her parents' second family had become a warm unit:

> The 'second family' – still not much more than toddlers – romped with him, pummelled him and metaphorically tweaked his beard. How I envied them. So at the age of about fifteen, I started dutifully kissing Dad goodnight. Wasn't this normal behaviour for fathers and daughters? I wasn't sure. Every evening, before going up to bed, I steeled myself, approached his chair where he sat reading and kissed his cheek. Was he mystified, did this embarrass him, or did he even notice? He always looked up and said pleasantly 'Goodnight my child.' I wonder whether he ever realized how difficult this self-imposed ritual was for me?

In December 1956 Thyra and the two younger children returned to Britain. John and Jen followed in January 1957, arriving in the cold and making their way to their new home in Bedford. 'I hated this place,' she recalled. 'Low light, black dripping trees and the pervasive smell of wet wool.' For a while she went back to a school in Bedford where she sat exams to get more O levels and then went to college where she qualified as a secretary. In 1959 she met Mike Howe, an Irish electronics engineer who was ten years her senior. They married and moved into a house not far from her parents. Jen had two children in quick succession, a daughter, Bridget, in 1961 and a son, Ben, in 1962.

England did not suit either Mike or Jen so they emigrated to Canada in 1963 and thereafter saw her parents only intermittently, when they travelled over every three years or so. Jen visited her parents a few times in Britain but the distance meant that the trips 'home' were also infrequent. John Godber died in 1990 at the age of eighty. He was diagnosed with lung cancer and refused chemotherapy, saying that there was no point at his age.

'He died as he lived, with great bravery,' she said. 'Kissing him goodbye for the last time in the early morning darkness, before I left to catch the plane back to Canada, I tried to tell him for the first time ever, that I loved him. Sadly, without a hearing aid, he couldn't hear me. Four weeks later, he was dead.' It was only after her father's death that she began to think more about her childhood and try to understand better what had informed her whole life: 'There must have been a degree of post-traumatic stress but it was only years later, long after the event, that I could understand this.'

It took years for Jen to get to know her younger siblings and it was only after her sister Pen became a mother and, eventually, a grandmother that the two of them began to have a better understanding of one another. For these two women the war divided their family and shaped their futures in a way that her parents perhaps never completely understood.

Adaptability was the key to post-war reconciliation and when it worked well it made for a very happy homecoming. Marion Platt's parents were flexible and her mother Nora's strong character and determination to keep her home together even when her husband was abroad made Marion and her sister Betty's life easy. Marion's father, Bill Hillman, served as a bombardier in the Royal Artillery from September 1939 until February 1946 during which time he came home very infrequently and not at all after 1941. Bill had married his sweetheart Nora in 1937 and had two little girls, Betty born in 1938 and Marion in 1940. For a long time Nora was the only wife in her circle of friends who had a husband in the forces. She lived in Headington, Oxford, in the small house which they had moved into soon after they were married. For the first few years of the war little changed in the Hillman household except that Bill was away. Nora worked at the Wingfield Hospital as well as looking after her two daughters.

Although they had a Morrison shelter in the house they hoped and believed that Oxford would not be bombed and in that they were lucky.

Nora's brother-in-law was an air-raid warden in Coventry and saw the dreadful destruction wrought by the German bombing of that city in November 1940. His wife, Nora's sister Gladys, was an invalid, having suffered from rheumatoid arthritis since the birth of her second daughter, and he asked Nora to take her and the girls to their home in Oxford so that she would be safe from the bombing. This was a very happy time for Betty and Marion who loved Aunt Glad and got on very well with their two girl cousins, who were almost exactly the same age. 'We seemed to be constantly happy and giggling,' Marion explained. 'I loved Aunt Glad because she used to brush my hair and put ribbons into it. She couldn't help Mum much around the house because of her arthritis but they were very close and enjoyed each other's company so much. In a way it was like having two mothers. It was a very happy childhood.' The house was small with just two bedrooms but it was warm and welcoming and full of laughter. The women had to share bedrooms with their daughters, sleeping head to toe, and Marion remembers her aunt recalling that Nora would often get up in the night and go downstairs to the front room to write long letters to Bill, who was in Italy. Some nights Gladys had to sleep downstairs in the sitting room if she was in too much pain to get upstairs to bed but other than that Marion has no recollection of her aunt's disability affecting their way of life. Nora did all the heavy work, including digging the garden to plant potatoes and other vegetables.

Marion's overriding memory of the war was of her mother coping magnificently with a small home crowded with females. 'My mother was a great organizer. She was a good cook and was expert at keeping everything hot before it got on to the table.

During the war she grew vegetables in the front garden. I remember she planted them in squiggly lines.'

The one thing that bothered her in the garden, however, was that the metal garden gate was requisitioned for the war effort and she had, for a long time, no way of keeping the children in the garden. It is the kind of job that Bill would have seen to had he been there but eventually Uncle Jack, who was married to Nora's younger sister and who worked in Oxford throughout the war, made her a new gate. Her neighbour, Mr Taylor, was also very kind to the family and as he worked for the local hospital as a gardener, was able on the odd occasion to bring them vegetables from one of the gardens he tended. 'Financially and food-wise it was tight during the war,' Marion recalled, 'but it was the same for everyone else too. There was never a spare biscuit in the cupboard, for example, and we were often hungry but not starving. I remember my mother bringing back some crab apples from the garden of a pair of spinsters she worked for as a cook. She put them in the bath and hid them with a piece of material but we knew they were there and pinched them because we were hungry.' She remembers well how careful the children were with their clothes. Everything that was torn had to be mended and she had a vivid image of Aunt Glad, with her badly crippled hands, unpicking woollen garments and knitting them into socks or jumpers. 'Despite her arthritis she was a beautiful knitter.'

Marion recalls: 'I remember my father sending us ribbons for our hair from Italy and he wrote to my mum regularly, telling her about the flowers coming out in the spring and everyday things like that.' In return Nora wrote letters telling Bill about the girls' goings-on, how they were growing and thriving, how she had to push one pushchair and pull the other up the hill to their Manor Road nursery every morning. She never complained about anything she had to do to keep the family going but she told him the bad as well as the good things. On one occasion Marion was due to have her tonsils out but the operation had to be postponed as a batch of wounded soldiers had been admitted to the hospital. Bill wrote back: 'Sorry that Marion could not have her tonsils removed. Then it would have been over and done with while she is young. But Battle Casualties come first.' Marion's tonsils were removed in due course and this was reported back to Bill in a subsequent letter. 'Yesterday I received an air-letter from you. The first for 10 days. I was very glad to receive it. Glad to hear that Marion's operation went off well. What a brave little soul she was. A proper little soldier. Tell her Daddy is very proud of her.'

Both Betty and Marion are convinced that the very full and affectionate correspondence between their parents made Bill's homecoming much easier than if there had been no communication. He was nevertheless anxious about how he would adjust to life back home and wrote about this to Nora in a letter dated 3 May 1945:

> I wonder how many more of these letters I shall write? It can't be long now before it is over. It's finished here in Italy but you would not think so. Not a sign of celebration as yet. It makes me think, six years as a soldier. I am going to feel all out of place for a while. My life is going to take some readjusting. Just to think, no parades, no discipline, free to lead my own life. To sit with you by our own fireside and the kiddies. What fun we will have. To have their Dad back again. To be able to see other kids and say 'This is my Daddy.' Bless their hearts.

Just before the war in Europe ended Gladys and her two daughters went back to Coventry. For Betty and Marion this was very sad. They had grown up together over five years and for

Marion it was all she had ever known. Nora took them to visit their cousins in Coventry after VE Day and Marion recalls her shock at the devastation she saw as the result of the bombing. She clearly remembers walking round the ruined cathedral and seeing a number of children who she was told were refugees. One little girl, about three years older than Marion, was sitting on a broken bit of wall with her arm around the shoulder of a grubby little boy: "'E and I are Dutch,' the little girl said, by way of explanation. It made a deep impression on five-year-old Marion and seven-year-old Betty.

At the end of the war Bill Hillman stayed out in Italy to help resettle villagers in the remote country region where he had previously been fighting. Marion believed, on reflection, that this was one of the happiest periods of his life. He loved Italy and he felt close to the Italian people. He learned their language and all his life used expressions such as 'Mamma mia' and 'Salute' when proposing a toast. He continued to write to Nora and tell her of his work with the resettlement programme. In May he was moved to the Adriatic coast: 'worse luck, I hate that side of Italy,' he wrote. Eventually his work was complete and he was due to come home and be demobbed. 'I wonder what my reactions will be when they do eventually say: "Bombardier Hillman you are going home" – 2 words that mean so much to all of us . . . I saw my conduct sheet today, the first time since I joined the army. Not a blemish on it. How's that for being a good boy?'

Betty and Marion were playing out on the road when Bill finally returned in late 1945. They saw him walking down the road carrying his bags, his guitar slung over his shoulder, and smiling. They didn't recognize him immediately as their father but then someone pointed out who it was and Marion ran along behind him shouting: 'Daddy, Daddy, Daddy!' He did not recognize the little girl with flyaway hair that was calling to him but he saw Betty and scooped her up in his arms. Nora was delighted to have him home and proudly took him to the shops shortly after his return where he was regarded with suspicion owing to his dark tan that made him, Marion said, look very foreign. Their long years of separation had been bridged by a continual exchange of letters so that he knew all about how the girls had grown up, what they had been doing and even what their favourite things were.

'We never felt Dad was a stranger in the house,' Marion said. 'He was a well balanced man and never bore a grudge against anyone. He had a very good relationship with my mother who understood him and let him do the things he wanted to do.'

Bill loved his home and was pleased to be back in the house that he had left nearly six years earlier. They quickly slipped into family life once again and began to get used to the things that had changed in him, revelling in the stories that he told them about Italy. When he had arrived in Sicily he had bought himself a guitar which he carried with him on his back throughout the rest of the war. He carefully engraved every place he had been to in Italy on the guitar and it reads like a travel diary with such romantic names as Salerno and Amalfi, places that the girls had only heard about through his letters and seen drawings of that he had sent home to Nora. He had taught himself to play the guitar and the mouth organ in Italy, learning music by ear. He could also play the piano and accordion and was given to impromptu recitals, which Marion sometimes found embarrassing but secretly she adored her outgoing, gregarious father.

The great thing about my parents' relationship was my mother's ability to adapt to him. She was naturally quite shy, he more out-going. He got involved in all sorts of activities such as the boys' club, the local social club, in bingo and dance events and his archery, which he really enjoyed. My mother let him do all these things and never complained about his busy life. The only thing they ever argued about was decorating the house. Then there would be rows, if he hung the wallpaper upside down, for example. But these did not spoil the atmosphere at home at all.

At first, Bill, like many others, had difficulty in finding work. For a while he worked for the GPO fixing telephone lines and then went to work in the Cowley motor works. Marion distinctly remembered him shinning up telegraph poles in the winter of 1947 and taking her and Betty for long walks up to Shotover Hill to give Nora time to be with their new baby, a little boy, Billy, born that year. 'I can recall so clearly the feeling of snow going down my boots, that squeaky cold of the powdery snow getting into my boots and socks.'

Shortly after his return Bill decided he needed a shed in the garden, a space he could call his own where he could make things, mend things and be out of the house. In common with many men who came back from the war the shed in the garden was a solace and a comfort as well as a useful place to store tools. The shed was a gift from Uncle Jack, her mother's brother-in-law in Risinghurst. The shed was Bill's domain and he was able to make things for the girls such as a high jump for Marion, which they mounted on a piece of land opposite the house and which was enjoyed by lots of the local children. He worked on all sorts of things for the house and the garden and Marion believed that this shed provided him with privacy when he occasionally needed to be alone.

'My mother was the rock of the family,' Marion concluded, 'she allowed Bill to be himself and that was a great thing because he never had to struggle to settle down. He had all the freedom he ever needed.'

Other women, even those who had been married for a long time before the outbreak of war, found the readjustment less easy. Often these women had not had close family round them but had had to make do on their own. Independence, thrust upon women who had been used to being dependent on their husbands for everything, including all decision-making, was sometimes hard to relinquish after the war. Veronica Kerr, known to everyone as Toby, was one mother who found that her husband's return home interrupted family life in a way she had not foreseen and changed everything that had become stable during the six years of her husband's absence. Her daughter, Lindsay Munro, felt the effect of this and it impacted on her whole life. Lindsay and her twin sister, Margaret, were born in Australia in 1941. They were conceived before their father, Don Kerr, left to fight in the war in the Pacific and they first met him, and he them, in January 1946 when they were five and a half years old.

Don and Toby had married in 1936 and had had a first child in 1939 who died. After Don went off to fight, the twins were brought up by their mother in Brisbane, where the struggle to make ends meet was a constant one despite help from local support groups. As a child Lindsay was only dimly aware of the difficulties posed by her mother's situation and she remembered the early years of her childhood as happy. 'My mother was a very capable person,' she said. 'It must have been difficult for her but she looked after the house and we little girls really well and did everything for us. She made all our clothes and I remember that she deliberately made them too large for us so that one year we were walking around in baggy clothes, the next year they fitted quite comfortably but by the third year they were too small. I wore handmade clothes until I was an adult.' Eventually the family moved into a house of their own but not before Toby had received a telegram from the War Office telling her that Don Kerr was missing. For eighteen months she believed she was a war widow, although she never gave up hope that there had been a mistake and that her husband was alive.

As luck would have it Toby was right to be optimistic and a year and a half after the initial telegram a notice arrived from the Red Cross to say that Major Don Kerr had been identified as a prisoner of war of the Japanese and was believed to be in Thailand. Don, who had worked in a bank in civilian life, had enlisted in July 1940, at the age of thirty, and fought with the 2/10 Field Regiment A.I.F. in Malaya. He was taken prisoner on 15 February 1942 on Singapore. Three months later he left Singapore with A Force for Burma. He was a meticulous note-keeper and during the entire period of his captivity he kept a list of how and where people had died, stowing the papers in the heel of his boot. For three and a half years he was a prisoner of war and for nearly half that period nobody at home had any idea whether or not he was still alive.

When the Pacific war came to its end in August 1945 Don was kept back by the Allies to gather and produce evidence against the Japanese and Korean guards for the war crimes trials that were held in Singapore in 1946. As a result he was one of the last Australians to return home. His return should have been a joyous one. He had distinguished himself in the prisoner-of-war camps and returned with an outstanding record; his old bank had kept his job open for him; his wife and two little girls were housed comfortably in a working-class area of Brisbane and the time spent in hospital on his return had helped him to regain some of his strength and pre-war weight. The reality, however, was very different.

Lindsay's strongest memory of her father's return was his hatred of noise. He could not cope with the twins' chatter. Toby therefore fed and bathed Lindsay and Margaret, now five years old, and put them to bed before her husband came back from work at the bank. Having been so close to their mother for the first few years of their lives, they hated this new regime. Toby, who had been their mainstay, was now occupied with trying to make Don's life comfortable and adjust to a new life with a stranger who had come into their lives. They were no longer able to claim her undivided attention and their father was an unknown quantity: 'We couldn't bond with him,' Lindsay explained, 'because we were always separated from him as he couldn't bear any noise. We hardly had a chance to get to know him when he first came home. And he just didn't know how to handle two little five-year-old girls.' The twins, who were identical, were thrown together in their own company and because of that they made no effort to make friends at school. 'Had I had twins, I should have sent them to separate schools,' Lindsay commented with feeling years later.

There was another problem too. When Don came back, Toby was deposed and she was never given the credit that Lindsay felt she deserved for having kept everything going during the difficult war years. She had been a tower of strength and had shown such resilience when she was on her own looking after the twins and planning for the family's future. Now not only did she have to cope with having all her responsibilities abruptly taken away but her husband was suffering from nightmares, which disturbed the whole house. He had pins and needles for the rest of his life as a result of having had beriberi, the vitamin deficiency disease. And life at the bank was not easy. Men who had been junior to him before the war had been promoted above him and he never recovered from the fact that the six years he had lost in terms of his career were never made up. These younger men enjoyed better health than he did and thus more opportunity for promotion. It did not make for a comfortable home life.

In 1948 Toby had another baby. Donald Junior came into Lindsay's life when she was seven and she and Margaret were jealous of him from the word go. 'Donald was the baby my father had never had. We were five and a half when he first met us and he never formed a close relationship with us. Donald was the apple of my father's eye. He could do no wrong.'

Don did not ignore the twins, but he had no sense of who they were and how they fitted in to his life. Whereas Donald had come as a baby and his father could watch every development from his early smiles and giggles to him becoming his own person. He had missed all those precious stages with the girls and it seemed to leave an unbridgeable gap between them. Don was nevertheless ambitious for his daughters and encouraged them to do well at school. 'Dad insisted that we go on to a tertiary education so that we could support a family if the need arose in the future. He spoke endlessly of war widows who were struggling to support a family because they did not have an education. But it was a dispassionate involvement, merely the conviction that this is what would serve us best in the future.' And he was very definite about what they should not do: there was no way he would accept them becoming a teacher or a nurse, for example, although he never really spelled out the reasons for dismissing those two professions. Lindsay was determined to succeed at school and worked hard for her exams. In the event she was awarded a Commonwealth Scholarship that allowed her to study at university. She chose physiotherapy and was the top student in her year. She wanted above all to impress her father.

Lindsay felt that Don's post-war obsession with the army and with former prisoners of war took him away from them even more than his work in the bank. 'He never came to watch us playing sport although when Donald began to play sport, which he was brilliant at, Dad was always on the touchline cheering for him. We felt, rightly or wrongly, hard done by. Donald scraped into university to study veterinary science and my father paid for his studies.'

Toby never complained about her husband but Lindsay knew that their relationship had been scarred by Don's war experience. 'They lived parallel lives in the end. I know they slept in separate bedrooms after the war because my father used to be disturbed at night, he snored badly and was restless. He never slept well. He had frequent nightmares and would get up at four o'clock in the morning. They cared for each other but somewhere along the way there had been a fracture. It would not have occurred to them to split up, one didn't in those days, but their relationship was difficult.' Fortunately, Toby Kerr found companionship among the army wives with whom she had much in common, although Lindsay suspects that familial difficulties were never discussed. She enjoyed a lifetime of good friendships, many of which lasted until she died in 2004. Don Kerr was actively involved in the army for years after the war, receiving a CBE (Military) in 1963 in the Post-war Honours List and rising to the rank of Major General in the CMF, the Australian army reserve. Lindsay said:

Army slogans dominated our lives; it was something he was passionate about and he always enjoyed all things military. Dad was also fixated on my sister and me eating everything on our plate regardless of whether we liked it or not. We would then hear how Dad had had to eat leaves and pumpkin skin etc to get sufficient vitamins and we did not know how lucky we were to have such good food. We sometimes had a vile fish soup which I absolutely hated but had to eat. The day I was married, I vowed I would never again eat fish soup.

Don Kerr died of leukaemia in 1984, just two weeks after he was diagnosed with the disease. After Don died Toby initially found life difficult. Suddenly she had to cope again, to learn how to manage her money and restart her life as a widow forty years after she had had her independence taken away. It was a struggle and she relied on the family for support. Six years later a further sadness struck when Donald died very suddenly at the age of forty-three. Toby wept every day for her beloved son. For Lindsay this was a difficult time. Toby did, however, receive support from the POW community and for that reason she chose to stay in the house that she and Don had bought in 1963 rather than moving to live closer to her daughters. Her mother, Lindsay explained, was a formidable old lady. She had a great fighting spirit but something of the wartime attitude, a certain hardness born almost certainly out of her determination to cope, made her difficult to help.

Jean Hammond was an only child and for her the war years were relatively easy. She lived with her mother and grandmother in the country and was only dimly aware of her father's absence until his return home in April 1945. Graham Hose Brooker had spent five years in prisoner-of-war camps in Poland and Germany so she hardly knew him when he came back. Her memory of him was fleshed out by his photograph in uniform and the stories that her mother, Charlotte, and her grandmother had told her about him while he was away. He was a tall man, nearly six feet in height, but on his release from BAB (Bau- und Arbeitsbattalion) 20, a forced labour camp in Germany, he weighed just seven stone. He did not look much like the photograph in the frame.

Jean's mother, Charlotte, as mentioned earlier, fell down the stairs in surprise when she saw him walking up the garden path towards the house they were sharing. When Jean met him for the first time she did not know what to make of the stranger staring down at her, the man who would now be sleeping in her mother's bedroom while she was demoted to another room in the house. Of course, she knew that she had a father because she used to kiss his photograph every night before she went to bed. However, she was only two when her father left home so her memories of him were vague. For his part, Graham Hose Brooker did not recognize the eight-year-old who was busying herself around the house, unsure of how to approach him. 'It seemed to me that he had difficulty cottoning on to the fact that this slightly stroppy eight-year-old was the cuddly little toddler he had left behind all that time ago.'

Charlotte and Graham Hose Brooker had met over the phone in the mid-1930s. She was working in the telephone exchange of a company in the City of London, having grown up in the Camden Town area of North London.

Graham was working as a trainee surveyor when he chatted up Charlotte at the telephone exchange. He would have gone on to qualify as an architect had not the war intervened. Graham's own background was somewhat confusing to the family and it was an affectionate joke of Jean's that she later referred to him as 'the old bastard'. Graham's mother, a Scot, had worked as a nurse in the First World War and was not universally loved. She was tough but Jean always felt that anyone who had been a nurse in those circumstances would have seen things that would have made her strong. The man she lived with, who turned out not to be married to her, although this was only discovered after he died and she was anxious about qualifying for a pension, was not Graham's father. No one was sure who his father was but the fact that Graham had a double-barrelled name made Jean think that in all probability he took one name from his birth father and the other from his mother's subsequent partner. His Christian names also puzzled her: his full name was Earwacker Graham Wemys Hose

Brooker, which she presumed came from her Scottish grand-mother. At any rate, the fact that Graham's early childhood had been disrupted as he had been sent to foster parents as a young child and then to boarding school when he was seven, had left him with a chip on his shoulder which he never quite got over. All Jean knew about her father's family was that she was actively discouraged from getting close to them and she saw her grand-mother Brooker less than ten times in her whole life.

When Graham and Charlotte first married they lived in London in a flat with Charlotte's mother, Grace Tombling. Her mother, Grace Tombling, loved London and hated the country-side. 'Not for her trees and fields,' Jean remembered, 'she liked a tall front door leading down steep steps on to a street. She was a city woman through and through.' Life seemed to run smoothly and in 1937 Jean was born. Two years later the family was visiting friends in Peppard Common near Henley-on-Thames in Oxfordshire when they heard that war had been declared. Graham at once announced that on no account should Charlotte and Jean go back to London. He had joined the Terri-torial Army and was immediately called up to go to France with the British Expeditionary Force in September 1939. Char-lotte found herself rooms in a house owned by a woman who worked at a local sanatorium and there she, Jean and Grace, who left London under protest, spent the first few months of the war, moving later to another house in the area and finally ending up sharing a large house with a big garden, the Rosary, in Baskerville Road, Sonning Common, with a spinster called Miss Ham.

Graham spent the months of the Phoney War in France and in May and June 1940 fought with the French 10th Army against the Germans to defend the Maginot Line. By the second week of June they were trapped at the seaside town of Saint-Valery-en-Caux, 30 kilometres west of Dieppe. Graham was later quite cynical about this 'brave' battle, telling his daughter: 'We were running like hell to get away.' Unfortunately they ran out of land and eventually the 51 (Highland) Division surrendered to Erwin Rommel on 12 June 1940. Charlotte knew nothing of Graham's fate for six weeks after he was captured. All she knew was that he had not returned with the men who had been evacuated from Dunkirk and had been declared 'Missing'.

Finally in August 1940 she learned that he had been taken prisoner and was housed in Stalag XXA1 in Germany. She then began a correspondence with the War Office to establish how to get in contact with him. Many years later, when Jean was looking through her parents' effects in the attic, she found a scrap of paper headed simply 'Lille' on which was written in hand: 'Mrs or Mr, I inform you whom your son or your husband is prisoner, but ever in good moral. Also keep your courage and trust. Lots of luck to you xxx.' She has no idea where this mysterious message came from or when it arrived but it was clearly of significance to Charlotte who kept it among her precious memorabilia.

Although Graham was tall he was not physically as strong and fit as some other young men in the army and he suffered from the poor diet and hard work in the POW camps. He told Jean that the men were so desperate for their once-a-day cigarette that they would sometimes have to resort to smoking grass or hay if no tobacco was available. He also told her that there were escape parties in his camps but that he knew he would never be able to go through with an escape as his health would not permit him to run once outside the wire. However, he did help with escape planning, drawing maps and forging documents for the escapees. 'My father had very small, neat handwriting. It was so small, in fact, that he once wrote the Lord's Prayer out in full on the back of a postage stamp and you can read it clearly with a magnifying glass. Because of his training he knew all about maps and drawing, so that was the role he could fulfil for his fellow prisoners.'

Meanwhile, Jean continued to live in the country with her mother and grandmother. Charlotte was a capable woman and active in the village where they lived. Although she did not work for pay during the war she ran the house and cared for her lively little daughter and her mother who hated the countryside and longed to be living in London. Jean's memory of the wartime period is not an unhappy one. She cannot remember being particularly cold or hungry and although she was aware that her mother was not well off, she always had clothes and shoes for school and there was sufficient food on the table, although the lack of chocolate and sweets stuck in her mind. The houses where they lived had big gardens and she remembered having fruit and vegetables as well as food brought back from the sanatorium by their first landlady who worked in the kitchens. In their final house, the Rosary, where they lived with Miss Ham, they had plenty of space to themselves including their own kitchen: '. . . not that it had a tap, or anything. Water had to be brought in from the lean-to outside the house where there was a well and the only tap. We only had one bath a week and that was in a slipper bath brought into the kitchen. Mother did the washing on Mondays in the scullery where a great boiler to heat the water stood over a fire. It was lucky if the washing was dry by Wednesday. My husband has to this day a hatred of the smell of damp laundry that stems from the war.'

Charlotte and Graham corresponded throughout the war. Charlotte sent him photographs of Jean so that he would see her growing up and they discussed Christmas presents for her via their correspondence. 'In one letter I found out that she had asked him whether she could spend a sizeable sum on a copy of *The Wind in the Willows* for me and he had written straight back to insist that she did. Another Christmas I came downstairs and there was a lovely dolls' house waiting for me. He had told my mother to get that for me and later, after the war, he added things to it to make it even better.'

On his return his wife found him changed. One of the strangest of his foibles was his inability to eat his meals indoors. Jean remembers him taking his meals outside, eating in the porch when it was raining. At the time it did not seem odd to her, it was something she came to accept about her father, but later she wondered what had happened to him that made him feel claustrophobic at mealtimes. He also found it difficult to show affection towards anyone but Charlotte, whom he worshipped. Jean found this hard and did not understand the emotion boiling up inside her, which she realizes was probably jealousy. For six years she had been at the centre of her mother's life and suddenly, with the return of her father, there were other calls on her attention. Graham was very ill after the war and needed to spend time in the Battle Hospital at Reading. He never fully regained his strength but he did not complain about it as far as Jean could recall. 'I do remember, however, that we used to get tins of bully beef and fruit from the local US Army barracks after the war. I suppose my father must have made contact with them as he was picked up by the Americans in Germany once the prison camp he was in had been released. Certainly the food was welcome and I expect it helped him to get back to his normal weight.'

After the war Graham joined Berkshire County Council and eventually became assistant county planning officer, retiring with emphysema at the age of sixty in 1965.

My father never grumbled or moaned about the war, in fact he barely ever mentioned it. I think he had contact with a few fellow POWs after the war but not for long. It was not something he liked to dwell on. His attitude was that this had happened to him and now he had to get on and make the most of his life. My mother always gave the impression of being contented with her lot but I sense now that she had a lot to put up with. I remember on one occasion my father told her to 'take that muck off your face' when she had put on make-up and lipstick. Mother retorted that she had coped with bringing up a little girl for six years and living through the difficult years of the war so she would not take any criticism from him. He could shut up. To a certain extent she had the upper hand after the war and my father seemed to accept it. My mother was very sociable and liked company but my father did not and that could sometimes be difficult. But other than that I remember no real problems.

Jean never established a close relationship with her father. She recalled quite serious rows when she was a teenager. He would not let her wear nail varnish and she remembered walking into the house with her hands deep in her pockets to hide her painted nails. Charlotte hated it when the two of them argued but as far as Jean was concerned it was teenage tantrums on her part and lack of understanding of teenagers on his. She also remembered thinking that whenever he talked about the past he was not speaking of anything that was relevant to her. 'Now I kick myself that I didn't listen to what he wanted to tell me and I wish I had asked him more questions so that I might better have understood his situation. I know almost nothing about his family background and even less about his war.'

In 1961 Charlotte became ill. She had been treated by the family doctor for an undiagnosed stomach complaint that was exacerbated as she went through the menopause. When the old doctor retired and a new one saw her for the first time he diagnosed ulcerated colitis and Charlotte was rushed into hospital to have a colostomy. 'I remember seeing her just after the operation and thinking, oh goodness, she'll never get out of here alive, but a week later there she was, walking down the hospital steps. How she coped with that I will never know but I remember that she even managed to carry on with the old-time dancing that she and my father so enjoyed. She would wear pretty dresses to hide her bag and off she would go to the dances. She was quite an impressive woman.'

Graham Hose Brooker died in 1985 at the age of eighty and Charlotte four years later at the age of eighty-nine. Jean said:

I think my parents had a perfectly amicable marriage. My father worshipped my mother. He absolutely adored her and I think part of this had to do with his disrupted childhood but much of it had to do with the fact that she was a constant in his life. She had loved him, waited for him for five long years when other POWs had received 'Dear John' letters, and welcomed him home after the war. Towards the end of his life he became more possessive of her and he was actually a little jealous of his first grandson, Rex, because my mother adored him. Later, when our second son, Scott, was born my father was happier and got on well with him because they were quite like one another. My mother, for her part, was, now I reflect upon it, a very capable woman. She was a loving mother, a caring wife, a kind daughter, an adequate housewife (she preferred to go out to doing the housework) but she was amazing really and the way she coped during the war now strikes me as admirable.

According to Jean: 'My mother hated the Germans right up to the end of her life. It was the only legacy of the war that I can remember. It must have had a tremendous effect on my parents but they never discussed it and never complained about what might have been had they stayed in London and Dad trained as an architect. When my own son went into the RAF and found himself stationed in Germany I remember thinking that my mother would not have liked that at all.'

CHILDREN OF BAMBOO: THE FEPOW CHILDREN'S TALE

Sometimes the men got through their POW experience sort of intact or at least able to manage themselves, only to find that their wives took a nosedive when they came home and never really recovered enough to rebuild the relationship. Even as I'm writing this, my heart breaks for all the fine men and women whose lives were essentially destroyed by the unrelenting trauma of those years during and after the war. And nothing much was ever done, nothing much was ever published except about the physical damage sustained by malnutrition, disease and neglect.

Dr Patricia Mark, 2007

With a few exceptions, the young men who were captured in the Far East had more trouble readjusting to civilian life than any others. There were several reasons for this. First, they felt humiliated by their defeat at the hands of the Japanese and many felt bitter about being, as they saw it, thrown into a hopeless military situation. Secondly, by and large, they felt completely cut off from what was happening in the rest of the war and with communication haphazard at best, they were unable to have meaningful contact with their families. Thirdly, and perhaps most importantly, they were subjected to desperate conditions in which nearly one third of the men died and many who returned suffered from survivor's guilt in addition to chronic medical conditions and often mental health problems that lasted for years. For their families the return home was often painful. Inexplicable character changes and frequent bouts of depression made the task of welcoming these men particularly difficult.

The men who seemed to do best were those who had something to come back to, a wife or a family. This had given them something to cling on to during their captivity and a perspective on the ordeal they had to undergo. It was said that on the whole the men who survived their captivity best were those aged between twenty-five and thirty-five. They were considered to be at the peak of their physical strength and had some experience of life. For men who had left home as boys captivity sometimes brutalized them and affected many of them for the rest of their adult lives. They found it difficult to settle down, to live with the recurrent nightmares and chronic ill health. There was a higher rate of suicide in the first fifteen years after the Second World War amongst the Far Eastern prisoners of war than any other group of returning men. The psychological effects of their captivity were so little understood that it often took decades for them to come to terms with it. This naturally had an impact on those close to them and the children of these men frequently had traumatic childhoods. In researching this book the response from the families of the FEPOWs has been enormous. For every four letters I received or contacts I made, three were from families of former FEPOWs. For this reason this chapter is devoted solely to their experiences. I should add that some people who have contributed have never spoken before about the impact their fathers' experiences had on their lives and it has been a slow and painful process for them to allow their stories to take shape.

Jean Roberts's father, John, was a regular soldier with the 3rd Heavy Anti-Aircraft Division, based in Woolwich. Born in 1917, he had been brought up in Glasgow by a tough father who was 'handy with his fists'. John joined the army under age, giving a false date of birth, to escape the poverty of the 1930s. He met Jean's mother, Mary, in 1937, a day, she recorded in her diary, as being 'the day my life began'. He asked her to marry him but she refused, saying she would wait until he returned from what they feared was going to be a long war.

John's family name was Cameron. This was the name he used when he joined his first regiment, the Argyll and Sutherland Highlanders. He changed his name when he transferred regiments: 'All I know is that he transferred regiments by himself without informing the proper authorities, i.e. left one and joined up again using the changed name,' Jean said. 'The family story was that he deserted the Argylls and joined the Royal Artillery because he wanted to work with horses, however I don't believe that was the case.' When he joined the Royal Artillery he served using his middle name, Walker. In a letter written before the fall of Singapore he explained that he had had a bit of a scare when his old unit turned up in Singapore and he was worried that he would be recognized. Fortunately he was not. In April 1942 a telegram arrived for Mary, living in Dagenham, from her future father-in-law in Glasgow: 'Just received word John missing.' It was a bald statement of fact. Thousands of families received similar telegrams throughout the war but Mary was convinced John was still alive and began to write to the authorities for news of his whereabouts. It was eight months before she learned from the Red Cross that he was a POW.

> During the war my mother worked in the munitions factory in Dagenham making Bren gun carriers. She lived at home with her parents and, even though she wasn't hearing from John, she refused to give up on him and wrote him almost daily letters. They were newsy, chatty, happy letters about the family, films that she had seen (she was a keen cinema goer) and trips she had been on. There was always caring concern about his health, was he eating well etc. She also wrote letters to the Red Cross badgering them for news on his whereabouts.

Meanwhile John was sent from Singapore by the Japanese to work in various labour camps. First he was sent to Saigon. Then in 1943 he went to Thailand where he worked on the Thailand–Burma Railway, going as far up as Kinsaiyok and Nike, some of the most isolated camps towards the Burma border, hundreds of miles from the base camps at Kanchanaburi and where the food supplies were intermittent at best and disease was rife. Jean said:

> While in Saigon my father was tortured, beaten, and sentenced to death for stealing biscuits. On starvation rations he and another prisoner had taken the opportunity to steal some Japanese ration biscuits (like the iced gems that we can buy here). They were caught at the docks, badly beaten and brought back to camp tied up, where they were again beaten severely. The beating included the stubbing out of cigarettes on their naked skin. When the death sentence was given the British colonel, an enormously brave man called Francis Hugonin, intervened on their behalf. The death was to be a particularly painful and drawn out process as they were to

be tied to the camp wire with the biscuits festooned around their necks, until they died of starvation. After they had been standing outside the guard room for four days and nights Colonel Hugonin managed to get the death sentence commuted to 7 days without food whilst still tied standing outside the guard room and then they would be released. There is no way that anyone who has been through an experience like that can come out of it unscathed.

In his early letters to Mary immediately after liberation in August 1945 John begged her urgently to book the church so that they could be married as soon as he returned. He warned her not to cook rice and he apologized for his appalling handwriting, explaining that he had not had pen and paper in his hands for three and a half years 'thanks to our Jap friends'. Of the experiences of the last three and a half years he wrote nothing. There would be no dwelling on the past. His focus was on the future. He returned to Britain in November 1945 and, after a short visit to Mary in Dagenham, went straight up to Glasgow to see his parents, taking her with him. On his first visit home there was an argument about some family photographs and John's father beat him up. It was not an auspicious homecoming. Five weeks after arriving back in England John and Mary were married in the Methodist Church in Dagenham and settled down to married life in Romford in Essex. 'John seemed happy, if not determined, to settle into obscurity after the war,' Jean said. 'First he became a bus conductor and then he went to work at Fords. Although he cleared his army record and the confusion over use of two names was resolved after the war, he was always known as John Cameron-Walker.'

Jean was born in 1946, thirteen months after John and Mary were married. Two boys followed nearly ten years later in 1955 and in 1957 so that to all intents and purposes Jean's childhood was that of an only child and it was not easy. Jean was told by her mother that 'she shouldn't be here' and she grew up believing she was not wanted. 'My parents adored each other to the exclusion of us children,' she admitted.

Dad was kind and gentle but then he would turn in a flash and use his hands, his belt, sometimes using the buckle end, and he would be in such a rage that he wouldn't stop until he had burnt himself out, then a second later it was, for him, almost like it hadn't happened. My mother used to say it was not my father who was beating me, but the Japanese. Many times I went to school with belt marks. As a child I was frightened that I would not be believed about where the marks came from and I didn't like to undress at school. I suppose I got into the 'cycle of fear' that exists, and I was also ashamed.

The sad thing was that for years Jean believed her situation to be unique and convinced herself, as did other children of FEPOWs, that her family was not like those of her friends. There was a veil of secrecy drawn over the violence. It could never be mentioned yet she somehow understood that other people close to her parents were aware of what was going on. 'People did know about it,' she said, 'my uncle and aunt took me out to protect me. I understood this later on, when I was much older. But it was never discussed in front of me. On one occasion when I was about five my father was beating me with a bicycle pump and mother tried to stop him. She was hit and broke her finger, after which she swore she would never get involved again. I don't want to give the impression my father was a monster,' Jean said, 'it was just a part of my childhood. He was my family. He was sometimes kind, always generous, and a very gentle man, enormously compassionate. However that could all change in an instant.

I can recall many happy times with him but I was always on edge in case I did something to upset him.'

John loved babies and he was very proud of his boys. He used to give them little bits of his food to share from his plate, an almost unimaginable act of generosity for a man who had nearly starved to death during the war. 'This, however, was a mark of how much his sons meant to him, but it was also something that he would do for others. He could not bear to see anyone going without. He had issues with food in that he needed very little but he wanted his children to have plenty.' Jean, it seemed to her in retrospect, was born too early in the marriage and it affected not only her childhood but also her subsequent relationships with men. 'If you are not brought up with love and cuddles it is so difficult to learn it later. What you learn as a child you believe to be normal,' she explained. 'I grew up in awe of men and almost expected to get hurt. My first marriage did not work out. I let the enemy get too close to me.' Jean insists that her husband was a good man but she married for the wrong reason, as it was the only respectable way to leave home.

John Cameron-Walker died in 1992 at the age of seventy-five when Jean was in her mid-forties. For a few years she had been talking to her father a little about his experiences in the Far East during the war. After his retirement he mellowed and seemed marginally more comfortable discussing the past and answering questions that Jean had hardly dared to think of asking earlier. 'As a child I had known one or two little details, little snippets about his life as a prisoner. It usually had to do with food. My mother knew as much as I knew as a child about my father's past. No more. I knew not to ask questions and if I ever did ask I was told not to.'

Five years before he died Jean persuaded John to contact the National Federation of Far Eastern Prisoners of War. She discovered that he had been to reunions in the immediate post-war period, when the Federation was in its infancy under its president, General Arthur Percival. But, she explained, 'he had found it too "Jap Happy" in his words. He said that the branch he went to always started each meeting with *tenko* [parade]. He felt he had done too many *tenkos* already and wasn't prepared to do any more.' In old age he was more at ease and he seemed to enjoy the few reunions he went to. The overwhelming benefit of the Federation for John was the medical help it offered him. When he was asked to complete a questionnaire in order to get a disability pension, which was finally granted in 1987, he listed, according to Jean:

Malaria, Dysentery, Malnutrition & privation, Strongyloides, Hookworm, Depression (anxiety neurosis), Nightmares, Tinnitus (gunfire deafness), Dietary problems (sensitive stomach – he had a stomach ulcer plus a large inoperable growth in his stomach from an infestation in his stomach during captivity), Tropical ulcers, Nervous symptoms – results of beatings by the Japanese. He had a 'tic' which he said in another letter caused him embarrassment and left him open to ridicule. In addition there was an occasion in Thailand where he had his jaw broken and a spinal injury from a Jap beating him with a golf club. When you read the above you can forgive him anything. The saddest thing is that he wasn't alone. He was one of hundreds suffering exactly the same. Most of them, like him, in silence.

Through the then president of the FEPOW Federation, Harold Payne, John was introduced to the tropical diseases programme at the Queen Elizabeth Military Hospital in Woolwich where his conditions were treated. 'This all helped to bring me a little closer to my father,' Jean explained, 'but it was only after his death that I dared to go to the Far East and that was the real cathartic experience for me.'

In 2003 Jean went to Thailand to see the places where he had been held prisoner during the long years of the war. When she was there she met Rod Beattie, an Australian in charge of the Commonwealth War Graves Commission cemeteries at Chungkai and Kanchanaburi. Rod is also an expert on the history of the Thailand–Burma Railway and has made it part of his life's work to help families of men who suffered and died working on it to come to terms with their family history. He knows the exact route the railway took and has located the sites of almost every station and prison camp along its length in Thailand. He took Jean up to Nike and Kinsaiyok where her father had been imprisoned and explained to her the terrible conditions in which he had lived and worked for many months. This helped her to understand better what he had been through. She also found letters from her father telling Mary how he wanted to have a family when he got back to England and how he very much hoped to have a little girl. Piecing together her father's life after his death she began to build a picture of how events had affected him and turned him into the man he became. After her visit to Thailand Jean felt much closer to her father than she had ever done but, she admitted, 'I wouldn't have been able to go when he was alive because I'm not sure he would have handled it. I lived with a stranger for all those years but I understand him now and love him more than I ever could in his lifetime.'

In considering John again more recently she wrote:

I really want to add in a bit of balance. I feel that I have painted a picture of a monster, just telling you the negative, but I cannot stress to you enough just what a good person my dad was. He was hard working, a good provider, very much a family man and I am enormously proud of him. To me he was a hero, and I know of the courage and the fortitude that brought him through those darkest of times. I wish I had known earlier. It is inconceivable that anyone can go through what he did and remain unchanged. I would give anything to be able to talk to him again, even just once, if only to say 'Dad, I understand.'

She added: 'I have come to terms with the trauma it caused in my life. I am sure that is because I have been able to talk about it and work through it. The silence of these men meant that so many of them carried it to their graves. How we have let them down by not encouraging them to talk sooner.'

Mary Michael's family grew up not twenty miles from Jean Roberts's parents. Although they did not know each other as children, Jean later met Mary's younger brother, Kevin, and they became friends but as Mary lives in California the two women have never met, although they correspond.

Like Jean's, Mary's childhood was violent. But unlike Jean, Mary never formed an adult relationship with her father, which might have helped her come to terms with her turbulent early years. She left home at the age of seventeen and went to live with friends in London. Years and years of anxiety, tension and violence in the family home and fear of her father had driven her out. 'My dad was unaware that I had left home. I left during the day while he was at work. My mum knew but was a nervous wreck. I only took one very small suitcase with me including my school reports and certificates.' Mary married young and soon had three children. She, her husband and the children emigrated to South Africa when she was in her early twenties and after three years moved to California. 'My mother was obviously heartbroken that I left England with her three little grandchildren. We came back to see her of course and she visited us too but we were abroad and that was hard for her,' she said. Mary hardly knew her father in her adult life. She never visited him on her trips to England after she left home and she dwelt only rarely on her memories of her childhood until 2006 when she began to do research into her father's life in an attempt to understand more about what it had been about his past that had so barbarized a fundamentally good man. She began to write poetry in order to give voice to her feelings as the process of discovery developed. In her poetry Mary refers to the violence that dominated their family life and to the punishments given for no reason:

> Long lonely silences, no one must talk
> Not allowed to leave the house even to go for a walk
> Fighting and screaming could last all day
> Children not allowed to go out and play.

This poem was published on a website dedicated to the FEPOW community. It elicited a big response from grown-up children of former Far Eastern prisoners of war who could identify with the world she described. So many of them had spent their childhoods knowing their fathers were different but never daring to talk about it to anyone else. Who would understand? 'You may think this sounds quite extreme,' Mary wrote, 'but believe us it sure was no dream. It was the life lived by a few.'

Mary's father, John Forgione, was brought up in Belfast. He was born to an Italian father and an Irish mother in November 1919, the oldest son of six, three boys and three girls. His father was a second-generation Italian who set up and ran a thriving family business that made home-made ice cream for a number of parlours he owned throughout Ireland. Business was flourishing and John received a private education and enjoyed a privileged background in the 1920s and 1930s despite the general gloomy economic situation. After he left school he went to England to try to find work but before his twentieth birthday the Second World War broke out and he signed up with the Territorial Army, joining the 4th Battalion, the Royal Norfolks. His army medical record showed that he was fit, strong and had suffered from no significant illnesses. In 1941 he was sent out to the Far East and in February 1942 was captured on Singapore and imprisoned by the Japanese. John Forgione was sent up to Thailand to work on the Thailand–Burma Railway in June 1942: 'Along with everyone else he suffered all the terrible diseases caused by a lack of good diet, lack of rest and cruel treatment.'

When the war ended John was living in a godown in Bangkok awaiting transport to who knew where. By that stage he did not much care. He was in a very poor condition physically and when he was sent home he spent part of the voyage in the ship's hospital. On arrival in the UK he was given only a couple of months to live. He had been suffering from a variety of diseases including amoebic dysentery, stomach ulcers and beriberi. He had also lost hearing in his left ear resulting from the after-effects of malaria. He was twenty-six years old but his parents barely recognized the man they called their son, so badly had he suffered. He had aged physically and mentally and lost all his teeth before his thirtieth birthday. 'Before the war he enjoyed singing and playing the piano accordion but I never saw that side of him,' Mary wrote, '. . . it never returned from the jungles of Thailand. His family say he was never the same person again.' Although there was a warm welcome for him on his return he felt at odds with his surroundings. His parents had moved to London just before the war where their first home was bombed. He found he could not cope with all the changes. He found sleeping on a bed indoors uncomfortable and unfamiliar and the kindness and warmth of his family made things more difficult rather than easier for him.

After a short period at home he was transferred to the Royal Herbert Hospital in London where he spent the next two months undergoing treatment for his various diseases. It was while in hospital that John met Dorothy: 'My mother was a cute Corporal in the WAAF and was volunteering after the war in the hospital to care for the returning soldiers.' Dorothy had grown up in a wealthy family in Surrey, one of seven children. Her father was in the Admiralty and she had a strong sense of duty. Born in 1924, she joined the WAAF during the war and drove and repaired military vehicles, something that amused her children afterwards: 'Strange, growing up we never owned a car and my mum was the typical stay-at-home mum, looking after the house, her family, cooking, sewing, gardening and all the usual things women of that age group took for granted as their responsibility to do. She was however always very proud of the fact that she "held" the ropes for the barrage balloons that were intended to stop enemy planes from flying too low over London.'

When John left hospital he was still in no fit shape to work. His medical records in July 1946 show that he was suffering from amoebic dysentery, amoebic hepatitis, bacillary dysentery, aches and pains in joints caused by dry and wet beriberi, malarial headaches and had had thirty-four bouts of malaria in four years. Nevertheless he did recover sufficiently to start work on the railways some months later, a job he continued to hold for the rest of his life. In his army medical records there was a note that he was 'too interested in his own health issues', implying hypochondria, but Mary refutes this vigorously: 'He rode his bike to and from work, worked as much overtime as he could, and never stayed home sick. In fact, he was such a strong believer in carrying on when you don't feel well, that WE were not allowed to be sick either. And with that catalogue of diseases it is hardly surprising that he was concerned after the war about his health.'

John and Dorothy were married not long after he left hospital and moved into a top flat in the New Kent Road area of London in Southwark. Mary was born in 1948 and two boys followed: John in 1949 and Kevin in 1953.

As children we were aware that our dad had been a Japanese prisoner of war but in keeping with most others, that is practically all we knew, we had no idea of what it really meant, it was just something he had done during the war. We had no idea of the duration of his captivity and no knowledge of all the terrible things he had been through. We knew he had lost all his friends (that he did tell us) and that he had returned with serious health problems we were aware of, though it was never discussed. It must have been terribly hard to deal with the treatment they received on their return and lack of understanding of all that they had been through and how they were still suffering, with bad health and the mental aspect of all they had been through and seen.

Although his physical health was bad for John during the first months after his release, it was without doubt the psychological effects that caused both him and his family the greatest problems.

Family life was punctuated by fierce arguments and anger from John, outbursts that often had no explanation and were frightening to the children. He found it difficult to show his children affection. Hugs and kisses were always missing in their lives, and the sense that John could go off like a rocket at any given moment led them to fear their father. This, Mary concluded, was something that many children of former prisoners of the Japanese endured but at the time it was not something they could share with others. They simply knew that the atmosphere at home was different from that of their friends' houses.

Did my dad's POW experiences affect our family? I have to say a strong 'yes'. I remember many very traumatic experiences, that out of respect for my parents and relatives I would prefer not to repeat, but it was far from a peaceful family life and we children knew when to keep quiet and make ourselves invisible. The mood swings of ex-prisoners of war is now an accepted fact, but as a child to live through it and its consequences, is a very different matter.

Up until the time Mary left home in 1965 John was still waking at night screaming from the terrible nightmares that plagued him for his entire life. 'He shared with my brother that one of his nightmares was that he was on a boat with a lot of other young men, and that an island was in sight and kept getting closer and closer and he didn't want to go there . . . one can only imagine the terrible fear his sleep held for him.'

Dorothy never complained about her husband but Mary knew that her life with him was hard. Eventually it became too much for her and she divorced John in the late 1960s, after Mary had left home.

She never ever spoke badly about my dad during the marriage or after she separated (which believe me, was not a very easy time for her, and once again there were many 'uncomfortable' incidents that she had to suffer). The only thing she did do was to cut him out of the family photos she had, so there are many photos showing only my dad's legs. She never ever ran him down to us. While growing up, after various incidents, she would always use the excuse that it had happened 'because he had been a Japanese POW' and we grew up using that in our own minds as the reason every time there was an incident.

Both John and Dorothy remarried. 'Mum finally met some-one who treated her as the lady she most certainly was, and her remaining years were spent with someone with whom she laughed a lot and they were very happy together.' Mary is con-vinced that her mother still cared deeply for her father even though she could no longer cope with living with him: 'When my dad passed away in 1987, my mum's very special new husband took her to visit my dad's grave and she just cried and cried. They had both been through so very much together.'

Mary regretted that she did not have a chance to get to know her father and establish a proper friendship with him:

My recollections are those of a child and not having had a rela-tionship with him as an adult, I have no idea if he would eventually have mellowed with age and we could have enjoyed each other's company. Sadly, the war never ended for my dad, for it continued in our home and his mind, and I can only hope that if anyone read-ing this knew my dad, that they now understand why he was a little 'different'. To me, he is now remembered as a true and very special hero and my only wish would be that I could have told him so.

It was not only daughters who experienced difficult child-hoods in the families of former prisoners of the Japanese. Stephen Rockcliffe had a turbulent childhood that for years he believed was different from anyone else's. Certainly no one in his circle had a father who behaved like his.

My parents met when they were fifteen years old. My father was working in the rolling mills in Sheffield in the steel industry. His father had died when he was four years old and he had been brought up by his maternal grandparents, John and Beatrice Clixby. My mother was working as a touch-up artist for a photography company. Sidney could easily have stayed working in Sheffield as his was a reserved profession but he found that the glamour of life in the Territorial Army was more appealing than life in the rolling mills, so he signed up and was pulled into the army full-time and sent to Bovington Camp in Dorset.

Stephen was not born until after the Second World War but he has no doubt that the war had a profound effect on his parents' relationship and on his childhood as a result.

Mary Goddard, Sidney's wife, was born in Sheffield, the daughter of a train driver at the steel works. Her father was a veteran of the First World War and had survived although his two brothers and many of his friends had died in the trenches. When war broke out and Sidney left Sheffield to join the army, Mary moved from her job at the photographers to a production line at a Batchelors' factory canning and drying rations for the army. When Sheffield was bombed in the Blitz her house was damaged and had to be demolished although she and her family were unhurt. One of Mary's fellow workers at the canning factory was Sidney's Auntie Elsie, so she was in close contact with Sidney's family throughout the war.

After two years in Britain, Sidney Rockcliffe was sent out with the 18th Division to the Far East where he was captured by the Japanese in February 1942 at Singapore just after his twentieth birthday. He was a member of A Battalion, part of No. 2 Group, a force of about 650 men, who went from Changi Barracks, Singapore, to Ban Pong in Thailand by train in October 1942. From there they were force-marched 130 kilometres to Tarsau and then ferried by barge to Kinsaiyok, from where they worked on the Death Railway until by June 1944 he was in prison at No. 2 Camp at Nong Pladuk. From there he was transferred on board the hell ship *Teia Hioki Maru* to Moji in Japan and from there to Fukuoka No. 17 Camp where he spent the rest of the war working at the Mitsui zinc factory.

John Clixby died in 1943, convinced that Sidney had been killed in action. Sidney was released on 16 September 1945, a full month after the official end of the Pacific war, by US marines and transferred to a hospital ship in nearby Nagasaki harbour. He was so ill that he could not be sent home directly so was taken to San Francisco military hospital where he spent two months being treated for beriberi and other deficiency diseases. He finally arrived back in Liverpool in December aboard the SS *Queen Mary* and returned to Sheffield in January 1946.

'My mother waited for his return through those dark years, even though she did not hear anything from him until about eighteen months after his capture. She had had one or two young suitors who might have married her under different circumstances but instead of which she waited for my father.' What made Mary wait for Sidney is something she never discussed with her children but she did once tell Stephen that an old flame, who visited the house in the mid-1960s, was a man she might well have married.

When Sidney returned home there was great rejoicing. The neighbours held a street party and he was swept up in an avalanche of warmth and affection. But he was not the man who went away: 'He was an utterly broken man of just twenty-four years old. I spoke to an old neighbour who described him as a "shadow of a man" who still weighed less than seven stone even after three months of decent food. His back was covered in large scars and he had suffered from all manner of tropical diseases. Far and away his biggest problem however was the psychological damage that proved to be permanent.' Sidney and Mary were married almost immediately and the couple moved into his grandmother's house for the first period of their married life. 'I know for sure that my mother was deeply shocked by the person who returned. Dad really was a stranger in the house. Mother must have loved him very much before he went to war otherwise she would not have waited for his return. But life with Dad was difficult in the extreme. Most of his life he was prone to violent outbursts, the slightest thing would tip him over the edge.'

Everything in Mary's strict upbringing had brought her to believe that marriage was for life and that it was her duty to be a good wife, come what may. 'How my mother put up with my father, I will never know,' Stephen said. 'He used to suffer from terrible nightmares, he could be violent and I would sometimes hear him in the night throwing furniture and smashing cups and saucers. We children could only run and hide but mother was always in the middle. I'm not sure that anyone other than a fellow child of a Far Eastern prisoner of war could understand what it was like having a complete stranger in the house who you called "Dad".'

In 1948 Sidney got a job working for the railways and from then on he worked long, hard hours: 'My memory is that my father worked fifteen hours a day, seven days a week without a day's holiday. It seems, now, to have been his way of coping with his problems but as a child I just felt we were different as a family. We never had holidays like other children and our father was always at work.' Around 1955 he went to work for the bus company as a conductor, and later in the receipting office until he took early retirement in 1982 on grounds of severe heart problems.

In all Sidney and Mary had seven children, including twins, born between 1946 and 1958:

Dad obviously had a deep psychosexual dysfunction like many FEPOWs and I think it was a very serious problem for both him and Mother. Again I think Mother 'did her duty' so to speak. Thinking about it now convinces me that she did this to some extent through fear of Dad's temper as much as duty. I am also certain that Dad had a number of affairs, and I think this broke Mother's heart on more than a few occasions. But for Dad – these affairs were just for sex and nothing ever came of them. I think one has to realize that many, if not most, FEPOWs became obsessed with the idea that they had become permanently impotent during their captivity. This obviously had a great effect on the men's attitude towards sex on returning to their families.

As Stephen grew up he learned quickly how not to irritate his father, who used to 'go berserk' if the children annoyed him. He got used to not speaking when his father was around for fear of upsetting him but this had the result later in life of making him afraid to speak in public. He remembered on one occasion as a teenager getting very angry about something his father had said or done and Mary turning to him and saying: 'Look, you've got to remember your dad has no idea what it is like to be a teenager. At your age he was being shot at and then he had it beaten out of him by the Japs.' Such comments, however, were never properly explained and it was not until he was an adult that Stephen learned more about his father's war years. And it was later still that he talked to other members of his extended family about his father:

My Aunt Jan is my mother's youngest sister by twenty-two years. She told me a few things I didn't know: one being that she was terrified of my dad and obviously worried about my mother's situation. Another was when once my dad had lost his temper and had taken it out on one of my brothers. Dad had broken down and spent a few days in deep despair at his inability to control his temper. Quite how my mother coped with all this is difficult to comprehend, but I think it was done through a deep sense of duty. Mother understood perfectly that no one could go through the FEPOW experience and return to normality as if it had never happened.

'My mother was a legend in her own family,' Stephen said.

She was a tiny waif of a woman but she was strong in herself. Her marriage was so peculiar that she had to learn the rules from scratch. It was different from anything she had been brought up to expect. But she coped and was wonderful. People came to her for advice on all sorts of matters. She knew every childhood disease and she would look after the neighbours' children so that the house was always full of kids. I think it was her way of coping. In some ways she was almost two different people. She was quite happy looking after a house full of children and chatting to her friends during the daytime, but when Dad was home she became very quiet – like treading on eggshells trying not to upset him, she would make him cups of tea and always made his meals but would never dare challenge him over anything.

Stephen Rockcliffe said he is not bitter about his father but about the circumstances of the war that broke him.

I have had to come to terms with all this in my own mind and the key has been understanding what Dad was subjected to during those dreadful three and a half years. What I feel about Dad now is that his life was utterly wasted in so many ways. He could and should have been a much more successful person but it is as if he had to give his all just to survive. In some ways his release at Nagasaki in September 1945 may have been the end of captivity, but it was the start of another battle, that of learning how to live again. It is a sad fact that Dad, like so many others, never fully reclaimed his life and his troubled mind was always back in the POW camps where so many of his friends died and where he fought for his own life for three and a half years. Of course this also affected my mother who I have no doubt wanted a much better life than she had. She would have expected Dad eventually to recover fully when they were married but the wounds were too deep. I always thought it very significant that towards the end of his life Dad used to drive my mother nuts by talking endlessly about the Second World War – about the Germans, Italians, French, Americans, even the Indians – but he would never ever mention the Japanese and his own captivity. To anyone else this may sound bizarre but it just illustrates what a complex and deeply disturbing set of emotions these men had to come to terms with. If only I had known all this when I was young I'd have understood my father more. I live with the guilt of not understanding his situation when I was young but I now admire greatly his toughness and sheer bloody determination to survive.

Stephen also acknowledged the strength of his mother: 'Women like my mum were part of a story that I feel is only just beginning to be understood. They were in a unique situation and received no help whatever from either the services or health professionals. These women were the victims of one of the most heinous crimes ever perpetrated and they suffered their entire lives.'

It would be wrong to suggest that every family of Far Eastern prisoners of war endured such traumas as those of Mary Michael, Jean Roberts and Stephen Rockcliffe. Martin Percival's father was also a prisoner of the Japanese and his story is so different that it is included here to offer another perspective.

Martin was nineteen when his father died in December 1982.

His brother David was seventeen. They kept the family house for two years while David did his A levels and Martin got his first job.

> Fortunately I had the presence of mind to keep all my father's books and papers referring to his years in the war. Initially I did nothing with them. My father had often spoken to me and my brother about his life as a prisoner of war in the Far East and had always emphasized the positive side of his experiences. For example, he held few grudges against the Japanese and always admired them for what they achieved in the post-war years. Whilst he never had a chip on his shoulder about the Japanese, he had nothing good to say about the Korean camp guards who he always regarded negatively due to the poor treatment they gave the POWs.

Frank Percival was born in Paddington, London, in May 1918. His mother died when he was nine and his father, William Percival, who was the editor of the local newspaper, the *Willesden Chronicle*, remarried so that Frank was brought up by his father and stepmother. At the age of seventeen he left home and went to work as a medical orderly in Norwich, showing a determination to take charge of his own life. When the war broke out Frank applied to join the RAF but was turned down. 'I don't know the reason for this but I suspect that the RAF was inundated with young men interested in joining what must have appeared to be the most glamorous arm of the services,' Martin said. In December 1939 he joined the York and Lancaster Regiment and in July 1941 he transferred to the Royal Army Service Corps and was posted abroad two months later, sailing on the *Empress of Canada* from Gourock in Scotland. He arrived in Singapore at the end of November 1941 and saw active service in Malaya and Singapore before he was captured in February 1942 when the island fell to the Japanese. A month later he was reported missing in the *Willesden Chronicle*.

Frank spent his captivity from June 1942 in Thailand, working in various camps on the Thailand–Burma Railway. He was aboard the first train that crossed the famous viaduct at Wampo. The train derailed and was held up for thirteen hours as the engine hit an overhanging rock at the north end of the viaduct, one of many dramatic incidents to punctuate his captivity. Three days after the derailment, on 7 May 1943, Frank was reported in the *Willesden Chronicle* as a prisoner of war. It was not until July 1944 that William Percival had a personal communication from Frank, by means of a postcard. A month and a day later William died but Frank knew nothing about that.

During his captivity Frank succumbed to a variety of tropical diseases including malaria and pellagra and in October 1943 he was sent to Kanchanaburi base hospital suffering from pleurisy. He spent the remainder of his captivity in a variety of camps in Thailand before being released by the British in Takura camp a week after Japan surrendered. He travelled to Bangkok and from there went by plane to Rangoon where he boarded the HMT *Orduna*, arriving in Liverpool five weeks later on 19 October 1945 in the middle of a dock strike. From Liverpool he headed back to London. It was not a happy homecoming: 'Didn't you get my letters?' his stepmother enquired. 'Your father died in August 1944.' It must have been a terrible shock.

Both his father and stepmother had worked as air-raid wardens during the war, and in an effort to reduce the amount of flammable material in the house they had thrown out all his papers including the pre-war programmes from his favourite football club, Queens Park Rangers. It was as if his early life had been obliterated and his stepmother told him frankly that they had not expected him to come back from the war, as if this went some way to explaining why all this precious material had been destroyed. After six weeks at home Frank was admitted to the Queen Alexandra Military Hospital in London where his medical report recorded his various tropical illnesses and the fact that he now weighed 10 stone 12½ lbs but that his lowest recorded weight as a prisoner of war had been 7 stone 9 lbs. In February he went to the doctor to complain about pains in the balls of his feet. This was caused, he was told, by wearing shoes and walking on pavements.

Frank was released from the army in June 1946 and set about finding a job. He began to work in local government and made his way up through the system, eventually moving all over the country to pursue his career. During the early 1950s he met a former army nurse, Margaret Martin. The daughter of a miner from Scotland, Margaret was a no-nonsense woman. She married Frank in 1953 and the two of them did not seem to expect to have any children. In 1955 Frank was admitted to the tropical unit of Roehampton Hospital where he underwent an operation for hookworm. In 1963, two years after she had lost a little baby girl in the late stages of pregnancy, Margaret gave birth to Martin. Two years later David arrived. By now Frank was forty-seven. The family was living in Fareham at this time and Frank was working for Southampton City Council.

From his early childhood Martin remembered his father talking about the war and his life in prison camps. 'He was quite open about it and it was never an especially negative experience when he described what he had been through. He was always relatively matter of fact,' he explained. Martin was eight years old when he noticed books on his father's shelves with interesting-sounding titles such as *Railroad of Death*, *Naked Island* and *Knights of Bushido*. Frank bought most of the books that came out about the war in the Far East and was happy to answer Martin's questions. In 1972 the Oscar-winning film *Bridge on the River Kwai* was re-released in cinemas in Britain. Frank took Margaret and the boys to see the film. Martin remembered enjoying it very much but Margaret was horrified and thought it quite unsuitable for the children. It was after seeing the film that Frank really opened up to Martin about his past. The film was a useful way of talking about different aspects of captivity in detail and Frank told the boys anything they wanted to know.

Later the same year the family went on holiday to Tunisia and Frank taught both the boys to count to ten in Japanese.

I know now that all this was really very unusual. Most people who were prisoners of the Japanese kept complete silence on the subject of their imprisonment and never spoke about it even to their wives. But for some reason my father was fairly relaxed about it and was happy to talk to us. I feel now that it was a very positive experience both for him and for me. I never felt he was putting a shine on the story for our benefit, it was just how he viewed his past.

When Martin was ten his mother Margaret died. Frank took early retirement and brought the boys up by himself. He used to be there when they left to go to school and was at home when they arrived back. He took them to football matches, which they all loved, and there they would meet other members of the family. 'Queens Park Rangers has been the glue that has kept the male members of our family together over the years,' Martin said. 'My grandfather was a keen QPR supporter too. In fact the relationship goes back to the 1890s.'

In 1979 Frank took the boys to Canada for a holiday. It was in Vancouver that Martin saw for the only time his father revisited by his wartime experiences. They had gone to see a dolphin show at the Vancouver aquarium and the audience was made up in part of a large group of Japanese tourists with their children. There was a lot of excited chatter and shouting in Japanese, which upset Frank and he told the boys he needed to go back to the hotel. 'I remember that that night he was very disturbed. We were sharing a room and he had terrible trouble sleeping and I think probably had nightmares. I couldn't really make it out at the time but I think it was the shouting and jabbering in Japanese that suddenly awakened old memories in my father and he was full of anxiety. I could see it was bringing back very bad memories for him.'

In the autumn of 1982 Martin was due to go to university but his father was seriously ill so he decided to stay and look after him. In retrospect he was very glad he had opted to spend what turned out to be the last two months of his father's life at home. 'I suspect my father knew he was dying and he talked a lot during those weeks. He talked about his past, about the war and we managed to tie up a lot of loose ends so that by the time he died I felt those weeks had been of inordinate value to me, far more so than if I had gone off to Hull to take up my studies.'

One of the things that Martin learned was that his father had been very involved in the Far Eastern Prisoners of War Federation from its inception in 1947 until 1957 when he moved away from London. Over the following years he lost touch with the organization. It seemed to Martin that once the children came along Frank cut ties with that part of his life. It was only in 1980 that he finally made contact again with the organization. Martin also learned that Frank, against official orders, had written an account of his internment on the passage home in 1945 and this was published on the front page of the *Willesden Chronicle* on 9 November 1945 under the title 'Your God's Stronger Than Ours'. 'There was a little part of my father that chose to ignore authority and I think that probably came from his time in the prison camps. Although there were one or two British officers he admired, on the whole he thought that too many of them pulled rank and got out of a lot of the hard work. So when he was told he should not speak to the press or talk of his experiences I suspect he deliberately ignored the command.'

Martin later discovered that his father had written other articles which he submitted anonymously to the FEPOW newsletter in 1981. 'I think he would like to have been a journalist had other circumstances prevailed but after the war he did not have that opportunity. I found these articles and thought I recognized my father's style and then confirmation came and I realized he had probably also written quite a lot immediately after the war.'

Another discovery, which surprised Martin more than his father's writings, came through a conversation he had with a cousin who had known Frank and seen a lot of him in the immediate aftermath of the Second World War. 'When I came across this cousin again many years later he was astounded that my father had spoken to me about his POW experiences,' Martin recalled. 'He told me that when Dad came home he would not speak of what he had been through. He <u>never</u> talked about the prison camps or the Japanese. He was absolutely amazed that my father had been so open with us boys.'

Martin is convinced that his father managed to come to terms with his POW experiences after he returned to Britain for two reasons. First, Frank was independent and unattached, which meant that at first he did not have anyone emotionally attached to him to take into consideration. Secondly he had a career to concentrate on as well as a wide circle of friends, a passion for the theatre, cinema and football and, later, a strong and loving wife. The fact that Frank had already struck out on his own four years prior to the war and had some experience of living alone and getting on with his own life helped, Martin felt, to give him a sense of independence and something to look forward to on his release.

For Martin the war had two opposing impacts on his life. On the one hand he was aware of it during his childhood, because his father talked about it so openly, but on the other hand it did not have the detrimental effect on his family life that it had for so many FEPOW children. In an article published in 2007 Martin wrote: 'At that time, not knowing any other children of FEPOWs, I assumed that others shared similar tales with their children. I have since learned that this is generally not the case and that in fact I have been very lucky in that I have a relatively rich store of memories and artefacts from my father relating to his time in captivity. Fortunately I had enough presence of mind at the age of nineteen not to just throw all of this away when he died.'

10

THE WINDS OF WAR: THE
POST-WAR CHILDREN'S TALE

I know so very little about my father's life, to be honest. He
had no dependants and had been brought up in Trowbridge
with his aunt and uncle, although I know that my grandfather
used to write letters to him.

Keith Andrews

For children born after the war it was not so much readjustment
as understanding the past that proved their lives' challenge. While
many had perfectly normal childhoods, a number were able to
look back on their parents' marriages and conclude that but for
the Second World War life could have been very different. How
different they will never know.

Juliet Curry first learned about her father when she was fifteen
years old. He was Alfred James Bestow, referred to as AJ in the
family, but he had adopted the name Carington-Bestow as an affec-
tation when he was in his twenties working as an actor-manager at

the Nottingham Playhouse. He was born in Nottinghamshire in 1905 and was brought up by his widowed mother and four or five maiden aunts who doted on him and indulged him during his childhood. In those days the Nottingham Playhouse was an amateur theatre and Alfred was unpaid. But he was his mother's only boy and she was wealthy enough to provide funds.

Alfred met Juliet's mother, Ruth Winifred Lytle, at the Playhouse in about 1930 when they were both in their mid-twenties. Ruth was a part-time amateur actress and elocution teacher who also worked as a chauffeur for her father who was a successful insurance agent. She was the oldest daughter, with two younger brothers who were eight and ten years her junior. In her twenties Ruth had raced Alvises and Bentleys at Brooklands and it was she, not her father, who taught the two boys to drive. She was often seen dressed as a man and the three of them were known affectionately as 'the three Lytle brothers'. Juliet explained that Ruth was given cross-dressing roles in any Shakespeare plays they put on, mainly because she could fence well, and she would often walk around wearing men's clothes and a monocle. 'She always said she had a straight up and down figure which meant she could successfully pass [herself] off as a man and she was quite tall for the age, about 5 foot 7 inches, so that helped with the disguise as well. When she was racing the cars she would often take part in the men's races in her masculine guise, as well as racing as a woman in female clothes, because there were of course women's races in those days too.'

Intoxicated by Ruth, Alfred was convinced that she was wealthy because she drove a large American Chrysler and wore beautiful Parisian dresses. The car belonged to her father and her dresses were made for her by her clever seamstress mother. Ruth in turn believed Alfred was rich because of the life he led in the theatre. They ran away together in 1934 and married in secret but it was only when it came to paying for their hotel that they realized that neither of them had any money to settle the bill. Their parents were furious and refused to speak to them. It was not an auspicious beginning to a marriage. Their first daughter, Rosalind, was born in June 1936, and they scraped by on Ruth's earnings as an elocution teacher. When war broke out in 1939 Alfred applied to join the Royal Navy but was turned down on account of his eyesight. He was completely surprised and shocked to learn, at the age of thirty-five, that he was colour blind. Apparently he saw green and blue as grey. '"You never saw the turquoise suit I got married in?" Ruth enquired of him when he told her what the problem was. "What turquoise suit?" he replied. "You always wear grey!" Imagine how it must be to be colour blind and not be able to see the greens and blues of nature. And it was so sad for my mother because she loved to wear turquoise and blues.'

Alfred was unwillingly conscripted to work in an armaments factory in South Wales for part of the war, returning to Nottingham to work in a small-arms factory until 1945. 'As far as I know my father was away from home for the full six years. Even when he came back to Nottingham he was living in the city whereas my mother was living in a little cottage on the green in Kinoulton some twelve miles south-east of the city.' Ruth continued to teach elocution but the pay was a pittance and she had very little money to live on. She became a volunteer for the Red Cross as a fundraiser. She was also a local ARP warden. Juliet said: 'I remember her telling me that she had a tin hat and she used to sleep in her wellington boots. The farmland around Kinoulton was planted with lights to distract bombers from the armaments factories in Nottingham so there were often local air-raid warnings.'

When Alfred returned to Ruth in 1945 he brought back a

bullwhip and informed Ruth that 'This is how it is going to be from now on.' Before the war, Ruth told Juliet, Alfred had been cultured and well read. He was nicknamed 'Plato' by his colleagues at the Playhouse. After the war he was rough. He drank and swore and had an unpleasant temper. When Juliet was born in 1946 Alfred left. Her mother told her she had been 'a horrible mistake'. Alfred wrote to Ruth the day after the baby arrived saying that he would try to get to visit her the following day. He never came. He ran off with the woman who owned a local cafe and Ruth was left to fend for herself and her tiny baby.

In March 1946, when Juliet was just a few weeks old, it began to snow. Kinoulton village was on the side of a hill in the Belvoir Vale and the valley soon filled up. 'My mother said that there was so much snow that it came right up the door so it was impossible to get in or out of the village. At some stage there were airlifts but it wasn't enough or the right sort of food to feed a newborn baby.' Ruth had to watch her little girl becoming malnourished. By the time the snows melted Juliet was diagnosed with rickets, a vitamin deficiency disease that left her needing callipers for several years.

Alfred would appear for brief moments in Ruth's life and then disappear again. He came once to take away his clothes from the house and on the odd occasion he would collect Rosalind and Juliet in her pram, and take them into Nottingham. Rosalind's only recollection of these visits was sitting on a doorstep waiting for her father to come out of this strange house and take her home. She had no idea there was another woman in Alfred's life and that he was living with her.

Eventually Ruth succeeded in getting a divorce and moved to Bournemouth. The doctors told her that salt water was a good treatment for rickets and Juliet recalls being dunked into the sea daily and forced to do a five-mile walk every weekend to combat the effects of the disease. Juliet walked in callipers until she was five and thereafter in built-up shoes. Ruth took a flat, subletting one of the rooms to foreign students to cover the rent. She began to build up her portfolio of teaching, beginning once again with elocution but then broadening her range to include English, history and geography at local private schools where the pay was minimal because she was not qualified. 'My mother was an actress and she had a great sense of drama. She was a good teacher, resourceful and incredibly hard working,' Juliet explained. 'But she never learned to cook and we were fed, as I remember, on a diet of cheese on toast, unless there were students in the house to cook for.' Juliet and Rosalind, while she was still at home, were left alone for long hours while their mother worked. Ruth was a tremendous fighter. 'Money was always tight and I remember once she sold her wedding and engagement rings to buy me a pair of surgical boots. These were not available on the new National Health Service and of course I needed a new pair every year. After that the opals went and my mother's other jewellery for these horrible, brown, clumpy boots.'

Rosalind did a secretarial course on leaving school, married at twenty and moved with her new husband to Southern Rhodesia (Zimbabwe). Juliet was ten years old. 'I remember it was like a death when Rosalind left,' she said. 'We were very close and suddenly she was gone from my life. I somehow knew I would never see her again, at least that's how it seemed to me then. Without Rosalind's financial input my mother could not manage to pay the rent so we had to move into a bedsit.'

Juliet loathed school and was told she was unresponsive and lazy by her teachers. In fact she was badly bullied for being partially disabled, and because she could not run the other children tormented her. Often her upper body was black and blue with bruises from where they pushed her around between the desks in the classroom. She hid these bruises from her mother by always taking a bath on her own but one day Ruth saw them and marched her down to the school to complain to the headmaster. He denied any knowledge of bullying, as did the other children and their parents. This left Juliet dreading going to school and hating it even more when she was there. She left her secondary modern after taking GCEs and took a job in the local library educating herself in her free time by going to evening classes in a variety of subjects including French, painting, bookbinding and English literature. She did a correspondence course for three years to obtain the qualifications to get into library school, which she did at twenty, leaving the bedsit in Bournemouth. Ruth had by this time emigrated to Southern Rhodesia. 'The strange thing was that my mother always told lies about me. She had been to a very good school herself so she could never admit that I had been to a secondary modern. She would tell people I'd been to the grammar school even though I had failed the eleven-plus. And my college became a university in her mind. I don't think she ever really understood what I did professionally either.'

After qualifying as a librarian Juliet got a job with the firm J. Walter Thompson, then the largest advertising agency in the world, working in their marketing library. She found she had a facility for writing and reportage and eventually she successfully ran her own company and enjoyed a life of freedom, independence and respect from her peers. One day, Ruth, who had spent five years living in Southern Rhodesia to be close to Rosalind, reappeared on Juliet's doorstep in London and ended up living on her sofa for three years. She had come back, she told Juliet, because she was concerned about her pension entitlement. 'She was a terrifying woman and I was frightened of her until she died. She had had to be strong to survive and she had very little affection for me but I admired her too. When I was twenty-nine I wanted to get married and Mother's presence on the sofa became impossible so I went to a housing association. They found my mother a council flat in Marylebone where she lived until she died in 1999 at the age of ninety-three.'

It was only when Juliet was grown up that she learned more about her early life and the terrible conflicts that had taken place around the time of her birth in 1946. To her Alfred was a complete unknown. He had been cut out of all but one family photograph, which she saw as a child but which her sister took with her when she left home. The photograph was of Alfred and Rosalind in 1938. Juliet did not see the photograph again for over forty years and when she did she found it overwhelming: 'It is the only record of him I have, except the odd play programme and my birth certificate. I think these things only hit you when you have children of your own. Then you can imagine the lost youth of the man (well, actually he was about thirty-four to thirty-six), as by the next year 1939/40 he was in a munitions factory, and was never to enjoy family life again.' At the time she was growing up his name was almost never mentioned within the family and if it was he was referred to as AJ. All she knew about him was that he had remarried at some stage after the war the woman he had run off with the day after she was born.

She learned later that this woman was unable to bear Alfred any children. She did however have money and when she saw Juliet in her pram with her pretty fair curly hair she persuaded Alfred to fight for custody of her so that they would have a child. They would be able to pay for Juliet to have the surgery that they believed was needed to deal with the effects of rickets. Ruth found herself going to court to fight for custody of Juliet. Alfred very nearly won as Ruth had been hysterical at the thought of losing her little daughter and the barrister had suggested that Ruth was neurotic and not a fit mother to look after a child.

Fortunately a female barrister came to Ruth's aid and they won the case, but it was a close shave. Such were Ruth's pain and anger at this battle, won only, she said later, by a dramatic demonstration of 'womanly appeal', that she and Rosalind decided to tell Juliet that Alfred was dead. So for the first fifteen years of her life Juliet had believed that her father had died some time after she was born. Then one day she opened a letter, by mistake, about the contribution he was supposed to make towards her upkeep – £1.00 per week. When she asked her mother, Ruth simply told her that Alfred was 'alive, yes, and in the Nottingham phone book'.

It took some time for Juliet to untangle the web of untruths that had surrounded the early part of her life. At one point she considered visiting her father in Nottingham to confront him but in the end she felt that the episode would cause more pain to her than to her father. 'What would I have done?' she asked, 'kicked him in the shins? How would that have helped? So I let it be. My mother was both a mother and father figure to me. I didn't know what it was like to have a father. After all, you can't miss what you don't have.'

Juliet married Roger Curry in 1976 and they had two children, a girl and then, in 1991, a boy. Ruth was appalled that Juliet was having a baby at forty-four but when the little boy was born she was enchanted by him. They called him James. Ruth told her that they had chosen Alfred's second name. Juliet had only ever heard him referred to as AJ and had no idea that his second name had been James.

Like Juliet's, Chris Best's father had a civilian role during the Second World War. Held back from joining up on religious rather than health grounds, he nevertheless had as traumatic an experience as many fighting soldiers and the legacy of his war years greatly affected his only daughter's childhood. It was not until 2003 that Chris made a 12,000-mile journey to Japan to try to lay the ghosts that had haunted her father for the last fifteen years of his life. By then her father had been dead for over forty years but it had taken all that time for her to piece together the past.

'I've received one letter card from you recently,' Malcolm Ingleby-Scott wrote to his fiancée, Patricia Whalen, soon after his release from a civilian internment camp in Japan in September 1945.

I know you've written lots but the Nips have blocked everything which might have made a prisoner's lot a little happier . . . I am hoping you'll find me less like a skeleton than I was a few weeks ago. I don't know when I'll arrive home. What with being on trains, hospital ships, destroyers, planes etc I'm literally in a daze so you'll forgive me for writing feebly. I'm all taut inside. Freedom after more than three years of hell makes one feel dizzy.

Malcolm had just turned thirty-six when he left Britain in January 1942. Born in York in 1906, he was the last in a male line of Shetland seafarers who could trace their ancestry back to 1720. His male ancestors had been Arctic whalers, fishing off Greenland, Baffin Island and the Davis Straits. Malcolm's grandfather had died at sea so his grandmother would not let her own son follow in the family tradition. He had worked on the railways. Malcolm trained as a draughtsman in Sunderland but like his forebears he had sea legs and was at his happiest when he was allowed to sail. In an attempt to square the circle he decided to train, in the mid-1930s, as a radio officer, combining his education with his passion for the high seas.

When it was clear that there would be war he was determined to do his bit. The family was Quaker and the religion discouraged its followers from fighting so Malcolm decided the next-best thing he could do was to join the Merchant Navy, which he did in 1939, being employed by Marconi as a radio operator. He made several voyages to the Caribbean and the United States and in January 1942 set sail from North Shields, now in Tyne and Wear, aboard the SS *Kirkpool* as the ship's radio officer, his destination Cape Town, and on to Lourenço Marques, now Maputo in present-day Mozambique. From there they were ordered to sail to Montevideo with a shipment of coal to supply the British fleet. It was while they were sailing in the South Atlantic that the *Kirkpool* was torpedoed by a disguised German raider named the *Thor*. The ship was sunk with the loss of sixteen lives and the remainder of the forty-six-man crew abandoned ship: 'I was blown off the ship and wounded in the leg and swam for ages before being picked up and arriving in Japan months later,' he wrote to his fiancée in September 1945 by way of explanation.

Before he had sailed Malcolm had become engaged to Patricia Whalen, a deputy matron at a nursery school in Sunderland. He had met Pat through the youngest of his five sisters, Marion, who was also a nurse. Pat had been brought up in a strict Roman Catholic family and, although both she and Malcolm had been out with other partners, this felt to her like the most important relationship of her life. She told Chris years later that Malcolm had walked over to her before they even started dating and said: 'I'm going to marry you.' Pat knew he would be going abroad with the Merchant Navy but she promised him she would await his return, whenever that came. She coped with those dark years by continuing her work at the nursery and volunteering for the St John Ambulance service: 'I had a feeling from the time he went away that he was alive. I always knew he would come back,' Pat had said. When the news reached Sunderland that the *Kirkpool* had been sunk and that Malcolm was posted 'missing presumed dead', she refused to believe the news and continued to hope that she would eventually hear that he was alive. In April 1944 she heard from Malcolm's father that the Red Cross had sent a telegram to say that he was a civilian prisoner and was interned at a place called Fukushima. She wrote immediately and Malcolm received her twenty-five-word postcard in August 1944.

Fukushima camp in northern Japan comprised ninety-eight men, twenty-nine women and thirteen children, all civilians and seamen, who were kept in unpleasant conditions, five people to a cell. Malcolm was released in September 1945 and sailed back to Britain via Australia aboard the HMT *Andes*. He knew that the experience of Fukushima had changed him and he tried to warn Pat that she should not expect too much of him: 'You will find me a changed man,' he wrote to her from the ship in Yokohama harbour. 'I am not the happy person that left you in January 1942.' When Chris asked her mother what she had said to Malcolm when she first saw him she replied that they had barely spoken, she had simply flung her arms around his neck and hugged him. They went straight back to his parents' house and made arrangements to be married as soon as possible.

Malcolm and Pat were married on 29 February 1946 in St Mary's RC Church in Sunderland. His family, being strict Christadelphians, could not attend a Roman Catholic wedding so her half of the church was full of family and friends whereas on his side there were only about three well-wishers. By now Malcolm was thirty-nine and Patricia thirty-four. Two years later, Chris was born, their only child, named after his late sister. Chris knew almost nothing of her father's life before she was born and he never spoke to her or her mother about his life in captivity. Chris remembered only that the word 'Fukushima' was spoken in hushed tones at home but she had no comprehension of its significance until long after her father had died.

The relationship between Malcolm and Pat was mainly

contented although there were troubles at times. His experiences in Japan had changed him in many ways. Pat found him unsettled, depressed, anxious and he found it almost impossible to hold down a proper job. After the war he was desperate to emigrate. He found Britain cold and impoverished and told her he wanted to spread his wings and try something new. But Pat hated the prospect of upheaval and change: 'My mother was a home-bird and she did not like the idea of life in Australia. She had been brought up a Roman Catholic, he a Quaker, and this led to strains in their relationship as they struggled to reconcile the different values of their two faiths.'

For the first year after the war Malcolm did not have to work. His old employer in the north-east, Marconi, gave him time to sort himself out, improve his health and find some stability. Chris discovered later that her father had kept a diary, or rather a log, in those post-war years. Instead of recording his feelings and emotions about day-to-day life he kept a meticulous list of everything he ate at every meal. He was obsessed with food – a sharp reminder of the effect that three years of starvation had had on his mind. When the time came for him to go back to work, his employers decided that he was not fit to go back to sea, so he worked part-time for them but was unable to settle. Eventually, in 1950, when Chris was nearly three, he found work with the Poor Children's Homes Association in Newcastle upon Tyne organizing fundraising events. This was work he enjoyed but the ghosts of his past would give him no peace and he began to drink. 'He only had one person that could understand his experiences in Fukushima, a former shipmate who had been in the camp with him and with whom he could share his experiences. Drink seemed to be a way out for him, a way for him to forget.'

Chris says: 'I remember as a child being woken up in the middle of the night by my father screaming in his sleep. He used to shout out "Don't beat me! Don't beat me!" The dreams and the screaming escalated in the mid-1950s and I remember one day he came home smelling very strange. I realized he had been drinking heavily. I was aware he had been going to the doctor's more frequently and that one of the reasons was that he was having black-outs.' Later Chris found out that her father had been given a disability pension after the war and when she read his medical records years later she found an entry that stated: 'Condition unchanged. 20 per cent disabled arising from: effects of detention (psychoneurosis).' The PCHA 'let him go', Chris explained, and after that Malcolm went into a deep depression. He would sit in a chair and not move or talk. How did Pat cope with this?

My mother was stoical. She had had a rose-tinted view of their relationship when he got back from Japan. She thought she knew him. And she loved him: that is for certain. There was a great commitment on her part and she was determined to stand by him. She never worked, of course, that just was not done in those days and being thirty-four when she married him she felt she was lucky to have found a husband. She did admit to me on one occasion, however, that she found the physical side of marriage difficult. It was also hard for her to see her two sisters who had married well and were enjoying a life with sufficient money and yet there was my father, unable to earn money for the family. It must have been very hard for her.

As her father never spoke of his time in Japan, Chris was frightened of his sudden anxiety attacks during her childhood. Her mother never explained to her why he was like he was nor did she explain his terror of earthquakes, which had frequently occurred in Japan. Chris just knew that something had seriously affected him in his past and that he was not like other fathers. She accepted the situation because she knew nothing else. Eventually Malcolm was given some treatment for his depression and anxiety. Then someone suggested that as he was trained by Marconi as a radio operator he should get a job in the local ambulance station. This was, Chris recalls, a very happy period for him. 'He was the old Dad again. Happy, enjoying his job and he even stopped drinking.'

For eighteen months the work at the ambulance station kept him cheerful and then the black-outs started again. His doctor established that he had dangerously high blood pressure and decided that Malcolm should be sent to St Mary's Hospital in Roehampton, where thousands of former prisoners of the Japanese had received treatment in the post-war years for tropical diseases and psychiatric problems. He left Newcastle in the summer of 1959 and was away for four weeks. 'That was the longest month of my life,' Chris explained; 'he had never been away from home before and suddenly he wasn't there. I went to school and carried on life with Mum but it was very strange without him.'

When Malcolm returned to Newcastle at the end of the summer he was in quite good shape but not yet able to go back to work. Three weeks after Chris's twelfth birthday in November of that year she and Pat came back from a trip to town to find that Malcolm was not in the house, where they had left him. They heard from a neighbour that he had been taken into hospital with a suspected coronary. A week later, on the following Saturday, she and Pat took two buses across the city to visit him in hospital. He seemed to be in quite good spirits. When they got home Pat said that she did not feel well. At about six o'clock in the evening she complained of a terrible pain in her chest, as if a great weight were crushing her ribcage. Chris was terrified and said she would call the doctor. Meanwhile, Pat lay in bed in agony. Then, about twenty minutes later, she called to Chris to say she was feeling better, much better, that the pain had gone and her chest felt lighter. She would like a cup of tea. An hour later there was a knock at the house door. A policeman was standing on the doorstep. He had come to tell Pat that Malcolm had died shortly after six o'clock that evening. 'There was always a great empathy between my parents, despite their differences and troubles, and I am convinced that some link told my mother that he was dying, just as a dream had told her fifteen years earlier that he was still alive.'

Malcolm died on 29 November 1959. Chris wrote in her short history of her father's life: 'Malcolm never recovered from his experience in the camp, and was later diagnosed as suffering from what we now call "post-traumatic stress disorder". The effects of cardiac beriberi and shrapnel wounds coupled with PTSD finally took their toll and he died of a coronary thrombosis. He was 53 years old.' The average life expectancy for survivors of Fukushima camp post-war was fifteen years.

The years of Chris's adolescence were not easy. Pat was distraught after Malcolm's death and she sank into a deep depression. 'I would get home from school and find her with her head in the oven and the gas switched on. It was a very difficult time. She was menopausal as well as in mourning and the combination left her with mood swings up and down until I was in my mid twenties.' Although Pat was attractive and several suitors made overtures to her she was not interested. She would say to Chris: 'I was married to your father and that's enough for me.' It was not until Pat was eighty-seven that she began to talk to Chris about Malcolm. Chris was by this time fifty, married with her own son and working full-time as an educational psychologist. 'Mum was losing her sight by then and was in fact completely blind as a result of senile macular degeneration by the time she died. When I asked her why she had never spoken to me about my father after his death she explained that she would have felt as though she were betraying him.'

Once Pat had begun to talk about Malcolm all sorts of questions that had been in the back of Chris's mind since her childhood were answered. She learned about the brief, happy period before the war when Malcolm and Pat met and were deeply in love. She heard about her mother's determination to wait for Malcolm's return, regardless of the insistence of others that he had died in 1942. And she learned, of course, about the terrible years after the war when his psychiatric problems became manifest and their lives were forever affected by the after-effects of his captivity. When Chris began to ask questions within the family about her father's mental health problems she established that there was no hint of psychiatric illness or mental disorder in any branch of the family. His condition had been entirely brought on by his three years as a prisoner.

The war completely destroyed my father's life. And my mother's actually. I wasn't so directly involved as I had not known them before the war and was distant from it. But my childhood, like that of the children of other survivors from Fukushima, was completely affected by their experiences. One thing that made me realize how the whole family had been affected by Malcolm's experience was my Aunt Marion's reaction when I bought a Japanese car, a Toyota. She absolutely hit the roof.

Before Pat died in 2000, at the age of eighty-nine, Chris told her that she had decided to go to Japan and visit Fukushima to see for herself where her father had been imprisoned. To her surprise Pat was dead set against her going: 'I think your father wouldn't want you to go,' she told her daughter. But Chris was not so sure and told her mother that on the contrary she was convinced her father would have wanted her to go, that he would have wanted her to know and understand a little better. In 2003 Chris found a photograph on the Internet of the convent at Fukushima with a man standing on the roof waving a white flag:

Suddenly this place came alive for me and I decided I had to go there and see it for myself. I wanted to find out what it was like for my father to be incarcerated for three and a half years. My son offered to go with me but I felt it was something I had to do alone – I wanted to lay the ghosts to rest. I wanted to understand what it felt like going to a strange place, not being able to speak the language or know anything about the culture and environment, just as my father had done. After the visit I felt anger and hatred towards the Japanese – but it only lasted for a few hours and then I felt at peace. It was something I felt I had to do, I knew it wouldn't be pleasant but it had to be done. It was important for me to understand what my father had gone through and I did.

Since her first visit to Fukushima Chris has been able to understand not only her father's story better but also those of others who were in the camp. She has come across many stories of men who were at least as damaged by their experiences as her father had been. She explained:

I met a crew mate who was on my father's ship when it was torpedoed. He was so shattered by his experiences as a prisoner of war and so ill with diseases during his captivity that he has never managed to sleep in a bed with his wife. He had suffered from chronic dysentery during captivity and this continued to trouble him when he came home. If he got anxious he would find he had soiled his bed. He was so frightened of doing this when he was sleeping with his wife that he never dared to sleep in a bed with her. It is amazing that such women were able to stand by their men under what can only be described as abnormal and extreme circumstances.

Chris is not bitter towards the Japanese but she is bitter about the war that destroyed her parents' lives. 'In doing the research I have done over the last few years I have come to realize what a dreadful thing war is. It has such a devastating effect on the long-term prospects for survivors and that is something that is little understood and seldom discussed. I think only children of prisoners of the Japanese can really understand what we went through during our childhood and how our lives were affected by what happened to our parents.'

Chris Best has thought, written and spoken about her parents' experiences in the post-war era and she admitted that although it took her a long time to come to terms with things after the war, she now feels at ease. Through her work as an educational psychologist she has seen a lot of children who were in a far worse situation than she felt she had been and this helped to give her a perspective on her own life as well as helping her to advise people who came to her.

Celia Kerr's life has been shaped to a great extent by what happened during the war but she had never really pinned down before how it all pointed back to the moment of her parents' separation in 1940.

Celia described her family as completely dislocated and fractured by the Second World War. A once happy marriage was disrupted by separation and the cracks that appeared during the war years were never healed. Celia's parents, Tom and Ann Reed, were married in Newcastle in 1928 in their mid-twenties. Born into a working-class family, Tom worked hard and by the outbreak of the war had become chief clerk for the Cooperative Society. Two boys were born in 1929 and 1935 and a little girl in 1937. Tom Reed was declared unfit by an army medical board on the grounds that he had problems with his ears. He continued to work in Newcastle and took on the responsibility of a special constable during the war. As the city was a target for German bombing, Ann and Tom decided it would be wise to evacuate the boys. They were sent to Kendal in Cumbria. Ann was distraught and persuaded Tom that she should go to Kendal to be with them, taking her baby daughter.

For four years the family was divided by just ninety miles. Without a car Tom had to rely on the cross-country train service, not improved during the war, to visit his wife and children. During four years he managed a once-yearly visit. Celia said:

My mother loved living in Cumbria. It was a much easier way of life there during the war because they did not feel rationing in the same way. My mother had an allotment so she had fresh vegetables to eat. In fact she used to take pride and joy in sending home food parcels to her family in Newcastle. And in Kendal she developed a sense of independence. The three children grew used to my mother's ways and lost touch with my father.

In 1944 Tom Reed thought it would be safe for his wife and children to return to Newcastle. The risk of bombing had receded and he wanted to be reunited with his family. 'Reading between the lines I gather that at this point the family began to unravel. My sister did not know this man who was her father and it seems never grew to like him. Meanwhile the two adults found themselves strangers to each other. Both had lived the way they chose and obviously found it difficult to readjust.'

They had another son in 1945 and in 1947 Celia was born.

I grew up thinking that Kendal must be a magical place because of the way my mother and older siblings talked about it so much. Because my parents had frequent loud arguments my youngest brother and I had difficult childhoods. These arguments were a feature of family life until my father's death in 1970. My mother ran a somewhat chaotic house, which my father hated and complained about. She would do things that seemed to me designed to annoy him although I think she found him impossible to satisfy at times. Although he became successful and even at one point chaired the Milk Marketing Board it did not make her happy. She was proud of him, yes, and we had lots of things that my friends did not have. We had a fitted kitchen and central heating in about 1960, for example, and there was no shortage of money, but there was no obvious love between my parents. They were both strong characters and neither found it easy. I will never forget the time my eldest brother told us that he could actually remember our parents 'cuddling each other' and the rest of us fell about laughing. None of us could imagine that kind of behaviour.

My sister changed her surname to Kendal in her forties because the years she spent there were the happiest of her life. I think it is significant that I never saw the Lake District until I was almost eighteen. When I did it felt like home and my husband and I moved here on his retirement over thirty years later. After Mother died my eldest brother expressed the view that it would have been better if our parents had divorced at the end of the war. Their lives changed completely when they got back together.

Perhaps I should add that part of the unhappiness in my childhood was to do with two very strict but inconsistent parents, both determined that I should not turn out as headstrong as my sister. I grew up hearing my parents telling my older siblings never to darken their door again and I secretly sobbed my heart out fearing

I'd lost them forever. Invariably forgiveness came at Christmas. I managed my own foolish sabotage by becoming pregnant at seventeen and telling no one until five months had passed. After the birth I kept my son with the support of my family. Those were grim, shameful years for an unmarried mother. There is no doubt in my mind that the family was repeatedly fractured by the effects of the war and continues to feels its repercussions. I believe it has had a profound effect on the whole structure and fabric of our society.

Like Celia, John Porter made Cumbria his home. Now in his early sixties, John is an Anglo-American mountaineer. He is also a poet and a wonderful storyteller. His father, Eric, was Cumbrian born but now lives in Canada. He might have been able to look back in his old age with pride on his war. He was, after all, in what many believed to be the most glamorous arm of the services: the Royal Air Force. Yet he cannot.

Born in Barrow-in-Furness in 1917, Eric Orwell Porter was the second son of a local council official, Herbert Porter, and his wife, Evelyn. He was educated at Barrow Grammar School and was a bright pupil. His older brother, Ivor, was the fair-haired blue-eyed boy of the family, the focus of his father's energies and ambitions. Eric was destined for a job in the local post office with a view to staying in Barrow to look after his parents as they got older. Life as a future family caretaker did not appeal so, at the age of fifteen, Eric made other plans. Keen to continue his education and hone his fine intellect, he applied for and won a prestigious scholarship to RAF Cranwell at Sleaford in Lincolnshire where he began as an apprentice in the early 1930s. As the decade drew to a close and war became inevitable he accepted that he would have to fight. 'My father was a man who just got on with whatever job was to be done,' John explained.

At the outbreak of the war Eric was a navigator but within weeks he was training to be a pilot. He was much liked both in the officers' mess and amongst the ground crew, where his humble background meant he was seen as 'one of them'. John has sometimes wondered whether the reason Eric was a bomber pilot and not a fighter pilot had something to do with his working-class roots. 'My father never had a chip on his shoulder, though. He knew that he was good at what he did and his intellect was exceptional so he had no need to feel inferior. He had read and understood the training manuals for all the aircraft he flew. He really knew what he was doing.' Eric later told his son that of the class that graduated in 1939 only one out of thirteen was still alive after the Second World War. 'I think this must have affected my father and contributes to what I believe is probably survivor guilt.'

Within two years Eric, at the age of twenty-two, was a squadron leader, flying for coastal command in a bomber squadron. He saw action all over Europe flying bombers mainly over the fjords of Norway but also over Malta, where he was stationed for a while, and the Middle East, before being sent out to Canada to train pilots. This was an unexpected reprieve from the war and came about when one of his lungs collapsed as he took off in a Lancaster on a mission. He overcame the pain and managed to get the plane safely back on the ground. A doctor specified an extensive period of rest, hence the posting to Canada. While there he met Mary Dennison, the only daughter of a Canadian nurse and her American husband, John, who had been at one time the mayor of Springfield. The family could trace their ancestry back to the *Mayflower* on Mary's father's side and were related to James Monroe, the fifth president of the United States, on her mother's. Eric and Mary had a brief romance and were married very quickly, a wartime union, John believed, when both were looking for comfort and fun. Eric was dashingly good-looking with a wicked sense of humour. Their first child, Mary Evelyn, was born in October 1942 in Truro, Nova Scotia. 'I was born two months premature,' Mary Evelyn wrote in an email after John encouraged her to get involved in telling their family story, 'my dad arrived the night after I was born and came straight to the hospital (because I was premature my mother had me in the hospital). Dad had been taken off flying for several months and was training new pilots – RCAF as well as Americans, Australians, New Zealanders and others. Because of his sick leave, Dad was there when I was an infant.'

When Mary Evelyn was about a year old Eric went back to flying sorties in Europe and Mary decided to go to England to be closer to her husband. 'This is the beginning of my memories,' Mary Evelyn wrote. 'We sailed to Liverpool and I remember boat drills on deck, once a week. One night the porthole blew open in a storm and there was water all over the cabin.' They stayed with Eric's parents until April 1946.

> Both my grandparents played various instruments and my grand-mother wrote children's songs. My grandfather had taught himself Greek, wrote a novel in Greek and also a number of poems, 'The Shadow on the Wall' being the most well known, published in several anthologies. I remember playing 'Jack be Nimble, Jack be Quick, Jack Jump Over the Candle Stick' with Grandad. At the word *over*, Grandad would lift me up and swing me over the candlestick.

At that stage Eric was flying from a nearby airfield and Mary Evelyn remembers him buzzing the cottage in Barrow on the way back from a mission to let them know that he was all right. The great drama of the period as far as she was concerned was when Eric accidentally ran over her kitten on his motorbike. 'Of course

I was far too young to comprehend the larger reality of the war but I do remember that when there were air-raid warnings over Barrow and Dad was staying at the bungalow at Green Road he refused to come into the shelter, preferring to stay in his own bed. Apparently, there was little or no tension between my parents at this time. My uncle Ivor remembers them as being happy in Green Road.'

In 1946 Mary decided to return to the United States. She was expecting her second baby and John was born in Massachusetts later that year. 'It is my understanding that mum did not want to remain in England; I would guess partly because of the poverty and privations in England at that time, but also because Mum's parents were fairly well off and had a nice home in a pleasant neighbourhood of Springfield, Mass.'

It was here that tensions began to develop. After the war Eric wanted to get out of the RAF as quickly as possible. Although he would later tell John he had enjoyed his time as a pilot and that the war had been, for him, one of the best times of his life, he was eager to start a career. He arrived in Massachusetts in 1947 and moved in with his parents-in-law. Mary Evelyn remembered that period clearly: 'my mother's mother had a nursery rhyme that she would say to me: "*Fee, Fi, Fo, Fum* I smell the blood of an Englishman." My grandmother would chase me around the living room as she said this. I can remember my father becoming so upset that he almost cried. My mother asked her mother to stop saying this rhyme and I guess she did, but I know that there was conflict between my dad and his mother-in-law.'

For about three years the family lived with Mary's parents. In 1949 John Dennison died and his wife developed cancer.

My mother discovered that her parents were deeply in debt and once the debts were paid off there was very little money left. My father was working near Boston at this time and we did not see him much. My mother took my grandmother back home to Nova Scotia to die and we then moved to Cincinnati, Ohio, where my father had been transferred by General Electric from their plant in Lynn, Mass. This was in 1950.

Eric found the family a rented apartment: they were never again to live as a family in a house that they owned. 'My Dad went through a tremendous depression. I remember him crying at the kitchen table. At one point he disappeared and my mother found him living in a one-room flat above a bar in a Boston slum when he had been temporarily shifted back to Lynn. My mum was also depressed. She hated Cincinnati. We had very little money and I remember Mum washing sheets in the bathtub.' John summed up his own memory of that period:

This part of my parents' life must have been very difficult for my mother. My recollection is that my father was seldom at home. He was always being moved around for his work and we hardly ever saw him. I think it was more difficult for my sister than for me because I barely knew him. My mother was a saint to put up with my father. He lacked any real appreciation of her loyalty and his wicked sense of humour could be cruel. They used to have terrible arguments but now my father would argue that they had had the perfect marriage.

Mary Evelyn began to develop her own psychological problems and her parents sought help:

I don't know what the psychiatrist advised, but in December 1952, I was sent back to England to attend boarding school. My mother used all the money that had been set aside in a trust for me and my brother to put me in the school . . . Unfortunately, I continued to have psychological problems which followed me into adulthood. On holidays at first I lived with my uncle Ivor, Dad's brother, and Aunt Ann, but there were problems because Aunt Ann did not like me. She invented punishments for me. Once when I was slow to get ready, she made me go to a pantomime in my underwear so that I had to keep my coat on during the entire show. Aunt Ann was later diagnosed as a schizophrenic and died in an institution.

To Mary Evelyn's intense relief she was sent to spend the holidays with her grandparents in Barrow-in-Furness. 'What joy!' she wrote. 'Apparently the concern of my uncle and my mother had been that my grandmother was not well educated and had a Cumbrian accent, but to me she was a loving, caring grandmother.' Mary Evelyn remained in England until she was thirteen when she and her grandmother sailed back to the USA. Life in the United States did not settle down as the family might have hoped. Mary Evelyn was still described as mentally unstable and was sent to a boarding school in Canada. It was a disaster for her. She was more advanced academically than the children of her own age and was teased for her strange accent and her habit of referring to people as Mr and Mrs. 'Neither my mum nor my dad appeared to understand in any way what was wrong with me. I began to rebel wearing make-up and tight pants and so naturally I was punished. My father was going through another period of depression and crying at night. My brother thought I was just strange.'

Eric had always had a great passion for the outdoors and would take first Mary Evelyn and then later John on long walks in the countryside. Mary Evelyn remembered the conversations on these occasions:

Dad told me there were only two people he had loved in his life: '. . . one a man and one a woman . . . my co-pilot who I looked up to and respected and your mother'. Then he would say something about his co-pilot being killed on a mission in Norway. Sometimes he would talk about a fellow pilot who came back from a mission and went into the infirmary complaining of a headache and when he took his helmet off the top of his head came off with it. He always told me that there is nothing more important than supporting your buddies. Dying is not that important but living with the shame of letting down your comrades is.

As John grew up and showed an interest in outdoor life, Eric became more engaged with him, taking him out into the New Hampshire countryside, and sharing his love of the mountains. On those walks he would sometimes talk obliquely about the war, telling him how hard it had been, particularly when crews did not return after missions. Yet he never wanted to have anything to do with the RAF in later life; reunions and the social scene did not interest him. Later on he refused to become involved in putting together a book about the history of his squadron. For him that part of his life was finished with. Eric would never be drawn on the details but John was aware that his time in the RAF had had a very profound effect on his life.

John's interest in climbing grew so Eric encouraged him. 'He used to think nothing of leaving me on the side of the freeway at five in the morning in a blizzard so that I could go ice climbing with my older companions.' Later, when John began climbing in the Himalayas and the expeditions became more dangerous, friends were lost, dying in the high mountains: 'You develop an ability to make light of difficult situations. One day you might be having tea with climbers at a high camp and the next day one or more of them might not return, an accident perhaps, but people die. My father would say that my climbing drove my mother to drink, but I don't think so.' The losses that John experienced, albeit under very different circumstances, gave him some view of how his father had coped with the death of colleagues during the war.

One thing that obsessed Eric was LMF, lack of moral fibre. 'Anybody who cracked up was classified LMF – probably a fate worse than death for most. He told me he could always spot when pilots were going to be killed. "They would weaken and go to the bar," he claimed. But he also said that some people were grounded <u>because</u> of their drinking – a way around being labelled LMF.' Eric seldom drank and later in life became teetotal.

In 1967 John was called up to join the US Army to be sent out to Vietnam:

When I was drafted and had missed all the appeals set up because I was climbing in Alaska (as a full-time student, all I had to do was get my forms returned on time), I thought I had only the choice of jail or going to Vietnam. It was my dad who convinced me to take out British citizenship. We did that at the consulate in Boston in less than forty-eight hours and I was gone. He did give me a grilling though, and it has stayed with me ever since: 'If you do not go, someone will be called to go in your place. That person might be wounded or killed or suffer your fate. Can you live with that thought?' I must admit that even at the time it had me hanging in the balance – he was absolutely right and I did not want to be classified by my dad as LMF. But I disagreed so much with war that I chose to go to a completely new country at twenty – no friends, no chance of return I thought. He has many times reminded me of that awful truth and of course someone did suffer my other fate, but he has never gone so far as to classify me as LMF.

When Eric retired from General Electric he and Mary moved to Canada to a farm which she had inherited from her mother's family. The farm was in a part of Nova Scotia where life was similar to that lived by Scottish crofters of the past. Eric took up running and ran dozens of marathons, setting records for his age group and sometimes almost beating John, fit, strong and thirty years his junior. They both ran the London Marathon in 1980 and Eric ran his last half marathon in 2003 at the age of eighty-six and his last full marathon about five years before that.

What John cannot say is whether his father's character was changed by his experiences as a pilot in the Second World War. What he is sure of, however, is that to have been a squadron commander in his early twenties represented a peak in his life and one he could never better. 'I am amazed at his tenacity and his love of life. He still lives on his own and is fiercely independent. He never celebrated his own successes and I do wonder whether his determination to cling on to life has something to do with his survivor's guilt.'

In assessing the effect of the war on her family, Mary Evelyn wrote:

The most pervasive effect of the war on my family has been separation. I was in the UK when John was growing up, then he left the US at twenty. My parents were at once joined and separated emotionally by the war. I believe that my mum and dad had an understanding of a shared view during the war and that living in the US after the war shattered that. Americans just didn't get it. Yes, many young Americans had gone off to war in the Pacific and America shared the tragedy of loss with Europe, but the war had not touched the mainland of the US.

A few years ago we watched a show featuring the folk singer Pete Seeger and Dad wrote the only poem I remember him composing. It is very simple: 'He was shaped by the songs of peace and I by the winds of war.'

Speaking about her mother she is frank:

> The effects of the war on my mother . . . 'Chin up.' Never talk about illness or unhappiness. My mum became an alcoholic. Dad did not allow either my brother or me to come to see her when she died because he held us at least partially responsible for her troubles. The effects of the war on my brother? He left the United States to avoid being drafted to fight in Vietnam. My father believes that he shirked his responsibility and condemned others to fight in his place. My brother became a world-famous mountain climber proving to himself that he has the courage to face life-threatening conditions just as Dad did even though the setting was not a war zone.

John was horrified by this description: 'No. I have no ambition to prove anything – never did – that is anathema to me. I do believe that achievement has value, but ambition is the road to hell. It was just called climbing back then.'

And of Mary Evelyn herself: 'I became a coordinator for Amnesty International, learned fluent Spanish and Portuguese and went undercover into Argentina during the dirty war of the 1970s collecting the names of torturers, the disappeared and the location of secret detention camps. In that way, I proved to myself that I have the courage to face life-threatening conditions just as Dad did.'

She added: 'It is strange, it is almost as if I have been waiting for someone to ask me these questions most of my life.'

11

THE LEGACY OF MY FATHER

I could have loved him even more . . . if only I had understood.

Di Elliott

If the war damaged some children's lives it also had the effect of making others determined to understand more about what their fathers had been through. The three women featured in this chapter all had fathers who were taken prisoner by the Japanese and all three have made successful attempts to put their experiences to good use for the benefit of other people who were in a similar situation.

In October 1945 Carol Smith was in her classroom in Great Yarmouth when the headmistress walked in and said she wanted to see her. Like generations of children before and since, she was terrified and wondered what on earth she had done wrong. Her heart in her mouth, she followed:

Outside in the hall, one of my aunts was waiting and, standing me on a nearby large trunk, she put my coat on. I asked where I was going and remember her reply: 'Your mummy needs you.' I recall entering our house and seeing my mother sitting on the old wooden chair in front of the cooking range; she was crying. My grandmother and another aunt were there and one of them lifted me up on to her lap. My grandmother told me: 'Mummy is crying because your daddy will not be coming home any more.' The enormity of her words was lost on a five-year-old, who didn't know who or what 'daddy' was.

Carol had no recollection of her father. She was born in 1939, the second daughter of Ida May and William 'Bill' Smith. Her older sister, Olive, was four at the outbreak of the Second World War and six when Lance Corporal Bill Smith sailed to the Far East with the 6th Battalion, the Royal Norfolk Regiment. He was captured in Singapore and was sent from Changi on Singapore Island with F Force to work on the Thailand–Burma Railway. Ida heard that her husband had been taken prisoner at Singapore but she never heard anything else from him until the fateful day in October when she learned he had died, and she subsequently discovered he was buried in Burma. She never knew what had happened to her husband and as she had last heard that he was in Singapore, part of her refused to believe that he could have been in Burma, a thousand miles away, and she harboured a hope that he would one day return.

Carol's memory of her early childhood was of her mother's sacrifice in keeping her two daughters fed and warm. After Ida learned of her husband's death she became ill and extremely thin: 'Looking back we were terribly poor. My mother had only a war widow's pension, which was a pittance,' Carol wrote, 'but I can never remember ever being cold or hungry: I think my mother went without food so we could eat. We lived in a house that had been bombed. It had no roof on the top storey. We lived with aunts and cousins and my memory of my childhood is a happy one.' However, she remembered her mother having mixed feelings about Christmas and birthdays. She loved Christmas time and enjoyed all the old family traditions, making her own puddings and cakes, but it was these happy times that also made her sad. She and Bill had shared a birthday and were the same age. On their birthday, 28 October, Carol remembered she once locked herself in her room. 'I think she couldn't cope with the memories that this anniversary awakened in her but she wouldn't talk about it in detail so I didn't understand and certainly didn't equate it with the death of my father. I asked her once why she did this. She just replied: "When you grow up and meet someone you love, you will understand." '

As she grew up, Carol would occasionally be asked about her father and she would simply reply that he had died during the war. Those words, she said, meant very little to her.

Carol's mother died in 1993 and she was sorting through her personal effects when she found a box full of letters, photographs, poems from her father and documents sent by the War Office. It struck her how little she knew about him. In one letter written from Malaya shortly before he was captured, Bill had written: 'Give my love to my Olive and my baby Carol.' 'I wept. These words were from a father I didn't know and now it was too late.' Her sense of loss was enormous and she regretted not asking her mother more about the young man she had married before the war. But like so many children she had grown up more concerned with the future than wanting to know about the past. She married Ron Cooper in February 1960 and was busy with a young family and her house in Norfolk and had little time to think about her late father.

Then in 1994 something extraordinary happened. It was Friday 16 December, she remembered. Ron showed her an article in their local paper about a diary that had been auctioned in Hull,

> a diary written by a local soldier during his two and a half years in a Japanese prison camp. I read the name and address of the soldier and realized, with a tremendous shock, that I was reading about my father. The article gave his name: Lance Corporal William Smith, and the address where I was born in 1939: No. 13, Row 11, Great Yarmouth. The article mentioned my mother and sister who were both dead, but I knew neither of them ever knew the diary existed. All they had known was that my father died in a Japanese prison camp and was buried in Burma.

Carol contacted the man who had purchased the diary but he refused to sell it to her. He handed it over to the Royal Norfolk Regimental Museum who kindly agreed to send her a transcript although they would not let her have the original.

> Reading this copy was a traumatic experience. The whole diary was written as a letter to my mother, with many moving and loving poems. Despite what he was going through, he always remembered our birthdays with a loving word and prayed and dreamed of coming home. But he never came home. I wept when I read of his determination to stay alive. To the very end he was so sure that, although so many were dying all around him, *he* was going to make it, *he* was going to come back. He was starving, he was very ill, his few clothes were filthy, but he still managed to write in the diary: 'Don't worry Ida darling, I'm coming back to you one day.' The last entry in the diary was 8 December 1943, when he wrote, 'having another bad attack of malaria'. He was then in a camp called Tambaya in Burma. He died nine days later on 17 December. I was to learn later that

he had died of malaria, malnutrition, diphtheria and cardiac beriberi.

Bill Smith had been a fit, strong 26-year-old soldier when he left Britain in October 1941. Two years and two months later he was a wreck of a human being unable to cling on to life. Carol learned that he was one of the men considered by the doctors to be so sick that he could not be evacuated to the hospital camps downriver as he would almost certainly die on the journey.

He had been ill even before he went up to Thailand. He had had diphtheria, which had weakened his heart, so that on the long march up towards the Burma border he would fall behind the rest of the party. As a result he never had a mate and now I know how important it was for men to have 'mates' to help them when times were difficult, maybe just to get them a bit of extra food when they were ill. Well that seems not to have been the case for my father and it is very sad to reflect on that.

What was poignant above all else for Carol was that her mother had not known of the diary which would have thrown so much light on his life after he was captured. And she felt that Ida would have taken comfort in the poems that Bill had written to her.

This extraordinary discovery of her father's wartime diary changed Carol's life. In her own words, up until then she was just an ordinary housewife with a husband, three grown-up children, a house and a garden. Now she had had her whole world turned upside down and things would never be the same again. She felt she owed it to her mother to get possession of the diary and set about doing so. In 1996 a BBC producer, who had heard about Carol's story, asked her to make a documentary with him. Initially Carol agreed as she hoped it would mean she could get some media attention and 'then someone out there might have the answer to the endless task of trying to acquire the diary for my family'. Filming commenced and the producer, Dick Meadows, approached the man who had bought the diary in Hull two years earlier. He succeeded in persuading him to sell it to her for £300. 'It was worth every penny,' she wrote.

In November 1996 she went to Thailand for her first visit, accompanied by the documentary team. It was an emotional trip and she was often in tears as she stood where her father and thousands of other men had toiled in the jungle to build the railway. 'Standing in Hellfire Pass where 700 men died of brutality in a few short weeks brought choking tears. There were more tears again when early one day I climbed into one of the original metal trucks which had transported hundreds of prisoners from Singapore to Ban Pong in Thailand.' Bill had written in the diary about the extreme discomfort of that journey when men were packed thirty to a truck for five days on the 1000-mile journey up the Malayan peninsula, days spent with little food and few stops, when men suffering from dysentery had little choice but to relieve themselves where they stood. Already at 8:30 in the morning the sides of the trucks were almost too hot to touch. What would they have been like at midday and in those cramped conditions and squalor? she wondered.

In Kanchanaburi Carol met an Australian called Doug Ogden who was making the same journey as she was, retracing his own father's footsteps. It turned out the two men had been in the same prison camps in 1943. Doug's father had died at Songkurai, close to the Burma border, and is buried in the Commonwealth War Graves Commission's cemetery at Thanbyuzayat in Burma (Myanmar) with Carol's father. Together they went up to Hellfire Pass to see where the railway had been cut through sheer rock in the jungle. 'As we talked, Doug was overcome with emotion and started to cry. I put my arms around him and we just sat and hugged each other.' Doug's father, Jacob Donovan Walker Ogden of Oakleigh in Victoria, had died in August 1943, four months before Bill Smith. The discovery of their joint quest forged a special bond between them and later, when Carol was unable to get into Burma on her British passport, Doug was able to lay flowers at her father's grave and sent her photographs of his visit. It was the first time she had ever seen her father's headstone.

'The whole journey from Kanchanaburi to the Three Pagodas Pass on the Burma border was one of emotion,' Carol wrote, 'passing through camps like Nike where my father wrote: "It seems like it will never end, but one must keep smiling and eating the rice. I pray to God that it won't be long now, over 2000 have died so far since we left Changi."'

One thing that struck Carol on her visit to Thailand was the lack of any memorial from the British government to the men who had died not in battle but of disease, neglect, malnutrition and brutality. Standing under a baking sun in the beautifully laid out war cemetery at Kanchanaburi she felt 'a dreadful injustice when I realized that nowhere along the length of the railway had I seen a memorial, a plaque or a stone from the British government, honouring the thousands of British servicemen who had died there. The cemeteries were beautifully kept but I felt that my father and all those who had suffered deserved a more fitting tribute.'

So, on her return to Britain, Carol began, at the age of nearly sixty, what has become her life's work. She determined to create a lasting memorial to the men like her father who had not returned from their captivity in the Far East. She began to bombard the government, MPs and officials with letters enquiring why there was no memorial to the prisoners. The reply she received was clear: 'It is not the policy of the government to erect memorials to servicemen. Any memorials have to come from private fundraising.'

She put an advertisement in her local newspaper in 1997 calling for the children and families of Far Eastern prisoners of war to join her in asking the government 'to pay these men the honour they truly deserved'. The response was encouraging and in November 1997 she founded the Children and Families of the Far Eastern Prisoners of War (COFEPOW). Seven years later there were over 700 members from all over the world, from as far afield as Australia, Taiwan and Borneo but also from Europe and America. COFEPOW became a charity and through Carol's single-minded determination and dogged persistence a building was erected at the National Memorial Arboretum in Staffordshire and opened to the public in August 2005 on the sixtieth anniversary of the end of the war in the Pacific. The building is a memorial that commemorates all FEPOWs, not just those who died. When asked what drives her she replied:

> I work hard and I work long hours for what I believe in. I will always feel guilty that I lived most of my life not knowing how my father suffered and died and never really giving him too much thought. Now he is so often in my thoughts and always in my heart. If I ever have doubts about what I am trying to achieve, I look at his photograph. Then I read the motto on a small bookmark that I took from the hotel near Hellfire Pass and the 'Death Railway'. It says quite simply: 'One step at a time you may walk over the highest mountain.'

Carol's personal mountain has been the creation of a remarkable memorial to the Far Eastern prisoners of war and her reward comes from former FEPOWs who thank her for creating the memorial building. 'Over the past three years since the building opened I have received many, many acknowledgements from FEPOWs. Some confess to being in tears when they see that the story of their three and a half years of suffering will not be forgotten.'

In April 2001 Carol succeeded where she had failed in 1996 in getting permission to visit Thanbyuzayat War Cemetery in Burma. It was a journey she had wanted to make ever since she had discovered her father's diary:

> We had to stop at many checkpoints to have our passports inspected but finally we reached Thanbyuzayat. I stopped at the local market and purchased armfuls of fresh flowers for both my father's grave and others. They probably didn't last long because the heat was intense but it was the first time in my life that I was able to buy something for my father. Only the children of POWs buried in the Far East can understand and feel the pain caused by the knowledge that their fathers – that most of them never knew – died agonizing deaths, all alone, thousands of miles from their families.

On her visit to Thailand in 1996 Carol had taken a small casket with some of her mother's ashes in to bury in her father's grave, but because she was unable to enter Burma, she could not fulfil her wish. She gave the casket to Rod Beattie, who is responsible for the Commonwealth war cemeteries in Thailand, and he promised to get in touch with his Burmese counterpart and arrange for an interment. On this visit to Burma she took another small casket of ashes and began to bury them in the grave. When the gardeners saw her they rushed over to explain that Bill's grave had already been opened a few years earlier and the first casket placed in the grave. She felt an enormous sense of gratitude towards the people who had respected her parents' memory fifty years after the war.

Carol is convinced that by visiting her father's grave she has carried out her mother's wishes:

> When I first found out about my father on discovering his diary I never dreamed that I would actually be able to visit his grave nor travel into Thailand to see where he had been as a prisoner. As far as my mother was concerned Burma was a closed country half a world away and by the time it opened up she was not fit to go there. But I know without doubt that she would have wanted to go. She kept all the letters she received from the British Legion, in reply to hers, constantly asking if they were arranging visits for widows to Burma. Sadly when it was possible she was not strong enough to make such an arduous journey. So what she wanted to do, I have done in her place.

In 2007 Carol went back to Thailand for a further visit and spent a week with Rod Beattie retracing the steps her father and other prisoners had taken with F Force.

> It is one thing to read a list of camp names but something else to visit the places and feel the atmosphere for oneself. One day I saw a woman washing her clothes in the river while her little children splashed around naked in the water. This was the kind of scene that my father too would have witnessed. Later I found myself standing in the jungle and wondering whether the prisoners lay on their beds and heard the lovely noises of the jungle, the birds and the bull frogs. As I watched the butterflies I thought how beautiful this place is and yet for a few short years in the 1940s it was hell on earth. All the horror is washed away now but it <u>was</u> there.

As a postscript to her short memoir of her father she quoted a poem that he had written to her mother just before he joined the army, which Carol had found in her mother's papers after her death. 'It was written on a very small piece of paper and was in a tiny envelope addressed to his "Darling Ida". It reflects what a truly wonderful person he was. My life would have been far, far richer had he lived.'

> There is no hour that passes by
> But some sweet thought of you
> Shines like a lamp on high
> To light my whole life through
>
> There is no day, but at its end
> My prayers for you I say
> That God will guard and keep you
> Forever Mine Alone, Darling Ida May

Carol Cooper's story is a remarkable one and through her energy and foresight many children of former FEPOWs have been able to understand more about the stories of their fathers' lives. But she also wants people to understand what women like her mother went through. For years Ida mourned a man she had been married to for just seven years. The war had robbed her of her husband but also her children of their father. Carol concluded: 'If we don't do this research now the younger generation will not have the stories to understand what people went through in the war. It is so important to keep this part of our history going.'

Another, equally impressive daughter of the wartime story is Di Elliott. I first met Di on a research trip to Australia in 2006. We spent many hours on the balcony of her lovely house in Canberra talking about her work for Australian POWs. For the last fourteen years she has devoted herself to researching not only her father's life but also the lives of other men who were imprisoned in the Japanese POW camps.

Di and her husband Paul went to Thailand in 1997 to visit their daughter who was working at the Australian Embassy in Bangkok. They planned to attend the Anzac Day dawn service in Hellfire Pass and to present the museum about to be built there with a collection of some of the one hundred books that she had been amassing for their proposed library. Unlike Carol Cooper's memorial building in Staffordshire, the museum at Hellfire Pass was funded by the Australian government who had bowed to pressure from former prisoners of war, led by an indomitable man called Tom Morris. A plaque had been unveiled in 1987 at Hellfire Pass and ten years later, on Anzac Day, Di witnessed the first sod being turned to mark the commencement of the building of the memorial museum. Sadly she could not be there to see the museum opened officially by the Australian prime minister in April 1998 because days after the 1997 ceremony Di, Paul and their daughter were involved in a major traffic accident that very nearly killed Di. Her life hung in the balance for several weeks as she underwent surgery in Kanchanaburi for severe injuries to her spine.

The hospital is close to what remains in operation of the Thailand–Burma Railway. On many occasions I lay in the bed drawing from the strength of my dad and those other incredible POWs who had toiled there fifty-four years previously. As I struggled to survive I concluded that many of them had come home after suffering far more horrendous conditions than I was suffering. I was in a modern hospital with modern drugs, plenty of food and the most caring doctors and nursing staff one could wish for. The only thing that I and the POWs had in common was the care we received. They too had amazing doctors and medical orderlies who took such care with their patients when practically all they had to offer were their healing hands. I am convinced to this day that when I was at my lowest point I received assistance from some forces more powerful than any medicine. I certainly felt a presence that helped get me back to Australia.

Di's recovery has been a slow and painful process, with other operations carried out in Canberra, but she has continued with her research into the POW story.

Her interest in the story of her father's experiences as a POW during the Second World War began three years earlier in 1994, almost twenty years after his death at the age of sixty-nine. As a child she had known nothing of what he had been through and had never thought to ask about the man who was to her 'just a cranky old bastard who, for some reason, was always sick and miserable. Our lives seemed to be disrupted so often because of him and I always wondered why I had to be the only one with a miserable father.'

Di's father, Fred Howe, was born in March 1906 in Uralla, New South Wales. He married Elsie in 1926 and they had six children, two of whom had died before the war. Fred was working as a telephone linesman when he enlisted for service on 1 June 1940 at the age of thirty-four. At that stage his children were aged between one and eleven years old. He joined the 2/19 Battalion of the AIF and was posted to their Signals platoon. He was sent to Malaya where he fought in the Battle of Muar against the Japanese (18–22 January 1942) and then at Bakri and Parit Sulong on the Malayan peninsula. 'The battle almost decimated the unit and ended even more tragically when they were unable to carry their wounded with them. Forced to make a rapid retreat, they left behind 110 wounded Australians and 35 wounded Indians at Parit Sulong. The Japanese massacred all but two of the men left behind.'

Fred and the other survivors of the 2/19 Battalion were taken prisoner on Singapore on 15 February 1942. Six months later he sailed on the *Celebes Maru* with A Force, under the command of Brigadier Varley and Lieutenant Colonel Charles Anderson VC, to Burma. As a POW he worked for the Japanese on various projects including, of course, on the Thailand–Burma Railway where he remained on maintenance gangs until the end of the war, when he returned to Singapore via Thailand, arriving back in Australia on 20 October 1945 aboard a New Zealand hospital ship, the *Tamaroa*. Di was born three years after his return so that she was almost a generation younger than her oldest siblings.

She says: 'I cannot recall exactly when I had first learned where Dad had been during the war but I do know that it was many years after his death. As a child I remember him marching on Anzac Day and getting drunk afterwards, so I knew he had been to the war. I also knew it had something to do with Japan because Mum would not allow anything "Made in Japan" into our home.'

In 1994 Di made up her mind to find out all she could about her father and through doing so, she hoped, she would understand aspects of her own life that had been shaped by a difficult environment at home. 'My very early memories of my dad are of his heated arguments with my mother. I do not recall any physical violence but the raised voices were certainly very threatening to a young girl. I also recall his heavy drinking which, in most instances, led to the arguments.' Fred was persuaded to give up alcohol but this merely made him very irate with others who drank and in particular with his son who was drinking heavily at this stage. Di's brother was violent and her father blamed himself for all his problems, saying that he had been absent for a crucial part of his son's life and that this had led to all the problems. Tragically for the family, the problems did not resolve themselves and Di's brother eventually died in 1991, by his own hand.

Fred worked hard, she remembered, but he was also often ill, suffering with severe gastrointestinal problems that were almost certainly caused by disease and malnutrition during the war. 'I remember him being always very ill and moody. There were many times when he would lock himself in his bedroom and I was forbidden to go near him. Mum told me that it was his malaria back again. You would not know from one day to the next how to approach him. What you would say one day would be fine but say it the next day and all hell would break loose.'

When the children invited people back to the house her father did not like it and Di had the impression that he wanted his family all to himself. If people came round unexpectedly he would invariably retreat to his shed in the garden and when things were really bad for him he would take himself off with his fishing rod and disappear until long after dark. All this was part of her childhood. Unexplained and unfathomable.

One thing that made an impression on Di was her mother's ability to cope with her father. She had, Di realized, taken on the role of a carer as well as that of wife. She seemed to understand what he had been through and she never complained about what she had to do for him. Things were particularly bad in the last year of his life, Di recalled:

He suffered from horrendous haemorrhoids and the doctors didn't seem to be of any help in this matter. He always had diarrhoea and on a lot of occasions he didn't make it out of his bed to the toilet. This was when my mum took over. I never once recall her complaining about the work she had to do and a lot of it was not pleasant. As a matter of fact I don't ever recall her complaining, no matter what he did. I guess she understood it all. This is where my pain comes in, if only *I* had understood.

What Di experienced was shared by many children of service-men from the war, prisoners or not. Silence. Few men were willing to talk about the war to their families and ex-prisoners of the Japanese were more silent than almost any other group of men. 'Did they want to protect us or was it their way of protecting themselves?' she asked. 'We hear now that they were told to come home and forget what happened to them and their mates and get on with their lives. Their families were told when they did come home not to ask them any questions about what might have happened to them.' Di could accept this but why had the rest of her family kept silent?

'What I don't understand is why my brothers and sisters, who were all born before the war, didn't talk to me about that time in their lives. I was not born until three years after Dad came home so I was totally in the dark. Did my brothers and sisters not know much either or did they block out that part of their lives?' When Di, in recent years, did find out something about her father and related it to her sister she replied: 'Yes, I knew that.' She was surprised and could only conclude that the reason she had not been told was because she had not asked. 'My brother who was only one year of age when Dad went to war has recently spoken to me of his memories of Dad's return home. Then aged seven, he was terrified of this 'person' who was coming into his life for what felt like the first time. When he saw him alight from the train he was most relieved to see he just looked like any other man.'

Since Di began her research she has learned so much about what had made her father like he was. The three and a half years in Thailand and Burma had robbed him of his good health and to a certain extent his good humour. It was with great sadness that Di realized that she had barely known him and certainly never understood him. There was so much to discover, and the trips to

Thailand, when she walked along traces of the railway, helped to put the story into perspective.

> I have been in the company of men who worked there during those walks and I have found myself imagining that it is my dad talking to me of his experiences. How I envied my friends whose dads were relating their experiences. If only it could have been my dad telling me. How I wish we could go back and I could tell my dad that now I understand. I was not always the daughter my dear old dad deserved. I could have been more patient with him and forgiven him all the things about him that I didn't much like. I could have even loved him more – if only I had understood.

In her determination to find out about her father Di has spent the last fourteen years reading everything she can about the POWs of the Japanese, and not just those on the Thailand–Burma Railway. 'I have met and now claim many of these men as my very special friends. These men have a quality not found in others. I will admit that when thinking back to my dad, at times I can recall this quality in him too, but I was too focused in those days on his moods and illnesses. I can recall an amazing gentleness and a faraway look in his pale blue eyes and this I have seen in other ex-POWs.'

The first book Di read about the railway was Hugh Clarke's *A Life for Every Sleeper* which was published in 1988. It contains photographs taken during the construction of the railway and is one of the most remarkable records of that episode as it gives such a vivid first-hand account of what went on. One of the men mentioned in the book was Tom Morris from Canberra, who, like her father, had been a member of A Force. She wondered if she would be able to find him and if so, whether he would be prepared to talk to her about his ordeal. 'Well, I made one phone call and all the answers were "Yes". I arrived on Tom's doorstep with a bunch of flowers and a million questions. I was shaking so much it is a wonder the flowers had any heads left on them. Tom was so generous and actually lent me a copy of his personal story about his time as a soldier and as a POW.'

This was a great start for Di's researches and she and Tom and indeed his family became very close. 'I was devastated when Tom died on 25 June 2003 having rung me that very night to say goodbye.' For eight years, however, Tom encouraged Di to learn more about the whole POW story. He suggested books for her to read and answered as many of her endless questions as he could. Her library now has over 300 books and she has made four trips to Thailand and has met dozens of former POWs and their families.

At the outset of her research she came across a surprise stumbling block and one that very nearly knocked her off course. When she talked about going to Thailand for the first time her brother-in-law Hilton 'Tod' Morgan became very angry. He said she was only going to Thailand as a tourist and that a fortnight after her return she would forget everything and, anyway, how could she possibly understand what it was all about? Tod had himself been a prisoner of the Japanese and had been in Changi and then later in Japan. She was so taken aback by his anger that she nearly called off the journey for the sake of family harmony but then she thought: 'No, I know why I am doing this, he is quite wrong. Damn it. I was going, even if it meant he never spoke to me again.' She went to Thailand and Tod did indeed not speak to her for over a year. Finally, when he heard that she was intending to travel to Singapore to find out more about the whole story he relented and called her to say that she did, after all, seem serious about learning more about Fred.

From that day in 1995 until my brother-in-law died in 1999, every time I spoke to him I was told more of his wartime history, which also included stories about my dad, as at times they had worked closely together during the battle. He also related things to me about my father after the war and the effect of being a POW had had on both of them. He especially felt sorry for Dad following their return to Australia. My brother-in-law was living in Sydney where there was a facility for ex-POWs to visit during times of difficulties in coping with their being back home. There they could meet men in the same situation and talk. But for Dad, living in a very small country town, this facility didn't exist and it is felt this was the reason he tried to solve his problems with alcohol.

Di also learned that Tod believed that her father had saved his life during the final battle on Singapore Island and that when they returned home he became good friends with Fred. The bond between Fred and Tod had become even closer when Tod married Fred's older daughter, Pauline, in 1950. This perhaps went some way to explaining Tod's outburst when Di first told him she was going to Thailand. Between the returning POWs there was a bond of loyalty, friendship and common shared experience which could not be broken. If there were some threat, as he might have seen it, to the respect in which he held his friend, then he was prepared to sacrifice family ties over perceived disloyalty to Fred.

As Di's understanding of her father grew so did the realization of the way he was regarded by other people: 'In recent years the men who worked for him have told me of their utmost respect for him and how they appreciated being able to work with him. They have also told me that at times he would be so sick at work that he would have to spend some time lying down in the lunchroom. We knew none of this at home.'

What began as a genuine interest in her father's past has become an obsession. But not a selfish one. Di works as a volunteer at the Australian War Memorial in Canberra and despite her continuing disabilities as a result of the car accident she helps other people who are researching the POW story to find what they are looking for. She is as devoted to this work as Carol Cooper is to the COFEPOW story and is widely regarded as one of the most respected experts on this subject in Australia, although she herself would be the last to admit such a claim. Fellow Australian Carolyn Newman, who edited a book about POW children's experiences in 2005 to mark the sixtieth anniversary of the end of the war in the Pacific, wrote of Di: 'She has become a focus and source of support for many of the offspring of POWs, some of whom have been desperate to discuss their own experiences with someone who understands. Di doesn't receive a cent for all this; all her work is voluntary. Her enthusiasm and energy for her projects are daunting.' What drives Di is similar to that which drives Carol Cooper, the knowledge that this was something so enormous and of such great importance to her that she would probably spend the rest of her life learning about it. 'What keeps me going is other people, mostly Rod Beattie. Also I received so much help from people like Tom Morris and Rod when trying to learn about my dad, I think I now have the knowledge to help others. When you can steer someone in the right direction it sure makes you feel happy and I know how those people then feel as I was there one day myself.'

Di is not only involved in helping other people to find out more about their family history but she also works on the historical side of the Far Eastern prisoner of war story, tackling the continuing problem of record keeping. Meg Parkes, working on a project at the School of Tropical Medicine in Liverpool, is looking at a different aspect of the FEPOWs' story, that of the effect of captivity on their health. The studies into this subject began as early as the 1950s when Professor Brian Maegraith was approached, initially informally, by Philip Toosey who, as head of his local FEPOW branch on Merseyside and vice-president of the FEPOW Federation, was inundated by requests from former prisoners for help and information about chronic health issues. The arrangement was formalized in 1964 when Toosey became president of the School and from 1968 Drs Dion Bell and Geoffrey Gill worked on a research project to assess the extent of continuing tropical disease within the FEPOW community. Meg was invited to join the research project in 2006 to collect oral history from surviving FEPOWs and this work will eventually be published. Her interest stems from her childhood as the daughter of a prisoner of war who spent three and a half years in Java and Japan.

When Meg wrote the introduction to her first book, *Notify Alec Rattray . . .*, she observed: 'As a child I had no cognisance of a world before I had existed and I grew up accepting, without question, my life and family as just "normal".' Over her adult life she became much more aware of her parents as individuals and as a result of her publishing the story of her parents' lives during and after the Second World War she has become, like Carol and Di, completely absorbed in the history of that part of the war.

She came to this through her work on her father's diaries, letters, photographs and documents while she was still in her twenties. In this Meg is unusual as she had the opportunity to discuss her parents' past with them long before they died, so that her knowledge of the war is shaped both by information written at the time and subsequent conversations with her father.

Her father, Andrew Atholl Duncan, was a young Scottish officer who was taken prisoner on Java in 1942. He survived to return home after three and a half years during which he had kept a secret diary recording all aspects of his captivity – its boredoms, irritations, joys and moments of deep despair. What is remarkable about his diary, Meg observed, is the fact that it was written in the firm belief that it would be read in the future. She felt strongly that the subversive act of hiding it from the Japanese helped him to feel that in some small way he was winning against them. 'What is clear,' she wrote, 'is that he wanted the contents to be read and what is more he believed that they would be.' Unusual among former prisoners of war of the Far East, Atholl Duncan had written up his diaries in a volume that Meg knew from her childhood as a large, bound black-clothed book entitled 'Diary of a POW' that sat on the family's bookshelves for as long as she could remember.

It was a transcript, she discovered in her twenties, of nine notebooks and diaries that he had kept while in captivity. When she saw the original notebooks she wondered why there were pieces of blue tissue paper stuck over certain words or passages, and was astounded to discover that her grandfather had edited the notebooks before the transcript was typed up. 'Do you mean that Grandad edited your diary?' she asked her father, incredulous, unable to believe that anyone could feel they had the right to do such a thing. 'Och well, Maggie,' he replied, 'I didn't care what he did. I wanted nothing to do with it. Dad was only trying to protect me I suppose, in case it was ever published. It didn't bother me.' Predictably it bothered Meg and she felt, as she reread the diary, that it had been done 'to satisfy a Victorian patriarch's sense of the decent'. So Meg began to transcribe the diaries anew. It took years as she was busy with her young family but she felt there was no hurry. It was a job that had to be done but it could be done slowly.

Over the years she spoke to her father about his diaries and asked him to elaborate on things she did not understand. He always tried to answer her questions but he never initiated conversations about that period himself.

Meg's childhood had been 'normal' in her eyes at the time. The second of four daughters, she grew up feeling loved, cherished and sharing a secure family home: 'we didn't want for the essentials. There was humour and wit, though often with a sarcastic edge to it. But it was tense, and at the time I never really knew why.'

Mealtimes, she wrote, were very fraught affairs. Atholl was strict and insisted on correct table manners – no talking with their mouths full or making unnecessary noises while they were eating.

> No allowances were made for youth or coughs and colds. Even friends (young and old) when visiting could get a sidelong look from Dad, or worse still, a sharp intake of breath between gritted teeth if they happened to be a noisy eater. It wasn't easy to please (and I wanted to please most of the time which is more than could be said of others round the table). Challenges to his authority became something of an art form in our household with Mum always 'piggy in the middle', trying to keep the peace, and a sense of proportion, while not undermining his authority in front of us.

This delicate balancing act was mirrored in many families after the war but Meg, as a child, was unaware of that. She merely felt there were tensions. Her father could erupt into a fit of rage with little warning and these outbursts were at first terrifying but later, when she was a teenager, embarrassing.

Meg's mother, Dr Joan Elizabeth Glassey, also had an extraordinary war, being catapulted by the necessity of the times into running a busy obstetric unit at Bradford Hospital at the age of twenty-four. She met Atholl Duncan while the two of them were at St Andrews University. She, the only daughter of a teacher from west Yorkshire, was studying medicine and he, the only son of a St Andrews family, in his second year of engineering science. Atholl was dashing, outgoing, a keen outdoor sportsman and full of energy. At school his list of sporting achievements was impressive, as was his list of hobbies. He was a young man bursting with energy. By his own admission he was not a particularly diligent student as there were too many other distractions – Meg names golf, cycling and 'making merry' as just three of these. By the time he met Elizabeth Glassey at the first Saturday-night 'hop' of the academic year they were both nineteen, Elizabeth newly arrived from Bradford. She was 'witty and intelligent with a well-developed sense of fun. She was also naturally modest, a discreet and attentive listener who had a quiet way of instilling confidence in others.' She had striking blue eyes, which was the first thing Atholl noticed. They fell deeply in love and were known to their fellow students as the 'twin souls'. They had two years of peace-time to get to know one another and enjoy freedom before 'the curtain fell'. 'The memories of these days would help sustain them when, all too soon, they were separated for who knew how long.'

Atholl, a member of the university Officer Training Corps, volunteered and took a commission in September 1939. He joined the Highland Light Infantry as a second lieutenant but was transferred in 1940 to a machine-gun unit with the Argyll and Sutherland Highlanders in France with the BEF. He came home on leave in May 1940 for a brief seven days during which he became engaged to Elizabeth. Back in France he found himself being picked up and evacuated from Cherbourg to Southampton. During the next few months he and Elizabeth were able to snatch brief days together but she was having to concentrate hard on her studies: 'Now that she was doing clinical training she was spending much of her time travelling to and from Dundee by train for lectures and hospital placements . . . On the rare occasions when time and petrol rationing allowed, Atholl would take his fiancée and his parents into the Highlands where he had spent holidays as a child.'

In January 1941 Atholl's papers came for him to report to Stirling Castle and within a few days he had sailed from Glasgow for the Far East, destination Singapore. This was the last time Elizabeth would see her fiancé for four years. Atholl was a good correspondent and his letters were full of descriptions of life on the ship. He was even able to send presents back home, including a crocodile-skin handbag for Elizabeth, a gift she treasured and which Meg now has.

Elizabeth also sent letters with regular updates about her studies, which he took great pride in, writing in September 1941: 'I am quite sure that next year at this time I shall be addressing you as Dr . . .'

Atholl was on Java by February 1942 and sent back news from GHQ that he had been promoted to captain. He received a telegram of congratulations from his parents. This was the last communication he had from his family until March 1944. He was taken prisoner in March 1942 and would spend three and a half years as a prisoner of war. He wrote in his diary on New Year's Day 1943: 'Stayed up to see in the New Year, the last person I saw in 1942 and the first I saw in 1943 was Elizabeth as I looked at her photo during the change. Well, 1942 has been the most disastrous year in my sweet young life and I can only hope that the New Year will see the return of peace to this war-weary world, and that we can return to all those so near and dear to us, and find them safe and well.'

On New Year's Eve 1942 Elizabeth still had no idea about his fate. Meanwhile, she had qualified as a doctor earlier that month and began work in January at St Luke's Hospital, Bradford, as a house officer. Her responsibilities were enormous, given the shortage of doctors, and before long she was running the obstetrics department almost single-handedly, 'an overwhelming responsibility far beyond her experience, though not as it turned out beyond her capabilities'. In May of that year she received news via Atholl's parents that he was no longer posted as missing but a prisoner of war. She began writing to him but she had no way of knowing whether her letters were getting through. But she assured him that every day was one day nearer to seeing him again: 'It will be wonderful when we do eventually see you again . . . It is bad enough now but nothing could be worse than those awful fourteen months when we never heard a word. I thought at times I would go mad.'

Atholl kept up his diaries, despite the enormous risk to him of them being discovered, and confided in November 1943: 'It's damnable to think that this war has come along and lifted such a large chunk right out of our lives at a period which is considered to be the best years of one's life.' By 1944 he had begun to take up studies in the prison camp, determined not to forgo a chance he felt he had missed at St Andrews. It perhaps seems extraordinary that 'studies' could be carried out in a prison-camp environment but in a place where boredom was as much a destructive force as starvation, it kept many men sane during the years of captivity.

Meanwhile Elizabeth was undergoing a different kind of endurance test. While her work at the hospital kept her very busy, her personal life was on hold while her fiancé was away. The hospital doctors were mainly men, the latter often called out of retirement as the younger ones were serving in the forces. Although the workload was relentless, Elizabeth recalled this period as essentially a happy one. There was always banter among the doctors, most of whom had trained in Edinburgh, so she was surrounded by Scots, a constant reminder of her fiancé's background. She told Meg years later that: '. . . despite the dreary accommodation and the vagaries of the food, all things considered the doctors were looked after. They were certainly better off than their nursing colleagues. Matrons ruled with a rod of iron in those days. There was to be no fraternizing with the doctors either. Mum thought that it was a dreadful way for fellow professionals to be treated.'

Thirty years later, when Meg was training to be a nurse in Manchester, she was struck by her mother's down-to-earth advice: 'No matter how much knowledge I acquired, how much technical wizardry I could utilize to do my job, the one thing that would matter above all else to the person lying in the bed was that they were comfortable. It is always the basic, simple things that really make a difference, whether it be a comfortable bed or someone who makes the time to listen, no matter how busy they are.' This was one of Elizabeth's greatest strengths and the thing that she was most affectionately remembered for by colleagues in the hospital. One junior doctor, who worked directly under Elizabeth, or Glassey as she was known to everyone in the hospital, wrote:

I was a newly hatched medical chick in September 1944 . . . with a fiancé I hadn't seen in nearly five years . . . and then I met Glassey — an inward sigh of relief that the Senior ROO [resident obstetric officer] was female — a fair-haired, smallish, smiling, chirpy-looking woman with a deepish voice and throaty chuckle and a welcoming handshake. After a week of residence I began to wonder how she had survived: for some time, weeks, she had run the whole of the Midwifery and Gynae block by herself, 24 hours a day and 7 days a week. I honestly don't know how she did it, broken sleep most nights and such responsibility and she radiated efficiency and competence. But there were two Glasseys and it was quite a while before I knew of the other one. The one whose fiancé was a POW of the Japs and who had to keep her love and anxieties and worry so deeply hidden. I never saw her break down.

In January 1944 an extraordinary event happened that provided Elizabeth and Atholl's family with the first tangible proof that he was still alive. The Japanese at Zentsuji camp had offered to let prisoners send radio messages to their families. The British refused as it was propaganda but the Americans accepted. Lieutenant George Armstrong, an American airman and Atholl's close friend, broadcast a message via Radio Tokyo. In this message to his wife Armstrong tried to give as much information as he dared about men who were his fellow prisoners. He was able to communicate: '. . . Notify Alec Rattray, 2111 Lincoln Avenue, San José, California, that A.A. Duncan is OK . . .' This was recorded in November 1943 and Rattray – an old friend of Atholl's father – received the message from the Short Wave Listening Post via postcard on 9 January 1944. He immediately contacted St Andrews with the news.

This turned out to be the first communication directly from Atholl (albeit via his friend). Finally they had word from him: now they knew that he was still alive . . . Imagine the joy that one sentence must have brought to them all. For Elizabeth and the family at least, the waiting was over; Atholl would have to wait a while longer, but very soon both he and they could begin to contemplate the possibility of starting to share life once again.

As this reality dawned on Elizabeth she became increasingly anxious. A persistent worry began to take hold. Meg wrote:

. . . if, God willing, Atholl did manage to hang on and survive whatever ordeal he was facing, he could return home in the not too distant future expecting to pick up their lives again. But what sort of life would the future hold for them? To what extent had he been physically and emotionally damaged? Would she recognize the man she loved so much or, worse still, like the person he had become? How could she possibly know how to help him recover and rebuild his life with her?

And of course she had changed so much in the four years he had been away. Now a senior doctor with a wealth of experience behind her, how would she settle down to a new life? These questions, faced by thousands of women, were unanswerable. They would simply have to wait and see.

The opportunity to find out finally came in November 1945. Atholl's ship, the RMS *Queen Mary*, docked in Southampton on the 18th, the day after Elizabeth's birthday. Three days later he was home in St Andrews: 'Elizabeth had travelled up a day or two earlier to be with his mother and father. Suddenly all the waiting was over. He walked through the door almost five years after he had left for the East.' At the end of 1945 Elizabeth gave up her job as a doctor in preparation for the move to St Andrews to start her new life as Mrs Duncan.

Two and a half months after he had arrived home Atholl and Elizabeth were married in a blizzard at St Barnabas Church in Heaton, Bradford. The wedding was attended by family, friends and five fellow prisoners of war. After a honeymoon in North Wales they returned to St Andrews and to the cottage owned by Atholl's father, which was to be their first home. At the beginning of April Atholl was interviewed by the dean of the Faculty of Science; he explained that he wanted to resume his studies but change to medicine. After some wrangling it was agreed that the first year of his science degree could be taken into account and he could start the second year as a medical student. Many of the students at St Andrews in the post-war era were mature students, ex-servicemen who had fought a long war. In his history of the university John S. G. Blair wrote: 'Although all these men and women, who for the most part had packed a lifetime's experience into four or five years, had often held positions of seniority and considerable responsibility, they were prepared in great humility to work for a university degree, for they were all aware, with a depth of insight unbelievable today, that they were fortunate and privileged to be at university at all.'

A number of Atholl's earlier friends were also back at St Andrews. All of them had had life-changing experiences but there was a real sense that they were making up for lost time. Meg's father was no exception in this. A friend wrote: 'Atholl was conspicuous in our class by virtue of his emaciation, this despite gaining 50 lbs during his long return to Scotland. Even at graduation on June 30, 1950 he still showed evidence of his captivity. Not once did he ever speak to me about his POW experiences . . . we never saw any of Atholl's hostility to his enemies but I can well understand how he may have reacted at home.' He threw himself into his studies with a determination that characterized the rest of his life. It was not all work, however. He loved the social life and their little cottage was often full of friends. One described these evenings: '. . . I well remember spending Thursday evenings round at Atholl and Elizabeth's, it was a regular thing, when we all swotted and Elizabeth offered what assistance she could. She was such a lovely woman and she did look after Atholl so well . . .'

This last phrase was the key. Elizabeth had her work cut out caring for her new husband. He was not the same carefree student she had known before the war and the dark rumblings of his wartime past were there from the beginning of their marriage. Why did Elizabeth Glassey give up her medical career so readily? She explained to Meg that on the one hand it was expected of her by Atholl, by her parents-in-law, and to some extent by society. And she was exhausted. Although she desperately missed the camaraderie of her medical colleagues and the day-to-day running of a busy hospital department she was physically and emotionally drained after three years working flat out. In the period of re-adjustment after the war, Elizabeth had to deal with her own problems in silence while she learned to deal with Atholl's needs which, she always felt, came above hers. Like many other former prisoners of the Japanese, Atholl had feared that the years of mal-nutrition and illness would have affected his ability to have children and Elizabeth had her own concerns about the levels of radiation she had been exposed to in the hospital. Kenneth Davey had writ-ten to his wife about this subject as early as September 1945:

> There's a lot of stories getting about that we fellows are impotent as a result of malnutrition (I've forgotten how to spell that one anyway). That is not true – no one really knows how we are affected but we have been advised by one MO to avoid pregnancy in our wives for at least six months because there is a possibility that a child may suffer some defect as a result of the conditions to which we have been exposed. In view of the doubt which exists I believe this to be good advice.

Neither could believe it when Elizabeth fell pregnant weeks after their wedding. Tragedy struck in late 1946 when their first son was stillborn. A year later their second son, christened Andrew Atholl Charles, survived for only twenty-four hours. It was a desperately sad time in their lives. Fortunately in 1949 Elizabeth gave birth to a healthy little girl, Patricia, the first of the four Duncan daughters. Atholl graduated from St Andrews the year after and took up his first post as an assistant to a GP in the village of Horsham St Faith, north of Norwich. 'It was while living in the nearby village of Drayton that Elizabeth suffered a miscarriage and then, in the ensuing obstetric emergency, very nearly lost her life. To have lost three babies in four years was terribly hard for them both but thankfully Trish thrived and was a wonderful distraction.' In total Elizabeth went through seven pregnancies in nine years, an indication of their desperation to have a family but an exhausting experience for a young woman already worn down by years of wartime working, rationing and readjustment to life. After the birth of their fourth daughter no further babies came: enough was enough.

In 1951 the family moved to the Wirral where they put down roots. Atholl was appointed junior partner in a practice in Moreton where he worked for twenty-nine years. Elizabeth joined him, initially on a part-time basis in 1964, and later as a partner taking responsibility for obstetrics, a role for which she was well qualified. She loved the work and was happy to remain as Mrs Duncan in deference to Atholl who was a senior partner and to avoid the confusion of having two Dr Duncans at the surgery. 'Why didn't she do her own thing?' Meg asked in her book. 'Well, I think the reason is really quite simple for despite the huge changes wrought for women as a result of the war, my mother's generation was not brought up to put themselves first. It may seem inconceivable to those of us who have followed but I do believe that was a large part of it. In later life she would occasionally vent her feelings to me about Dad's selfishness over something or other.'

Elizabeth was a much-loved doctor; after she died many of her former patients told Meg that she had been a wonderful support when times were difficult.

She always made time to talk to these women. She would offer them a cigarette and allow them time to talk through their problems. This was in the days before appointments and government health warnings about the dangers of smoking. The women were given as long as they needed. They appreciated her pragmatic advice and sensitive, wise words. These were ordinary women, some with large families and difficult home lives, who sought sanctuary in her surgery.

In addition to his work Atholl filled his spare time with endless activities which Elizabeth, often left alone to cope with her four little girls, 'accommodated with commendable patience and at times much needed humour as they absorbed most of the little free time he had in those days'. He took up golf, photography, stamp collecting, model making and engineering. 'His workshop was a haven for like-minded friends who helped him with all manner of engineering projects over the years,' remembered Meg. But the thing that gave him more joy than anything was the realization of his greatest ambition, which was to fly. Initially he volunteered to teach meteorology at the local Air Training Corps but soon became a regular at 631 Squadron, RAF Sealand Gliding School near Chester. 'This involvement with the ATC, or "squadders" as it was irreverently referred to by the family, lasted for thirty-two years and he loved it. It completely dominated his life, and ours, throughout my teenage years.' Now Meg understands better that flying was probably the one thing that gave her father a sense of freedom. In the prison camp he had been close friends with the American pilot, George Armstrong, whose radio broadcast had reached Alec Rattray. Armstrong taught Atholl about meteorology:

It strikes me now what a perfect hobby this was for a prisoner of war. Looking up at the sky was one thing the Japanese could not prevent him from doing. Dad always looked up when he heard a plane going over, right up to the end of his life. We used to joke that he knew the name and address of the pilot as well as the type of aircraft. All the cine films from our childhood are dominated by scanning shots of planes with a few children interspersed for good measure.

There is an impression throughout Meg's second book of the diaries that Atholl Duncan was determined not to waste a single precious second of his life, having squandered, as he saw it, three and a half years languishing in a Japanese prison camp. How much of this feverish activity had to do with suppressing the past with all its attendant horrors, and how much it had to do with feeling that life is for living, is difficult to say but there is no doubt that the drive to pursue his hobbies had, over time, a detrimental effect on Elizabeth. It is perhaps ironic that the book is entitled *A A Duncan is OK* . . . It was clear that Elizabeth Duncan was not. Meg wrote: 'My mother was amazed at his sheer determination to get back into life and to move forward. In those early years it was she who suffered a nervous breakdown, in silence and on her own; he was never aware of it. The stress of the war years took a heavy toll both emotionally and mentally; she couldn't share her anxiety, feeling that whatever she was going through was as nothing compared with what he had endured.'

Meg is clear that her mother was not subservient to her father but that she simply realized her own experiences were not part of his life: 'Mum was unable to share "her" war with Dad. Not that he wasn't interested, I'm sure he would have been, but more that she would not have wanted him to think that she had had a bad time of it. As she used to say, "How could I have done that? His war was so much worse than anything I'd experienced." How hard must that have been for her?'

As Meg grew up she became aware that her father was revisiting or dealing with his past experiences. 'His past gradually caught up with him and all of us who knew him closely felt the effects of it. None of us escaped.' If the girls ever complained, as teenagers, he would round on them: 'You don't know how lucky you are.' He would say, '*You* have had a youth. I spent *my* youth incarcerated in prison camps.' She went on: 'There was a searing resentment at the injustice of it all. He was angry at the wicked waste of his life, as he saw it.'

In 1973 Atholl had a heart attack and was grounded; he never piloted a glider again. Losing his hobby had a profound effect. In the autumn of 1979 he announced that 'they' were going to retire at Christmas. He was sixty-two. Elizabeth was not consulted. 'He never asked . . .' she told Meg, when her daughter wondered at her sudden retirement. 'I'd dearly have loved to slow down gently and keep on with the obstetric work for a year or two longer,' she told her. There was a streak in Atholl that defied anyone to question what he did or indeed suggest what he ought to do. In retirement his irrationality became more obvious and Elizabeth's patience wore thin. The girls often found the atmosphere at home tense and at times his behaviour towards their mother upset them: 'Mum spent her married life accommodating what Dad needed or wanted. She couldn't change the habits of a lifetime, neither his nor her own, so she did what she had always done, she just coped.'

In December 1996 Atholl was diagnosed with inoperable pancreatic cancer; in early January Elizabeth was rushed into hospital and was found to be suffering from lymphoma. She died on the afternoon of their fifty-first wedding anniversary, he died sixteen days later, on the fifty-second anniversary of the fall of Singapore, 'a somehow fitting date,' Meg noted. 'The whole family was devastated by their brutally swift departure, though for the two of them it was probably a blessing. Dad simply gave up once Mum had gone, life had no meaning for him without her.'

In summing up her parents and explaining her need to write the stories of their lives she concluded:

> Since first reading his diaries, I had been amazed at his perseverance and determination; what he had achieved in life was quite simply awe-inspiring. However, as time went by, I came to understand the enormous contribution my mother made to his success. Her need to make his life better dominated her own but, like so many other women in the same situation, it came at a high price. I don't want to paint too bleak a picture of my parents' marriage because they did love one another and they had happy times together but it was a difficult and at times a one-way relationship, especially as they got older. I feel it became Mum's life work just to help him to survive.

In publishing Atholl Duncan's diaries in her two books, Meg wanted to share with others her father's detailed account of his own battle to survive. But she also needed to shine a spotlight on the unsung efforts of women like her mother; those who have, throughout their married lives, quietly coped on so many different levels.

Since the books were published she has continued to research the FEPOW story and to give lectures. More recently, through projects like the oral history enquiry and helping to organize conferences for FEPOW families and researchers, she has endeavoured to bring the story to a wider audience.

All three women have given a great deal of time researching not only their own stories, but also the wider picture. It is a mark of the enduring fascination with the story of the Far Eastern prisoners of war and the legacy of those cruel years that there is still such an interest in trying to understand what it meant to the men and their families after they returned. For the women and children of these men the war left an indelible mark on their lives and although much of what came after was troubling, the positive side is that through understanding the situation better, people have been able to make more sense of their own past.

IN PRAISE OF GRANDPARENTS:
THE GRANDDAUGHTER'S TALE

Gran'pa's tales telescoped the years, making the events of his prime seem alive to us in a way no book possibly could. And his stories live on to the next generation.

Stephanie Hess

The relationship between a grandparent and a child is often less complicated and carries less baggage than that of the parent and child. It seems to be a combination of a mellowing of attitudes in old age and an uncritical trust. Questions that might have been unthinkable earlier can be posed by a grandchild. There is often a refreshing honesty in these relationships. Memories are still clear, if sometimes painful, but distance and other life experiences have helped to put things into perspective. 'Grandchildren have a sense that nothing is off limits. They seem to have the ability to put their finger on the pulse of family issues. Or perhaps put another way round, they tread where angels feared to tiptoe in the past.'

Children are perceptive and they share with their grandparents a luxury that most adults do not have – time. Time not only to talk, time also to listen and think. For children their grandparents' lives have been unfathomably long, stretching way back into history. The war years for children are something taught in school; for their grandparents they were something lived through. A vital and frequently life-changing experience. There is a lot to talk about. One grandmother, when talking to her ten-year-old grandson about her school being bombed during the Blitz, mused, almost privately: 'It's funny to think of it but I suppose Hitler is really part of history now. For me he was an evil man who was just part of my childhood.'

Mollie Lodder (whose story featured in chapter 6) said that her father always felt happy to answer her own children's questions about his wartime experiences. They loved to hear his stories and he took time to explain things to them that Mollie had never heard him speak of in detail before. 'With the grandchildren my father had immense patience and they could ask him anything they wanted and he would try to reply honestly and truthfully. They were very close to him in his older years and he took great comfort from their company. For them, of course, it was wonderful to hear these stories of a whole world they knew nothing about.'

Jean Kerr wrote:

I think there is also a sense that time and distance have helped to heal wounds. My own father was simply too busy to bother talking to me about things when I was younger and I suppose I was too busy growing up to be interested enough to ask him. But after he retired there was nothing he liked to do more than to reminisce about the past, especially the war, and my children adored that. They could listen to his stories over and over again. They never judged him, they just drank it all in and came back at him with perceptive remarks and questions. It was lovely to watch him opening up to them. My mother and I would stand back and wonder where this all came from but we never dared to ask him ourselves. It was as if the communication between my father and my children was a private matter that we were able to listen in on but could not interrupt.

One aspect of grandparents' stories is the sense of perspective achieved which is not always possible when those connected with it are bound up both physically and emotionally. There is no doubt that the effects of the Second World War have percolated down to the next generation and even on to those born long after the war.

Julie Gibb from Cornwall remembered being fascinated by her grandfather's war memorabilia:

My mother always told me I was never to touch anything in his study and never to ask questions. He didn't like talking about the war, she said. But there was a photograph of a cross with his surname on it and I wanted to know whose grave it was. I asked Grandpa and he told me it was his brother's grave. He had been killed nine days after D-Day. I didn't really know what he meant so I asked more questions. He sat me on his knee and told me so many stories that we were late for tea. Grannie was furious and called him an idiot for putting ideas into my head about the war but Grandpa just winked at me and put his fingers to his lips. It was our secret. I think he was pleased I'd asked him because he told me lots of things after that. When I told my mother she was amazed. She said that Grannie had never let Grandpa talk about the war because it reminded her of how much life had changed for her when he came home.

Rachel Thorn became aware while she was still young that the war had caused a serious rift between her grandparents, although it was not until she was much older that she had an understanding of what caused it. Rachel was twenty when her maternal grandfather, Ivor Flower, died. Her recollections of him are of a kindly, gentle man with a twinkling smile and a confidential wink that he would give her when his wife nagged him. Rachel's grandmother, Olive, was a more complicated person. She was a wonderful grandmother: a great cook and fruit bottler, she knitted beautiful sweaters, had home-made ginger beer in her larder, kept a lovely garden and was a stalwart of the local WI. But as a wife to Ivor she presented a different persona. 'She always nagged him, always found fault with him, she behaved towards him in a way that made you feel she found him tiresome.' Yet when Ivor died she was devastated, crushed by the belief that she had made his life miserable for forty years. She developed appalling back pain for which the doctors could find no obvious medical problem and Rachel was convinced that the pain came from the anguish and guilt she felt at her own lost opportunities and her constant nagging of her once beloved husband.

Olive was born in Bristol in 1920, the fourth of eleven children, and the first to be born in wedlock to her parents, something she admitted she found deeply shocking when it was revealed that her older siblings were illegitimate. She grew up in a tall, five-storey house in Cotswold Road, near Victoria Park, close to the industrial heart of Bristol with a view over the city. Her early life was not easy and at times, when things were hard for her parents, her mother had to scrub floors for other people. Arguments occurred occasionally, especially when the financial situation was worrying, and with eleven children to feed and care for there was little spare money. At the age of fourteen Olive rebelled against her parents, who wanted her to be confirmed into the local church, by joining the Salvation Army. The Salvation Army, which had been running outreach programmes in the slums, appealed to her more than the Church of England. It was a strange form of rebellion and probably had as much to do with distancing herself from her siblings as rebelling against her parents but she was happy with her decision and remained loyal to the Salvation Army until she was in her seventies. Its strict doctrines and emphasis on self-discipline, charitable giving and abstinence from alcohol, tobacco and gambling, among other things, chimed with Olive's feelings as a young girl.

Not long after joining the Salvation Army she met Ivor William Holman Flower, a bandsman in the Bedminster Corps. He was three years older than Olive and was working for the Bristol Tram Company. Ivor had been a member of the Salvation Army since the age of three and was, like Olive, firmly devoted to its principles of self-discipline and obedience to the church's doctrines. He was the only child of a conservative couple who had brought him up in what he later admitted were sheltered conditions during the 1930s. When the war broke out he enlisted in the RAF to be trained as a mechanic in the belief that if he was in at the beginning he might have some say in where he would be sent. By 1940 he and Olive were engaged and she was living with his parents when the bombing of Bristol began in earnest. When it was at its height they moved to Portishead but Ivor was stationed away and Olive had to spend time alone with her future parents-in-law. In 1941 Ivor and Olive were married in St Luke's Church, Bishopsworth, and had a brief honeymoon before he had to return to his unit in St Athan in South Wales. Olive fell pregnant and gave birth to a stillborn child in 1942, a terrible experience for them both, not least because she was living in a devastated city while her new husband was away for weeks and months at a time. Anxious to be closer to Olive, Ivor applied for a transfer and was sent to Colerne in Wiltshire so that he could travel more easily to Bristol when on leave. (Before the construction of the Severn Bridge the journey to Bristol was long and difficult.) Ironically had he stayed with the St Athan unit he might never have been sent abroad but in 1943 he was posted to India where he remained until the end of the war. In January 1944 Olive gave birth to a baby girl, Anne, who was later to become Rachel's mother.

Ivor's experiences in India broadened his horizons in a most dramatic way and he realized, quickly, how very sheltered his upbringing had been in Bristol. The poverty of India shocked him and in the photograph album he made during the war there were pictures of life on the streets that must have seemed to him very unfamiliar. Among the images was a photograph of a young woman breastfeeding her baby as she walked along the street and another of a polio victim with his legs in an ungainly position as he grinned for the camera. It all made a deep impression on him. Ivor told Rachel years later that one of the things that struck him in India was the way they chewed betel nuts, which gave them red teeth and red spittle.

In his letters back to Olive he would give her vivid but carefully worded descriptions of his everyday life, always presenting new and worrying images with such sentiments as 'I know this might sound unpleasant' so as not to shock his young wife. In one letter he explained how men in his billet would catch lizards and keep them as pets in order to catch the flies and bugs that made their lives so uncomfortable. None of it upset Olive as much as his confession that he had taken up smoking 'in order to keep up the camaraderie with the chaps'. This, Rachel explained, turned it for her grandmother. Olive was horrified and it was this single transgression for which she could never forgive him. It was something so vulgar, in Olive's eyes, that Rachel remembers growing up thinking that people who smoked were fundamentally evil. 'I don't know where this impression came from,' she said, 'but I suppose it must have come from my grandmother. She would never let Ivor smoke in the house and indeed he was never a heavy smoker but it was something she could never accept in him.'

Ivor did not see action in India and when he was demobbed in November 1945 he returned to Bristol full of his new experiences. On the return journey they had sailed via Durban in South Africa and he had fallen in love with the idea of emigrating there. When he came back to war-torn Britain he found it a profoundly depressing place. After the warmth and sun in India, winter in the south-west was most unwelcome. He told Olive he had set his heart on moving to South Africa but she would hear nothing of it. She, for her part, wanted to better her station and she urged her husband to retrain for improved career prospects. He refused. He had so set his heart on the idea of leaving Britain that he saw no value in retraining in Bristol for a job he knew he would not take. It was the first of many an impasse. When Ivor returned home he and Olive had no place of their own so they moved in with his parents and here, for the first time, he met his baby daughter, Anne. She was two months short of her second birthday and her clearest recollection of that time was her refusal to have anything to do with the man Olive called her father. Anne would not allow Ivor to hold her hand or cuddle her and she refused to recognize him despite the fact that her mother and grandparents had talked about him and shown her photographs of him. He was, in every sense, a complete stranger to her.

He was also a stranger to his wife. While he had been abroad, experiencing travel for the first time, Olive had been living at home and bringing up her little girl in an almost exclusively female environment. The fact that Ivor now smoked was the outward sign of a marriage damaged by the war. He never attended the Salvation Army church again although Olive continued to do so for another forty years. The gulf between them simply grew. Ivor went back to work in Bristol, this time for the Bristol Bus Company, which had replaced the tram company. A little boy was born in 1946. He was a sickly child, suffering from terrible asthma and eczema, and Olive decided that she did not want any more children. However, four years later an 'accident' happened and another boy was born. At this stage all five of them were still living in one bedroom in Ivor's parents' house, an untenable situation. Soon after this the family was rehoused in Henbury, on the other side of Bristol, some eight or nine miles from Bedminster. Anne, then seven, remembers this as being a good time but Olive was not happy to be so far away from her family. Eventually they moved back and were given a council house in Bishopsworth where they lived for the rest of their lives.

'If I knew then how things were going to turn out I never would have got married,' Olive told her daughter when she was grown up. She confessed that she once considered divorcing Ivor but it was something simply not done in the 1950s so she stuck at her marriage, nagging her husband and feeling bitter that she had not been able to fulfil her potential and better her social position. Her frustration was taken out on her husband, who she saw in some ways as an obstruction to the realization of her hopes. She never forgave Ivor for taking up smoking, and he had to take the dog for long walks in order to indulge his habit.

It was not until Ivor's aneurysm in the early 1980s, when he very nearly died, that Olive had a change of heart, Rachel recalled, and for the later years of his life the relationship was more mellow. She stopped going to the Salvation Army and joined the church in Bishopsworth where she and Ivor had been married in 1941, eventually taking communion in the mid-1980s.

The church was an enormous support to her for the rest of her life. Her grief when Ivor died was genuine. She felt an abject sense of sadness for all the times she had been so tough on him and the remorse never left her, leaving Rachel feeling a great sense of loss at what might have been had the war not intervened and damaged her grandparents' marriage almost beyond repair.

Rachel's story of their dislocated and fractured post-war life is not unique and gives a view of what many other grandchildren must have witnessed. But that is not the whole picture. The story of Stephanie Hess, who lives in South Africa, offers a different perspective.

Stephanie was born in Alexandra Hospital in Singapore in 1966, the second child of Dermot and Beattie Dunne. Her paternal grandparents had come from Dublin in the early part of the twentieth century, but she was brought up in Canada and the United States after her father retired from his job as an army surgeon.

> He was a restless spirit. New places and adventure called out to him and he followed, come what may. I suspect it may be a combination of circumstance and heredity — many of the Dunne siblings ended up in places all over the world. I think that the inclination for travel might already have been lurking in my father's heart, and was fuelled by the war. His thirst for knowledge seemed to be unquenchable and his ability to become bored quickly once he had achieved a goal dictated the pattern of our migratory lives. In the 1960s my father had a yen to see Singapore again. The family had left there in 1949. So he joined the RAMC with a view to studying tropical medicine and that is why I was born there.

Although separated by thousands of miles, the Dunnes were a tightly knit family with strong ties. Stephanie became close to her paternal grandfather, Joseph 'Joe' Benedict Dunne, during the last three years of his life when three generations of the Dunne family lived in Ireland under one roof. Joe entrusted her with one of his most prized personal possessions, a diary that he had kept during the three and a half years he was a prisoner of the Japanese.

Simon, the oldest grandson, also had a close bond with Joe. He shared a birthday with Joe's daughter, Eithne, known to all as Unie. 'She died of cancer at the age of thirty when my brother was just a month old leaving a most awful hole in my grandfather's heart. Apparently Gran'pa commented that he had lost a daughter but had gained a grandson.' John, the youngest, only really got to know his grandfather in 1978, when the family moved to Ireland. 'But his relationship with Gran'pa was special too – he was the same age my father had been when Gran'pa came back from the war. Gran'pa had an amazing heart. There was room for us all to be loved individually and uniquely. We, his family, were absolutely everything to him and we knew it.'

Before their move 'back home' in the 1970s Stephanie's parents had settled in North America where she and John were educated while Simon was at boarding school in Ireland, spending happy weekends with his grandparents at their home 'Kilcoursey' in Greystones, Co. Wicklow, south of Dublin. The family visited Ireland frequently to see their grandparents and Stephanie remembered being fascinated as a child by the old photograph albums and framed photographs that were displayed prominently in the house:

The sepia-toned images are an integral part of my mental make-up and were the vehicle which prompted many a conversation between me and my grandparents. One album, dating back to 1927, is covered in cloth bearing the pattern of Chinese coins; the other is black lacquer with a lovely scene in mother-of-pearl of a lady being pulled along in a rickshaw. These Chinese albums were propped up on display in my teenage bedroom and I would often leaf through the scenes that revealed a time when my grandparents were young and glamorous, and seemingly trouble-free. And even though the spines are cracking and some pages have come loose I still can't resist the call of the pages that were once turned by my grandmother's hands as she pasted in the precious images of her life.

For as long as she could remember Stephanie was aware that Gran'pa's health was a worry. 'Whenever he was "down" with a bout of bronchitis or pneumonia my parents would comment that this was the result of his years as a POW.' It was as if no further explanation of this statement was required. In 1976 a phone call came from Ireland to say that Gran'pa was gravely ill and it was feared he would not make it through the night. At the time Stephanie and her parents were living on a ranch in Illinois and she recalled the scramble to hire a four-seater plane to get them to Chicago, in the obligatory blizzard, so that they could catch a last-minute flight to Dublin. Everything about the journey stuck in her mind and in later years her mother, Beattie, told her how she spent the entire journey mentally repeating the words: 'Hang on Joe, we're coming, hang on Joe.' And hang on he did. 'My father arrived the next day, and we settled into a new life over the next few months of hospital visits, then nursing home visits, and finally visits to Kilcoursey. I think it must have been during those months that I began to get to know my grandfather on a deeper level. There were lots of chats and stories about the past, and memories of Singapore and of little Unie during her dancing days and at the Singapore Swimming Club.'

Eventually Stephanie's parents decided to move to Ireland to be closer to Joe, who was by now a widower, his wife having died suddenly and unexpectedly the year after his life-threatening illness. It had long been everyone's assumption that Eilish would outlive Joe but now the tables had turned and Dermot felt the need to be closer to his father. Beattie and the children stayed at Kilcoursey while Dermot commuted between the United States and Ireland. Living under the same roof as her Gran'pa meant that the bond which had been developing over the years of Stephanie's childhood was consolidated. She loved to spend time with him listening to his stories over and over again. He would tell her all about his time in Singapore before the war while they pottered about in the garden weeding and pruning. He would talk to her about his daughter, Unie, and this seemed to strengthen their relationship:

> Unie and my grandfather had had an incredible bond. It seems they were friends and allies to the last and delighted in each other's company. And it seems, according to my grandparents and parents, that I am the living image of her. Apparently at each stage of my development as a child I resembled Unie, not only physically, but in character as well, seeming to share her interests and talents in drawing and acting and dancing. She was as real a family member to me as those who were living – her memory was kept very much alive, most of the stories went back to the good years in Singapore before the war.

One of Stephanie's favourite tasks was to make Gran'pa his coffee: 'I wonder what concoction my twelve-year-old hands really produced, but Gran'pa never failed to go through the ceremony of taking up the coffee cup to give a lingering and appreciative closed-eyed inhalation of the brew. His first sip was always followed by a happy exclamation of "Ah . . . that's lovely."'

One of the tasks that she and Gran'pa undertook was to empty the maid's room, which she described as a pulsating entity off the kitchen. For years everything that was unwanted or no longer needed would be put into that room to be dealt with another day.

I don't know what prompted Gran'pa to face the debris of nearly thirty years or how it was that I came to be chosen to help him with the sorting but we waded in through cobwebby shapes with sleeves rolled up and got cracking. Beneath the surface layers of dust and abandoned toys and furniture lurked an undiscovered country inhabited by rotting boxes filled with fountain pens and jars of glue – the type that have the brush attached to the inside of the lid – lead pencils and headed paper from Dunne & McKenna.

They found shoeboxes filled with letters that coughed dust as the lids were removed, steamer trunks containing cocktail dresses with square padded shoulders in the garish colours that suited the bright, sunny east but which looked startling in the soft light of Ireland. These treasures seemed to Stephanie to be physical reminders of her grandparents' life in Singapore in that magical time before the war that to her was like a fairytale and to Gran'pa a distant but lovely memory of his youth. The one 'find' that Joe would not let Stephanie throw away was a wooden box filled with straw cradling six bottles sealed with cork and wax. They contained soya sauce, purchased in Singapore in 1949.

It took us days to sort through it all, and we both came out the other side of it feeling a bit battered by the unexpected emotion our 'tidy up' had provoked. The soya sauce remained behind triumphant, gloating over its success in surviving the culling. Gran'pa could not bear to let it go, and became quite agitated when I insisted that after thirty years nobody would want to consume it. But I backed down, it was his soya sauce after all, why shouldn't he keep it?

The great sort-out elicited further stories from the past, and inevitably, questions and answers about Gran'pa's time as a prisoner during the war. He was happy to talk about this and Stephanie's recollection was that he seemed to relish retelling the tales:

> Gran'pa only told amusing stories of his POW experience, or gave positive accounts of the kind gestures extended to him on occasion by the local inhabitants. I don't recall one horror story or bitter comment ever passing his lips. My brothers and I clamoured for his stories, thrilled each time the camp guards ended by having the wool pulled over their eyes by the resourceful, brave POWs. What fun it was to hear Gran'pa counting in Japanese, reciting his *tenko* number or uttering mysterious words. These were the stories of my childhood and I treasured them.

Joe Dunne was born in Dublin in 1907, one of nine children, whose father died when he was still a boy. 'His childhood years were spent in a city bubbling with unrest, and in old age he still remembered clearly the dramatic events surrounding the Easter Rising of 1916.' Life was difficult for the family after his father's death and Joe had to work to contribute to the family's income. In 1928 two things happened to change the course of his life: he met and fell in love with a beautiful young teacher called Eilish Beglin and he was offered a career in the Far East with Gestetner Ltd. Eilish and Joe conducted a four-year long-distance courtship while he worked hard to forge his career. He returned to Ireland in 1932 and married Eilish. Six weeks later they sailed back to the East and to their new life together.

Singapore was one of the most exciting cities in the Far East in the 1930s and Joe and Eilish made as much of the opportunities on offer as they could. 'Work was satisfying and exciting. Gestetner had branches in Malaya, Siam [Thailand], Java, the Philippines and Hong Kong, all of which Joe visited regularly. The world of the East, with all its magic and allure, was weaving its spell with each passing day.' In 1929 Joe joined the Straits Settlement Volunteer Force and became a member of the Scottish Company. 'Based on photographs taken at the time I can see he wore his kilt with pride!' Stephanie wrote. 'The Volunteers, more than any other group, were to impact on my grandfather's life, and until the end of his days he remembered his fellow Volunteers with great affection.'

In 1933 Eilish gave birth to their first child, a daughter, Unie. Five years later a son, Dermot, was born and the family was blissfully happy.

But there were rumblings from afar. Europe was plunged into war at the end of 1939, and the already frenetic pace of life for many in Singapore picked up a notch as fund-raisers and entertainments for the troops were added to the normal round of 'do's'. My grandmother's scrapbook of cuttings offers a glimpse into that whirlwind of activity dedicated to the war effort, but in a curious way the spotlight seems to focus largely on who was seen where, and more importantly, what they were wearing when they were there.

By December 1941 the Japanese were launching air strikes on Singapore. Suddenly the impregnable fortress no longer seemed invulnerable. Joe Dunne secured a passage for his wife and children on a steamer bound for Sydney and as he waved them off at the dockside he had no idea when he would see them again. He remained in Singapore fulfilling his duties with the Volunteers: 'For the second time in his life he found himself in a city of destruction and death, but unlike his childhood experience where he could only watch the events unfolding around him, this time he was able to take an active part in the fight to protect the city that had brought him so much happiness.'

Singapore fell to the Japanese on 15 February 1942 and Joe Dunne became a prisoner of war and entered a time he called 'the hidden years'. For fifteen months he moved between various camps on Singapore Island working as a labourer. The work was hard but the diet was even harder and it took a toll on his health. His hearing and sight began to deteriorate and in 1943 he was admitted to the darkened eye ward of the camp hospital at Changi where he spent almost two months in a state of semi-blindness as a result of malnutrition. In May he was moved to Japan on a so-called 'hell ship', the *Wales Maru*, on which he and 900 other prisoners were crammed in unimaginably squalid conditions. From Moji where they landed he was trained, ferried and marched to Hakodate main camp on the northernmost Japanese island of Hokkaido. Of the thirty-six Volunteers who had sailed from Singapore only six remained together in the next camp he was moved to, Kamiiso. Three men died as a result of the bitter cold 'augmenting the already high levels of anxiety about health and comfort. Snow fell between cracks in the roof and walls directly on to the sleeping spaces of the prisoners, and the water in the fire-buckets froze at night. In this new land of earth tremors and glacial chill my grandfather longed for those far away days in sunny Singapore – even Changi seemed like a distant dream.'

The labour on Hokkaido was hard. Joe was working with other prisoners at the Asano cement works when in June 1944 he had an accident in which he very nearly lost his leg. The incident turned out, Stephanie explained, to be a blessing in disguise as Joe was sent to the hospital for two months while his leg was treated. Given his poor physical state his foot was slow to heal and when he returned to Kamiiso camp he was put on gardening duties. By the time the end of the war came in August 1945 he had been moved again and was living in an isolated camp in the mountains. He was eventually freed a month later and among the precious items that he packed was a little bundle of notebooks and scraps of paper. 'It was a letter. Started in Singapore in 1942, the letter to Eilish became a chronicle of my grandfather's years of captivity, and in those pages he recorded a story of longing, faith, sadness, courage, love, and incredibly, humour.' This was the diary that he entrusted to Stephanie nearly thirty-five years later.

There was confusion at the end of the war as to what to do with the Singapore Volunteers and for a short period Joe was afraid he would be sent back to Britain while his wife and family were still in Australia. However, he managed to get himself to Sydney where he was reunited with Eilish, Unie and Dermot.

Unie was off at boarding school so it was just my grandmother and my father who lived together during the war. I know from comments made when I was a child that the Australian years were relatively happy years for my grandmother, in spite of the war and having a POW husband, and being separated from her family in Ireland, and losing friends and siblings to the cruel machine of the war. She loved the climate and rather enjoyed the freedom.

Gestetner reopened its office in Singapore in 1946 and Joe returned to take up his post. After the war he had months of medical treatment for his various conditions, including an operation on his foot following his accident in 1944 and treatment for his damaged eyesight and hearing. At first Joe and Eilish felt that Singapore was the right place to restart their lives but it proved to be a great disappointment. Too many of their friends had died or moved away. The ghosts of the past haunted the city and Singapore of the 1930s was now a distant memory. So, at the end of the 1940s, they returned to Dublin where Joe founded his own company, Dunne & McKenna, dealing in office supplies. He settled his family in the lovely Irish seaside town of Greystones and looked to the future.

> Those first years following the war were a time of readjustment. My father, at the age of eight, had no recollection of the man who had suddenly appeared in the household. Unie was no longer the little girl that my grandfather remembered, and he and my grandmother had to start all over again in every way. I have memories of conversations about this – it was difficult for my grandmother to defer to Gran'pa after nearly four years of making all decisions on her own. I think my grandparents had unresolved issues from before the war that suddenly became very real again once they were reunited, but I can see them both laughing together in old age at the memory of the rocky reunion. For better or for worse was the deal they had made, and they stuck with it. The war had stripped them of their house, their possessions and four years of their lives, but they were together again, which was more than many could claim.

Unie, Stephanie believed, soon picked up with her father where she had left off. In a letter written just after he returned from captivity her tone was as happy, chatty and gossipy as other letters written to her father before the war. For Dermot the readjustment was more difficult. 'I couldn't understand why my father sometimes seemed so resentful of his own father. As far as

I could see, Gran'pa had devoted his entire life to his family. Even in his diaries he wrote of his plans for his little "Dermot boy" and all the things they might do after the war but it somehow did not seem to have worked out as he wanted. It was very confusing for me.'

There is no doubt in Stephanie's mind that a large part of who her Gran'pa was stemmed from 'the hidden years'.

He had a marvellous sense of humour, was fiercely protective of his family, loved a 'good square meal' and enjoyed literature on the Far East, particularly the novels of James Clavell, who, it was often pointed out to us grandchildren, was a fellow POW at Changi. He couldn't bear to throw anything away and he derived the greatest pleasure from a good strong cup of coffee with lots of sugar and milk. His miraculous recoveries from numerous bouts of pneumonia in his later years were always summed up by the doctors with the comment that he was a survivor. The garden was one of my grandfather's favourite places to be. He would potter happily for hours, connected to the earth and the process of growth, enjoying a pastime in old age that had been a matter of life and death as a prisoner of war.

Joe Dunne died at the age of seventy-three.

The Christmas season of 1980 was overshadowed by another of Gran'pa's pneumonias. There had been terrible days of fevered hallucinations and the awful feeling of his eyes falling on us without recognition. And then came the gift of Christmas Day when he was bright and strong, sitting straight up in his hospital bed with colour in his cheeks and a happy air about him. We were delighted that he had turned the corner and returned from our day with Gran'pa breathing more freely than we had for weeks. It was with disbelief that I was awakened the following morning with the news that he had slipped away quietly in the night. In the wee hours he had called to the nurse for a cup of coffee and a cigarette – which incredibly she agreed to. He took a sip of his coffee, drew deeply on the cigarette, and leaning back into his pillow, happily sighed, 'Ah . . . that's lovely.' And he was no more.

For Stephanie there was a real sense that an era had ended and a link with the world before the war had died with him. As she lay in her bed while her mother stroked her hair, giving her the unbelievable news that her Gran'pa had passed away, she felt an almost physical sense of loss: 'It was such a shock when Gran'pa died. He seemed indestructible. At fourteen years old, for the first time in my life, I was faced with the awful finality of death.'

Perhaps in an attempt to feel that Gran'pa wasn't truly gone she made an effort to transcribe his POW diary which he had entrusted to her a few months before that final illness. Youth and grief were against her; the notebooks and scraps of paper were put safely in a drawer for another day. In 2006 Stephanie's ten-year-old daughter, Alicky, was asked to give a presentation on bias at school. She chose to tell her great-grandfather's story and the reasons behind the shocking treatment of the POWs by the Japanese. 'That was the year I spent transcribing my grandfather's diary, the year Alicky got to know him. She and I would curl up together in the evenings and I would read aloud the pages I had typed that day. Hearing his story put many things into perspective for her, and she still draws on the idea of his strength when faced with challenging situations.'

For Stephanie the Second World War shaped her life. The peripatetic lifestyle lived by her father, his wanderlust kindled by the war, gave her itchy feet. She and her husband settled in South

Africa in 2002, a place which was in the family psyche since her father first set eyes on

> the unforgettable and magnificent sight of the famed 'tablecloth' descending on Table Mountain. So strong was this image in the collective eye of the family that as an adult my brother Simon made sure to include Cape Town in his itinerary on his one-year round-the-world-trip that he embarked on in 1991. He stayed in South Africa, eventually meeting his future wife. 1996 was my first trip to this beautiful and sometimes frightening country. Roger and I were captivated and returned faithfully each year with Alicky to celebrate Christmas in the Southern Hemisphere. It didn't take long to decide that this was the place for us. I doubt any of us would be here if the war had not sent my family travelling far and wide.

Her Gran'pa's life influenced her too, in a positive way:

> By the time I got to know Gran'pa he appeared to be a man at peace within himself. The bumpy re-entry into the mainstream immediately following the war had given way to fruitful years spent building up a business and putting into effect the plans he had mulled over so often in those endless days of longing. Even the death of his beloved Unie could not break his indomitable spirit. In his final years he was able to observe his family with pride – his son was a highly qualified surgeon with a wife who was both beautiful and clever, and then we three grandchildren, I believe, were living proof that the fight to survive had been worth it.

If Joe Dunne had not talked about his war, however, Stephanie believed things would have been very different for her and, as a result, for her daughter Alicky:

Gran'pa has become the symbol of strength and dignity in adversity. He has shown her that no matter how hopeless a situation may seem one must never, ever give up. Gran'pa's ability to laugh, not only at himself, but at certain situations beyond his control, have directly helped Alicky handle her own challenges. He is a most vivid and real member of the family to Alicky (as Unie was to me) and is an extremely positive influence in her life.

But there would be no personal legacy for Alicky if Gran'pa had been silent about his war years. I would have had no stories to pass on to her, no diary to transcribe, and most likely no particular interest in a time and place so far away. It is through these stories and memories that the next generation can glean a sense of who they are themselves. Without these stories there is no past, no memory, just blank.

13

THE LAST WORD

I feel my mother did what she could for my father but she
never really understood him after he returned. I always felt so
sorry for my father but now I am older I can see things from
my mother's point of view. She was a brave woman and had
a hard time during the war and afterwards.

Catherine Butcher

For over sixty years families have dealt with the fallout from the
Second World War. This book has traced the stories of women
who felt it was time to tell their side of the story. For some it has
been a cathartic experience, for others it was an opportunity to
reassess the effects that the war had, and continues to have, on
their lives. It has also, necessarily, dwelt on the returning men's
story. When W. G. Harvey wrote his memoirs in the 1990s he
considered how pulling together the stories from the war helped
him but also how it had adversely affected his own family. His
memoir, he said, was a saga, written 'as a result of pressure by
my family and some friends and in writing it I have relived the

hardships and pain of the experience which, even 50 years later, are still vivid in my memories. My biggest regret was not that it marred my life, but [that it] also caused hardship and trouble to my wife and children. Much to her credit she never reproached me for it. Looking back I wonder if it was worth it or just an unmitigated folly.'

As Leonora Eyles and Norah C. James predicted in *Woman's Own* in 1945, it was to a large extent down to the women to rekindle the home and take responsibility for ensuring that family life went back to normal after the war. As Margaret Wadsworth foresaw, the war had 'hardened women's hands and women's hearts' and it is clear from Juliet Curry, Janice Taylor and Lindsay Munro among others that their mothers, in becoming fighters and survivors, had become hardened. They found expressing affection and even approval difficult; admired and respected by their daughters, they were also feared. The word often used to describe their mothers is formidable and it masks a perceived lack of warmth. This is a legacy that is seldom mentioned and little understood.

Elizabeth Rose had to focus all her attention on her husband in order to help him to get through his post-war health problems. 'I don't know how we managed all those years. But then, you'd be surprised how you *do* cope. Ken had fifty-six operations and was on dialysis for fourteen years.' Her daughter, Pam, has no doubt that this affected her life: 'It has made me think that in this world it is a question of get on or die,' she admitted. 'My mother does not like confrontation but I do. I have never had anyone else to look after me so I have had to fight my own corner. To be honest, Mother was so occupied with caring for my father that I used to feel a bit left out. But I adored my father and would have done anything for him.'

'Pam didn't have chances like other children,' Elizabeth agreed.

'There was never any spare money for her to go on holiday or do things like others did. But she has done very well in her job and has her own flat and has done all sorts of other interesting work.'

'My mother doesn't know half of it,' Pam retorted.

The families who appear to have coped best were those who scooped up their menfolk and welcomed them back into a thriving family environment. The Hillmans of Oxford, the Stampers of Northampton and Mollie Lodder in Stratford were all successful in rebuilding their lives. Although changed and sometimes scarred by the war, as Mollie was by widowhood, their post-war life was nevertheless characterized by an optimism that helped to mend fractures, heal wounds and absorb eccentricities.

For the children who were born after the war there was a legacy about which they knew almost nothing. Often their mothers had to take on a dominant role and become tough on behalf of their husbands.

Meg Parkes considered how her work has given her a better understanding of the childhood she and her sisters shared as daughters of a former Far Eastern prisoner of war:

> I think that learning more about the FEPOW story has helped to expose the fact that tensions and stresses in post-war family life were very common. That realization, and the knowledge that we were not 'the only ones', has helped many of us to come to terms with relationships within our families. Those men who recorded events at the time, and those who have finally decided to speak out about their experiences, deserve our gratitude.

Jen Howe, the daughter of John and Thyra Godber, summed up the experience for her in retelling the story of her relationship with her father:

I found myself thinking about parents – how within the context of their times, they do what they believe is the best thing for their children. And this led me to the conclusion that as each generation reaches maturity, they will inevitably pass judgement on their parents, forgetting that attitudes change and that one should never assess previous generations based on current thinking. And current thinking – with all its emphasis on political correctness – can be quite harsh. Whatever transpired, I know that my parents loved me dearly and did only what they felt was in my best interest.

And what of the future generations who will look back and wonder how the Second World War affected their families? Stephanie Hess has no doubt of the importance of the past on her life:

It began with me unwrapping the diary notebooks from their protective plastic covering one sad January evening when I was missing my mother, and missing Gran'pa and missing my childhood. I hadn't read the tiny script for a quarter of a century and emerged from the incredible tale two days later with a clear plan for the next year of my life. I would transcribe the diary. What began as a seemingly straightforward task soon became a multi-layered journey which continues to drive the direction of my life more than two years down the road. I was amazed and delighted to find that it was actually a realm of infinite possibility just waiting for me to explore.

NOTES

All quotations other than those listed below came from interviews, correspondence and conversations with the people featured in the book.

CHAPTER 1

p.3 'By the end of six years of war . . . and into the domain of "history".' Sir Carol Mather, *Aftermath of War: Everyone Must Go Home*, p.xii

p.3 'We were glad, but still our hearts refused to sing . . . from the nights of terror and fire.' Dame Barbara Cartland, *The Years of Opportunity 1939–1945*, p.265

p.4 'Victory does not bring with it a sense of triumph – rather a dull numbness of relief that the blood-letting is over.' Cecil Beaton, quoted in David Kynaston, *Austerity Britain*, p.9

p.5 'We were let loose at last . . . less than vindictive feelings towards the Germans.' Second Lieutenant F. J. Stewart, Unpublished Memoirs, p.95, IWM 88/20/1

p.5 'A completely new generation has arrived . . . With them you really feel five years have passed.' W. K. Laing, IWM Con Shelf

p.5 'I can't stop looking at them . . . sallow and yellowish.' W. K. Laing, IWM Con Shelf

p.6 'A young man is thrust into the army . . . walking about the world with quiet, strange eyes.' Trooper E. Pantony, IWM 83/41/1

p.8 'We must do it for the sake of the men . . . as quickly as ever you can.' Ernest Bevin in a speech at Wigan, 17 November 1943

p.8 'Young Sid's annoyed . . . in some stinking lodgings.' Mass Observation Archive, University of Sussex, D 5270, 27 August 1945 p.9 'The plan was all paper . . . the collective need.' Barry Turner and Tony Rennell, *When Daddy Came Home*, p.12

p.9 'In the last war, 1914–18 . . . precedence over all injuries.' Dame Barbara Cartland, *The Years of Opportunity 1939–1945*, p.56

p.10 'The return of personal interest . . . different sections of the nation.' Thomas F. Main quoted in Barry Turner and Tony Rennell, *When Daddy Came Home*, p.42

p.10 'have a human outlook . . . in need of help and advice.' Ernest Bevin quoted in Barry Turner and Tony Rennell, *When Daddy Came Home*, p.49

pp.10, 11 'Couldn't you speak to the men . . . will adjust themselves'; 'The padres looked at me . . . what we know through experience.' Dame Barbara Cartland, *The Years of Opportunity 1939–1945*, p.194

p.14 'We are completely foxed . . . find out bit by bit.' Lieutenant Louis Baume, Diary, 1 September 1945, IWM 66/310/1–2

p.15 'He had arranged a course . . . far too simple'; 'If I want to treat . . . principally by the woman.' Dame Barbara Cartland, *The Years of Opportunity 1939–1945*, p.196

p.16 'What will be the most important . . . now for the future.' Norah C. James, 'Back to Real Life', *Woman's Own*, January 1945, p.15

p.16 'and passed through experiences . . . may not be too easy.' Norah C. James, 'Back to Real Life', *Woman's Own*, January 1945, p.15

p.17 'That is woman's main task . . . better way of living.' Norah C. James, 'Back to Real Life', *Woman's Own*, January 1945, p.15

p.18 'So much depends on you, my dear . . . seemed beyond me.' Leonora Eyles, *Woman's Own*, 22 April 1945

p.19 'Don't expect to pick up . . . win the other's affection.' K. M. Catlin, *Home & Country*, June 1945, p.82

CHAPTER 2

p.22 'allowing seamen, NCOs . . . the letter was posted.' Peter Boyden, *Tommy Atkins' Letters: The History of the British Army Postal Service from 1795*, p.4

p.23 'Censorship Order and Regulations . . . defensive works.' Peter Boyden, *Tommy Atkins' Letters: The History of the British Army Postal Service from 1795*, p.4

p.23 'The stationery office . . . 26,000 bags of undeliverable mail.' Peter

Boyden, *Tommy Atkins' Letters: The History of the British Army Postal Service from 1795*, p.35

p.24 'In the planning for operation OVERLORD . . . as airstrips became available.' Peter Boyden, *Tommy Atkins' Letters: The History of the British Army Postal Service from 1795*, p.36

p.25 'Those letters have transported me home . . . who apologized for having no real news.' *Woman's Own*, editorial, 21 September 1945

p.36 'I read that . . . much for me to get back to.' A. G. Allbury, *Bamboo and Bushido*, Robert Hale, 1955, p.83; quoted in David Tett, *A Postal History of the Prisoners of War and Civilian Internees in East Asia During the Second World War, Volume 3, Burma, Thailand and Indochina*, p. 103

p.36 'Today, for the first time we have received mail . . . destroyed in the roaring inferno.' Warwick, November 1943, quoted in David Tett, *A Postal History of the Prisoners of War and Civilian Internees in East Asia During the Second World War, Volume 3, Burma, Thailand and Indochina*, pp.107–8

CHAPTER 3

p.45 'Two and a half years . . . There'll be trouble there!' Quoted in Barry Turner and Tony Rennell, *When Daddy Came Home*.

p.45 'They came home in various moods . . . thought they had a right to be there too.' Margaret Wadsworth, quoted in the epigraph, Barry Turner and Tony Rennell, *When Daddy Came Home*.

p.46 'bloody cocoa . . . get outside for a wee.' Maurice Merritt, *Eighth Army Driver*, Midas Books, 1981, p.176

p.47 'And so, instead of moping . . . a taxi home for happiness.' George Betts, *Autobiography of a Miner's Son*, Imperial War Museum, IWM 81/45/1

p.47 'The moment of walking through the door . . . far too large for me to consume.' Ray Ellis, Problems of Rehabilitation (A Return to Reality), IWM PP/MCR/388

p.48 'The phone call to my family was highly emotional . . . some gentle philosophizing.' C. L. Coles, RNVR, IWM 01/23/1

p.52 'From the really angry comments . . . having been completely airtight.' Mass Observation Archive, University of Sussex, D 5270, 3 June 1945

p.52 'Miss B went for her lunch at noon . . . the shop door at 10 o'clock.' Mass Observation Archive D 5270, 6 June 1945 p.52 'on chicanery and spivvery . . . were motivated by self-preservation.' Thomas Hanley quoted in Barry Turner and Tony Rennell, *When Daddy Came Home*, p.46

p.53 'We went to spend the day . . . possibly he had with Italian ladies.' Mass Observation Archive, University of Sussex, D 5443, 23 September 1945

p.53 'We eventually arrived in Liverpool . . . rolling stock all looked so small.' Harold Joseph Knowles, Unpublished Memoir, p.157, IWM 91/36/1

p.54 'When I eventually started to work . . . I'm getting back to a normal life.' W. K. Laing, Memoir 1945, IWM Con Shelf

p.55 'Many could not settle down . . . had a bad influence on domestic life.' Maurice Merritt, *Eighth Army Driver*, Midas Books, 1981, p.180

pp.57, 58 'I remember this shadowy figure . . . make an impact on me'; 'She was diabetic . . . this continued until she died.' Lyn Smith, *Young Voices: British Children Remember the Second World War*, in association with the Imperial War Museum, pp.376, 377

CHAPTER 4

p.73 'My mother, a wonderful person . . . stand in the way of opportunity.' Barbara Cartland, *The Years of Opportunity 1939–1945*, p.45

p.74 'This is just to send you my love . . . the meaning of – freedom.' Tony Cartland, letter home, May 1940, quoted in Dame Barbara Cartland, *The Years of Opportunity 1939–1945*, p.51

p.74 'I shall remember those hot, dry, sunny days . . . both her sons were "missing".' Dame Barbara Cartland, *The Years of Opportunity 1939–1945*, pp.52–5

p.74 'We had gradually been losing hope . . . for Tony was still "missing".' Dame Barbara Cartland, *The Years of Opportunity 1939–1945*, p.112

p.75 'Memories, however golden, cannot fill an empty place – a home that is suddenly quiet, a desk at which no one sits, a silence which remains unbroken by a voice.' Dame Barbara Cartland, *The Years of Opportunity 1939–1945*, p.113

p.75 'Another lady came up . . . to the poor mothers at home.'" Mass Observation Archive, University of Sussex, D 5270, 27 August 1945

p.79 'How remote the last six years are becoming . . . a general look of strain.' Mass Observation Archive, University of Sussex, D 5353, 22 August 1945

p.79 'He has been so thoughtful . . . all the senseless, formless cruelty.' Mass Observation Archive, University of Sussex, D 5353, 15 September 1939

p.79 'I missed Cliff very much . . . I'm mother enough to mourn my baby.' Mass Observation Archive, University of Sussex, D 5353, 18 October 1939

p.80 'It gives me a fear of the aftermath . . . remains to be seen.' Mass Observation Archive, University of Sussex, D 5353, 25 February 1941

p.80 'And he notices flowers . . . Everything evidently does come to them who wait!' Mass Observation Archive, University of Sussex, D 5353, 16 August 1941

p.81 'He got them out and I spread them . . . They look on it as 'Mom's party-piece'!' Mass Observation Archive, University of Sussex, D 5353, 25 May 1942

p.82 'I find my thoughts so often going to Cliff . . . and how he sees his 'luck' to continue.' Mass Observation Archive, University of Sussex, D 5353, 29 August 1945

p.82 'More and more does he seem to live in a world of his own . . . but not his time, company or 'consideration'.' Mass Observation Archive, University of Sussex, D 5353, 30 August 1945

p.82 'After demobilization, I lived in London . . . for two years as an art student.' Clifford Last in an afterword to Richard Broad and Suzie Fleming, *Nella Last's War*, p.301

CHAPTER 5

p.95 'It was easy to pick out the bereaved: the sad eyes above the smiling mouths.' Mrs E. J. F. Knowles, Memoirs Unpublished, p.100, IWM 91/36/1

pp.95, 96 'Just imagine the difference . . . the joy of seeing their children'; 'I know they probably had a difficult time . . . and here he was home'; 'It makes nonsense . . . educate the children, buy cars.' Jean Fry quoted in Joy P. Damousi, *Living with the Aftermath: Trauma, Nostalgia and Grief in Post-War Australia*, p.70

p.96 'Her endeavour to assist . . . their heads just above water.' Joy P. Damousi, *Living with the Aftermath: Trauma, Nostalgia and Grief in Post-War Australia*, p.21

p.97 'to make up to our children . . . the loss of their fathers had caused.' Jessie Vasey, quoted in *War Widows Craft Guild Circular* No. 8, February 1948, Melbourne Branch

p.98 'I used to dream, you know . . . quicker during wartime'; 'I had many . . . came up to him'; 'I always say . . . your first love is your only love.' Mary Ellen Simpson, quoted in Joy P. Damousi, *Living with the Aftermath: Trauma, Nostalgia and Grief in Post-War Australia*, pp.66–7

p.99 'We were only married for six years . . . decent human being.' Eve Harris, quoted in Joy P. Damousi, *Living with the Aftermath: Trauma, Nostalgia and Grief in Post-War Australia*, p.67

p.100 'How can I say this . . . through the years'; 'I don't know how . . . how he died'; '. . . the dreadful . . . my first husband again.' Joyce Tilley, quoted in Joy P. Damousi, *Living with the Aftermath: Trauma, Nostalgia and Grief in Post-War Australia*, p.79

CHAPTER 6

p.122 'That year was to be . . . yet there were waves of hope.' Dame Frances Campbell-Preston, *The Rich Spoils of Time*, p.87

p.122 'To talk of the future was theoretical . . . just like the women pictured in all wars.' Dame Frances Campbell-Preston, *The Rich Spoils of Time*, p.92

p.123 'I did not get the standard War Office telegram . . . and she kept me as sane as she could.' Dame Frances Campbell-Preston, *The Rich Spoils of Time*, pp.111–12

p.123 'Our ration today is coffee . . . I can see no end to this rot.' Letter from Patrick Campbell-Preston to his wife Frances, autumn 1940

pp.123–4 'Unfortunately the plan failed . . . I have never felt better in all my life.' Letter from Patrick Campbell-Preston to his wife Frances, 1942

p.124 'we were never able to express . . . had gone through was necessarily limited.' Dame Frances Campbell-Preston, *The Rich Spoils of Time*, p.153

p.124 'By the spring of 1945 we knew that at last the war was ending . . . prisoners might break out and stream home on their own.' Dame Frances Campbell-Preston, *The Rich Spoils of Time* p.203

p.125 'Poor old Fuff was wonderful . . . and there Patrick was.' Dame Frances Campbell-Preston, *The Rich Spoils of Time*, p.206

p.125 'Patrick has just walked in . . . a distant look comes into his eyes.'

'The more one sees of Patrick . . . he will very soon be himself again.'
Dame Frances Campbell-Preston, *The Rich Spoils of Time*, pp. 207–8

pp. 125–6 'When I came out . . . my friends had the same experience.'
W. K. Laing, unpublished papers, IWM Con Shelf

p. 126 'The first days were a rush . . . individually but nationally.' Dame
Frances Campbell-Preston, *The Rich Spoils of Time*, pp. 208–9

p. 126 'Mary Ann is a bit astounded . . . she and I slept together.' Dame
Frances Campbell-Preston, *The Rich Spoils of Time*, p. 210

p. 127 'The social market baffled him . . .the sniggers behind us.' Dame
Frances Campbell-Preston, *The Rich Spoils of Time*, p. 209

p. 129 'When he had his army check-up . . . technically he was dead.'
Dame Frances Campbell-Preston, *The Rich Spoils of Time*, p. 237

p. 130 'Before I could quite take in . . . and I was left gasping.' Dame
Frances Campbell-Preston, *The Rich Spoils of Time*, p. 268

CHAPTER 7

p. 153 'Women celebrated their new freedom . . . attribute of the harlot';
'Divorce rates had . . . to postpone marriage.' John Costello, *Love,
Sex and War 1939–45*, p. 11

p. 154 'Brilliant men . . . climax that makes you gasp.' John Costello, *Love,
Sex and War 1939–45*, p. 11

p. 154 'Illegitimacy rates were highest . . . by the extended absence of
their husbands.' John Costello, *Love, Sex and War 1939–45*, p. 278

p. 155 'I only knew and loved one of my three fathers . . . My brother and
I have been most fortunate.' Anonymous correspondent quoted in
Barry Turner and Tony Rennell, *When Daddy Came Home*, pp. 122–3

p. 156 'Men [who] came home and found their wives had been unfaithful . . .
there was no end to them.' Dame Barbara Cartland, *The Years of
Opportunity 1939–1945*, p. 147

p. 156 'No one has ever minded . . . I do believe what I say.' Dame
Barbara Cartland, *The Years of Opportunity 1939–1945*, p. 195

p. 156 'At first they swore . . . after all it's one of hers, isn't it?"' Dame
Barbara Cartland, *The Years of Opportunity 1939–1945*, p. 223

p. 159 'Suddenly the GIs were there . . . we couldn't have been more surprised.' John Costello, *Love, Sex and War 1939–45*, p. 311

p. 159 'We were half starved . . . it was rather pleasant, really!' John
Costello, *Love, Sex and War 1939–45*, pp. 311–12

pp.160, 161 'It is very easy to say what a woman should do or should not do . . . appreciate them or their cooking'; 'He is lonely . . . But they hadn't meant it to be like that, they hadn't really.' Dame Barbara Cartland, *The Years of Opportunity 1939–1945*, p.222

p.162 'When 1942 came in with the hit-and-run air raids . . . to forget the war for a few hours.' John Costello, *Love, Sex and War 1939–45*, p.29

p.162 'So began another part of my life . . . I didn't feel that I was doing anything wrong.' Correspondent quoted in John Costello, *Love, Sex and War 1939–45*, pp.29–30

p.163 'The post-war moral crusade . . . on the family and married life.' John Costello, *Love, Sex and War 1939–45*, p.357

p.163 'the moral life of America is in danger . . . We must accept the fact that total war relaxes moral standards on the home front and that this imperils the whole front of human decency.' President Hoover quoted in John Costello, *Love, Sex and War 1939–45*, pp.357–8

p.164 'The brutalizing and dislocating effects of war . . . as great a shock as joining the army had been.' John Costello, *Love, Sex and War 1939–45*, p.358

p.164 'When my husband finally came home . . . I could never have left the children.' John Costello, *Love, Sex and War 1939–45*, p.361

CHAPTER 9

p.221 'Long lonely silences, no one must talk . . . go out and play.' Mary Michael, *Growing up the Child of a FEPOW*, 2006 (www.fepow-community.org.uk)

p.239 'At that time, not knowing . . . throw all of this away when he died.' Martin Percival, *The Secret of Trunks in Family Attics*, *Researching FEPOW History Newsletter* No. 2, June 2007

CHAPTER 11

p.270 'Outside in the hall . . . didn't know who or what "daddy" was.' Carol Cooper quoted in Carolyn Newman, *Legacies of Our Fathers*, p.19

p.273 'a diary written by a local soldier . . . was buried in Burma.' Carolyn Newman, *Legacies of Our Fathers*, p.17

p.273 'Reading this copy . . . and cardiac beriberi.' Carol Cooper quoted in Carolyn Newman, *Legacies of Our Fathers*, pp.17–18

p.275 'Standing in Hellfire Pass . . . Ban Pong in Thailand.' Carol Cooper quoted in Carolyn Newman, *Legacies of Our Fathers*, p.21

p.276 'It seems like it will never end . . . 2000 have died so far since we left Changi.' Bill Smith, diary entry October 1942

p.277 'I work hard and I work long hours . . . you may walk over the highest mountain."' Carol Cooper quoted in Carolyn Newman, *Legacies of Our Fathers*, p.25

p.278 'We had to stop at many . . . from their families.' Carol Cooper quoted in Carolyn Newman, *Legacies of Our Fathers*, pp.25

p.281 'The hospital is close . . . back to Australia.' Di Elliott quoted in Carolyn Newman, *Legacies of Our Fathers*, p.41

p.282 'just a cranky old bastard . . . a miserable father.' Di Elliott quoted in Carolyn Newman, *Legacies of Our Fathers*, p.37

p.283 'I cannot recall exactly . . . into our home.' 'My very early memories . . . led to the arguments.' 'I remember him being always very ill . . . all hell would break loose.' Di Elliott quoted in Carolyn Newman, *Legacies of Our Fathers*, p.36

p.285 'What I don't understand . . . like any other man.' Di Elliott quoted in Carolyn Newman, *Legacies of Our Fathers*, p.39

p.286 'I have been in the company . . . if only I had understood.' Di Elliott quoted in Carolyn Newman, *Legacies of Our Fathers*, p.39

pp.286–7 'Well I made one phone call . . . and as a POW.' Di Elliott quoted in Carolyn Newman, *Legacies of Our Fathers*, p.38

p.288 'From that day in 1995 . . . problems with alcohol.' Di Elliott quoted in Carolyn Newman, *Legacies of Our Fathers*, p.40

p.289 'She has become a focus . . . projects are daunting.' Carolyn Newman, *Legacies of Our Fathers*, p.35

p.290 'As a child I had no cognisance . . . as just "normal."' Meg Parkes, *Notify Alec Rattray . . .*, pp.vii-viii

p.291 'What is clear . . . he believed that they would be.' Meg Parkes, *Notify Alec Rattray . . .*, pp.vii

p.291 'Do you mean that Grandad . . . It didn't bother me.' Meg Parkes, *Notify Alec Rattray . . .*, p.ix

p.292 'No allowances were made . . . undermining his authority in front of us.' Meg Parkes, *Notify Alec Rattray . . .*, p.viii

p.293 'witty and intelligent . . . the curtain fell.' Meg Parkes, *Notify Alec Rattray . . .*, p.30

p.294 'I am quite sure that next year at this time I shall be addressing you as Dr . .' letter from Atholl Duncan to Elizabeth Glassey, 9 September 1941

p.294 'Stayed up to see in the New Year . . . find them safe and well.' Atholl Duncan diary entry, 1 January 1943

p.295 'It will be wonderful when . . . I thought at times I would go mad.' Elizabeth Glassey to Atholl Duncan, 7 August 1943

p.295 'It's damnable to think . . . the best years of one's life.' Atholl Duncan diary entry, 7–9 November 1943

p.296 'despite the dreary accommodation . . . fellow professionals to be treated.' Meg Parkes, . . . *AA Duncan is OK*, p.54

p.296 'No matter how much knowledge . . . how busy they are.' Meg Parkes, . . . *AA Duncan is OK*, pp.54–5

p.296 'I was a newly hatched medical chick . . . I never saw her break down.' Dr Hazel Hinton in correspondence with Meg Parkes quoted in . . . *AA Duncan is OK*, p.60

p.297 'This turned out to be . . . share life once again.' Meg Parkes, . . . *AA Duncan is OK*, p.188

p.298 'if, God willing, Atholl did manage . . . rebuild his life with her?' Meg Parkes, . . . *AA Duncan is OK*, p.59

p.299 'Although all these men . . . privileged to be at university at all.' John S. G. Blair, *St Andrews University OTC, A History*, quoted in . . . *AA Duncan is OK*, p.164

p.299 'Atholl was conspicuous . . . how he may have reacted at home.' Ranald MacKenzie, letter to Meg Parkes, January 2008

p.299 'I well remember spending Thursday . . . she did look after Atholl so well . . .' Letter from Esme Leckie to Meg Parkes, quoted in . . . *AA Duncan is OK*, p.166

p.300 'There's a lot of stories getting . . . I believe this to be good advice.' Kenneth Davey to his wife Joy, 15 September 1945

p.301 'It was while living in the nearby village . . . a wonderful distraction.' Meg Parkes, . . . *AA Duncan is OK*, pp.166–7

p.301 'Why didn't she do her own thing? . . . selfishness over something or other.' Meg Parkes, . . . *AA Duncan is OK*, p.169

p.304 'The whole family was devastated . . . life had no meaning for him without her.' Meg Parkes, *AA Duncan is OK*, p.171

p.305 'Since first reading his diaries . . . help him to survive.' Meg Parkes, . . . *AA Duncan is OK*, p.172

CHAPTER 12

p.320 'His childhood years were spent . . . the Easter Rising of 1916.' Stephanie Hess in an article on www.malayanvolunteersgroup.org.uk

p.321 'But there were rumblings . . . were wearing when they were there.' Stephanie Hess in an article on www.malayanvolunteers-group.org.uk

p.322 'For the second time in his life . . . the city that had brought him so much happiness.' Stephanie Hess in an article on www.malayan-volunteersgroup.org.uk

p.323 'It was a letter . . . and incredibly, humour.' Stephanie Hess in an article on www.malayanvolunteersgroup.org.uk

p.324 'Those first years following the war . . . more than many could claim.' Stephanie Hess in an article on www.malayanvolunteers-group.org.uk

CHAPTER 13

p.329 'as a result of pressure by my family . . . or just an unmitigated folly.' W. G. Harvey, Memoirs, IWM 06/51/1

The publishers have made every effort to contact the copyright holders of material quoted in this work.

BIBLIOGRAPHY

PUBLISHED SOURCES

Adie, Kate, *The Kindness of Strangers* (London: Headline 2002)

Allbury, A. G., *Bamboo and Bushido* (London: Robert Hale 1955)

Barham, Peter, *Forgotten Lunatics of the Great War* (London & New York: Yale University Press 2004)

Best, Brian (ed.), *Secret Letters from the Railway: The Remarkable Record of Charles Steel – A Japanese POW* (Barnsley: Pen & Sword, Military, 2004)

Betts, George, *Autobiography of a Miner's Son* (London: Imperial War Museum)

Billière, General Sir Peter de la, *Supreme Courage: Heroic Stories from 150 Years of the Victoria Cross* (London: Little, Brown 2004)

Boyden, Peter, *Tommy Atkins' Letters: The History of the British Army Postal Service from 1795* (London: A National Army Museum Publication, NAM, 1990)

Broad, Richard & Fleming, Suzie (eds.), *Nella Last's War: The Second World War Diaries of Housewife, 49* (London: Profile Books 2006)

Campbell-Preston, Dame Frances, *The Rich Spoils of Time* (Stanbridge: The Dovecote Press 2006)

Cartland, Dame Barbara, *The Years of Opportunity 1939–1945* (London: Hutchinson 1948)

Condell, Jennie (ed.), *The Day the War Ended, Voices and Memories from 1945* (London: Weidenfeld & Nicolson 2005)

Costello, John, *Love, Sex and War, Changing Values 1939–45* (London: Pan Books 1985)

Damousi, Joy, *Living with the Aftermath: Trauma, Nostalgia and Grief in Post-War Australia* (Cambridge: Cambridge University Press 2001)

Dixon, Barbara, *Good Housekeeping Wartime Scrapbook* (London: Collins and Brown 2005)

Donaldson, Betty, *Once upon a Wartime: Tugs of War, Volume 8* (Barny Books 1999)

Garfield, Simon, *Our Hidden Lives: The Remarkable Diaries of Post-War Britain* (London: Ebury Press 2004)

Gilbert, Adrian, *POW: Allied Prisoners in Europe 1939–1945* (London: John Murray 2006)

Gilbert, Martin, *The Day the War Ended* (London: HarperCollins 1995)

Kynaston, David, *Austerity Britain 1945–51* (London: Bloomsbury 2007)

Longmate, Norman, *How We Lived Then: A History of Everyday Life During the Second World War* (London: Hutchinson 1971)

Marr, Andrew, *A History of Modern Britain* (London: Macmillan 2007)

Mather, Sir Carol, *Aftermath of War: Everyone Must Go Home* (London: Brassey's 1999)

Merritt, Maurice, *Eighth Army Driver* (Midas Books, 1981)

Newman, Carolyn, *Legacies of Our Fathers* (Melbourne: Thomas C. Lothian 2005)

Parkes, Meg, *Notify Alec Rattray . . .* (West Kirby: Kranji Publications 2002)

Parkes, Meg, *. . . AA Duncan is OK* (West Kirby: Kranji Publications 2003)

Roberts, Elizabeth, *Women and Families, An Oral History 1940–1970* (Oxford: Blackwell Publishers 1995)

Smith, Lyn, *Young Voices: British Children Remember the Second World War* (London: Viking Books in association with the Imperial War Museum 2007)

Summers, Julie, *The Colonel of Tamarkan, Philip Toosey and the Bridge on the River Kwai* (London: Simon & Schuster 2005)

Summers, Julie, *Remembered: A History of the Commonwealth War Graves Commission* (London: Merrell 2007)

Tedder, Valerie, *Post War Blues* (Leicester City Council 1999)

Tett, David, *A Postal History of the Prisoners of War and Civilian Internees in East Asia During the Second World War, Volume 3, Burma, Thailand and Indochina* (Wheathampstead: BFA Publishing 2005)

Turner, Barry & Rennell, Tony, *When Daddy Came Home: How Family Life Changed Forever in 1945* (London: Hutchinson 1995, Pimlico edition 1996)

Willis, A. U., Adam, R. F., Sutton, B. E., *To All British Commonwealth Ex-Prisoners of War* (London: War Office, 1945)

Far East (companion journal to *The Prisoner of War*), January 1945 & September 1945

Home & Country, Women's Institute magazine, June 1945

Royal Air Force *Java Letter*, February 1945

UNPUBLISHED SOURCES

Ball, Mr and Mrs E. G., IWM 05/57/1

Baume, Lieutenant Louis, Diaries 1941–45, IWM, 66/103/1–2

Betts, George, IWM, 81/45/1

Boxall, Major and Mrs G. C., IWM Con Shelf

Clark, Miss E. M., Maggie's War, IWM 94/10/1

Coles OBE VRD RNVR, Lieutenant C. L., IWM 01/23/1

Davey, RSM Kenneth, IWM, 65/106/1

Ellis, R. K., IWM PP/MCR/388

Griffiths, A. W., IWM 06/99/1

Harvey, W. G., IWM 06/51/1

Hopkinson, Diana and David, IWM, 86/3/1

Hounsell, Major General H., IWM 70/10/1

Knowles, Mrs E. J. F., IWM 91/36/1

Laing, Lieutenant W. K., IWM Con Shelf

Littleboy, Miss M. E., IWM 01/19/1

Littler, G. A., IWM, 65/6/1

Mather, Sir Carol, IWM, 02/692

Mortimer, E. G. A., IWM 97/12/1

Pantony, E., IWM 83/41/1

Penrose, Mrs P., IWM 94/27/1

Stewart, Second Lieutenant F. J., IWM 88/20/1

Vincent, Lieutenant J. D., IWM 65/107/1

Walton, Mrs N. C., IWM 88/2/1

Wootton, S. R., IWM P336

The North Staffordshire Prisoners of War Comforts and After-Care Fund

Trustees of Mass Observation at the University of Sussex kindly gave permission for quotations to be taken from diaries 5270, 5353 and 5443.

WEBSITES

Dictionary of National Biography www.oxforddnb.com
The Malayan Volunteers Group www.malayanvolunteersgroup.org.uk
FEPOW Community www.fepow-community.org.uk

PICTURE CREDITS

ACKNOWLEDGEMENTS

My sincere thanks go to everyone who has helped me during the various stages of this book: Betty Aldsworth, Keith Andrews, Winifred Beagan, Rod Beattie, Chris Best, Cynthia Brown, Catherine Butcher, Dame Frances Campbell-Preston, Maureen Cleaver, Amy Clifford, Doris Cole, Andy Cole, Carol Cooper, Juliet Curry, Betty Donaldson, Di Elliott, Ray Ellis, Roxanne Espantman, Gemma Gibb, Thyra Godber, Jean Hammond, Janie Hampton, Stephanie Hess, Denise Holden, David Hopkins, Jen Howe, Fred Jackson, Celia Kerr, Pauline Kiernan, Barbara Lamb, Barbara Lewis, Mollie Lodder, Valerie Loriga, Patricia Mark, Ian McCorquodale, Ena Mitchell, Jonathan Moffatt, Joy Newman, Meg Parkes, Gwen Parr, Martin Percival, Sue Philpott, Marion Platt, John Porter, Mary Evelyn Porter, Carol Rhodes, Anne Riches, Jean Roberts, Stephen Rockcliffe, Edna Roper, Elizabeth Rose, Pamela Rose, Anne Russell, George Schramm, Barbara Sinclair, Anne Stamper, Sue Stephenson, Janice Taylor, Valerie Tedder, Rachel Thorn, Bonita Walsham, Hazel Watson, Richard Webster, Jean White, Joanne Wilde, June Wingate, Maureen Worthington Hale, Mary Zacaroli.

Thanks are also due to individuals at the various collections I used: Peter Boyden at the National Army Museum; Commander Toby Elliott and Robert Marsh at Combat Stress; Peter Francis at the Commonwealth War Graves Commission; Roderick

Suddaby in the Department of Documents at the Imperial War Museum; Karen Watson at Mass Observation at the University of Sussex; Alison Wright at the Department of National Statistics; I should also like to thank my agent, Catherine Clarke, and her colleague, Michele Topham, my editor at Simon & Schuster, Angela Herlihy, her assistant Rory Scarfe, my father, Peter Summers, and my husband, Chris.

INDEX